The HOLLYWOOD JOB-HUNTER'S SURVIVAL GUIDE

by HUGH TAYLOR

LONE
EAGLE

THE HOLLYWOOD JOB-HUNTER'S SURVIVAL GUIDE:
An Insider's Winning Strategies to Getting That (All-Important) First Job...
And Keeping It
Copyright 1993 © Hugh Taylor

> LONE EAGLE PUBLISHING CO.
> 2337 Roscomare Road, Suite Nine
> Los Angeles, CA 90077-1851
> 310/471-8066 • fax 310/471-4969
> World Wide Web http://www.loneeagle.com

Printed in the United States of America

Cover design by Heidi Frieder.

Illustration by Lou Beach.

Front cover art copyright © 1993 Lone Eagle Publishing. All rights reserved.

> ®Variety and Daily Variety are registered trademarks of Reed Properties Inc., used under license. Used by permission.

> The Hollywood Reporter and The Hollywood Reporter logo are used with permission from The Hollywood Reporter and Billboard Publications, Inc., its parent company.

> The Hollywood Walk of Fame, its star, and logo are used with permission of the Hollywood Chamber of Commerce.

> The image of Mann's Chinese Theatre is used with permission from Mann's Chinese Theatre.

First Printing, March 1993
Second Printing, June 1993
Third Printing, January 1994
Fourth Printing, January 1996
Fifth Printing, September 1997

Library of Congress Cataloging in Publication Data
Taylor, Hugh, 1965—
> The Hollywood job hunter's survival guide: an insider's winning strategies to getting that all-important first job—and keeping it/by Hugh Taylor.
>
>   p.   cm.
>   ISBN: 0-943728-51-7
>   1. Motion Pictures—Production and direction—vocational guidance.
> I. Title
> PN1995.9.P7T285 1992
> 791.43'02302373—dc20   92-37828
>   CIP

Foreword

When Hugh Taylor told me he was writing a guide about how to get and do an assistant's job in Hollywood, the picture of a small book, something like *A Harvard Freshman's Guide to Wellesley,* replete with wise-ass comments, came to mind. I should have known better because I know Hugh Taylor. When I received the manuscript for this book I was impressed instantly by its comprehensiveness, its organization, and its good common sense about the subject.

Each of us has had or will have an entry level job. Hugh is correct. That first job is very important. In show business you have two choices. You can get a job where there are many indignities and few learning opportunities. Or you can get a job where there are many indignities and many learning opportunities. Too bad about the indignities.

This book is meant for those entering the business, and those already at work who would like to improve their performance. Hugh Taylor and his generation are tough competitors. Nevertheless, Hugh has performed a selfless act in making the depth of his experience and the fruit of his inquiries available to you in this book at a moderate price. Use this book. It is a weapon in the battle you are about to join.

Edgar J. Scherick
President and Executive Producer
Edgar J. Scherick Associates

Acknowledgments

I am deeply indebted to everyone I have worked with at Edgar J. Scherick Associates. This book was originally intended to be a training manual for that very special place. It is more than just a firm that produces movies. For decades it has been a virtual graduate school for young people starting out in Hollywood. The company has some impressive alumni, and expectations for performance on the job are very high as a result. I would like to express my sincere appreciation to Edgar, whose standards of excellence and spirit of mentorship form the soul of this book.

Several people had a direct impact on the creation of this book. Barbara Lieberman, Scott Siegel and Susan Cooper were all instrumental in encouraging me to get started and have the book published. For advice and support I relied extensively on Suzanne Young and Michael Barnathan. I would like to thank Sandi Carrillo and Mitch Engel for showing me the ropes early on.

Joan Singleton, my publisher, and Bethann Wetzel, my editor at Lone Eagle, guided me throughout the process of writing. I am also grateful for the help I received from many other people, including Chris Moore, Daniel Schwartz, Mickie Reuster, Adam Isaacs, Karen Swallow, Nan Blitman, Matt Mather and Larry Brothers. I thank Woody Allen for granting me permission to use quotations from his films in this book. Finally, I would like to thank all the people who gave their time to be interviewed for this book. They are David Kanter, Chip Diggins, Bill Todman, Michael Barnathan, Karen Swallow, Jenny Mintz, Cathy Stone and Karina Downs.

Hugh Taylor

Preface

When I graduated from college in 1988, I got a job checking the spellings of African countries for a desktop encyclopedia. I was not, as they say, on the fast track. But those classmates of mine who were, headed for a narrow, traffic-choked thoroughfare in downtown New York City. Its name: Wall Street. I had little in common with them. In school, I took courses like "Ibsen and Shaw," and "Philosophy from Plato to John Stuart Mill." They, on the other hand, opted for "Principles of Finance I, II and III" and, for a lark, "Intro to Fixed-Income Investing."

Why were so many of my schoolmates so single-minded? Because those dry economics courses were seen as the ticket to working for the financial behemoths of Wall Street—the sure and steady road to five-digit bonuses, weekends in East Hampton, and the chance to become a "Master of the Universe," as *Bonfire of the Vanities* author Tom Wolfe called these financial types. Upon graduating, these folks landed 90-hour-a-week jobs promising a foot in the door and, at the very least, a fair shot at carpal tunnel syndrome.

Those days of heading blindly for the ivory towers of stocks and bonds are behind us like a canceled sitcom. Now there's a new mecca for fast-trackers. It's called Hollywood. Today's Tinseltown job-seekers may not be all that interested in movies *per se*. But Sunset Boulevard is now infinitely hipper than Wall Street—or Madison Avenue for that matter. "Hollywood is to the 1990s what Wall Street was to the 1980s... (It's) where the action is," proclaimed *M Inc.* magazine last year. A U.C.L.A. film school prof lamented, in that same article, that his students didn't "care about the nature of film—what it is or what it does. It's just more glamorous than selling shoes."

To be sure, that's part of the picture. Film is definitely sexier than footwear. But there's something else at work here, something more reflective of our collective self-image. It goes like this: *Americans are used to winning.* In fact, we love it.

Being number one is as central to the Yankee mentality as freedom of expression, or light beer. I don't mean to imply that people in Finland and Senegal *like* to lose, not at all. It's just that, as nephews and nieces of Uncle Sam, we feel an undue burden to lead the league. Maybe it's World War II on the brain, or 30 years of being the world's economic heavyweight champ, or the aftermath of the 1980 Winter Olympics. Who knows? The trouble is, as the 21st century nears, that grand self-concept and the harsh realities of competing for global market share don't always get along so well. For over a decade, America has been enduring a painful comeuppance. Our manufacturers no longer monopolize world markets; our stock market isn't the only place to invest; and the U.S. trade deficit puts on a few more pounds every chance it gets. Across the vast seas, people are doing fine without U.S.-made products. Their Korean cars are fitted out with German stereos, and they are learning to become couch potatoes in the cool glow of Japanese TV sets and VCRs.

And therein lies the rub. The finest audio components in the world would go untouched if the only albums you could get were by, say, Ivan and the Polka-Magic Ensemble. Fact is, America feeds the rest of the world's hunger for entertainment like a zookeeper shoveling fresh meat into the lion's cage. Accordingly, we can still call ourselves a nation of winners. In Kenya and in Denmark, in Kazakhstan and Thailand, there are people who have never heard the words "General Motors." But you can bet that over there they *parlez* Madonna, Michael Jackson, and Batman with great fluency. *Fortune* summed things up pretty well in "America's Hottest Export: Pop Culture," a 1990 cover story. "[Foreigners] may not want our *hardware* anymore—our cars, steel or television sets. But when they want a jolt of popular culture—and they want more all the time—they increasingly turn to American *software*: our movies, music, TV programming, and home video, which now account for an annual trade surplus of some $8 billion. Only aerospace—aircraft and related equipment—outranks pop culture as an export." The most popular film of all time in Israel and Sweden is PRETTY WOMAN. Take that, Ingmar Bergman.

So, if you're considering a career in Hollywood, you're to be congratulated for adapting in short order to the rules of the new economy. You know where the money and excitement is—and the great glory of being number one. It's in producing HOME ALONE, in brokering the deal that has Bruce Willis get the bad guys in DIE HARDER, and in hooking up Ray Charles with the good folks at PepsiCo. Hey, I can't blame a 22-year-old who wants to work her way up from the mailroom at Creative Artists, and dreams of someday nudging aside Mike Ovitz. Why waste time on a sinking ship? I give you lots of credit for knowing where the action is. And where it's likely to remain.

Andrew Erdman
Fortune Magazine

For Irvin, Judith, Fanny, David and Janet

Table of Contents

Disclaimer: The information about companies, restaurants, hotels, and services listed here represent the ones that, in the opinion of the author, might be used in the average entertainment office. Inclusion or exclusion from these listings does not connote any particular status or lack thereof.

Introduction
We Are Here to Learn

This book is about getting from where you are now to where you want to be in the entertainment industry. The career track in the movie business is the object of much discussion and fascination. Yet the actual planning of such a career and one's day-to-day progression through the industry is little understood, even by those who are immersed in a job search or working at the entry level.

Since my tenure as assistant to one of Hollywood's top producers, a number of people have asked me how they can get a job in the movie business. My response to this question is always to ask them what ultimate career goal they have in mind. More often than not, their answer is, "I don't know. I just want to get in." One MBA student at Harvard approached me and said, "Hugh, I really want to work in production...By the way, what is production?"

So, we sit down and talk for while and try to determine what they might want to do in the movie business, what they will do at the entry level, and how they can parlay that experience into a promotion toward what they think they want. I give them my idea of what to look for in a job, and the possible paths they can follow toward their ultimate goal, be it producing, directing, talent management or screenwriting. We come up with strategies for finding the right job and keeping it. I have had this conversation with dozens of college students, a handful of lawyers, a professional photographer, a naval architect, a score of investment bankers and many, many people who are currently working in some branch of the entertainment industry itself and want to change jobs.

What is most striking about these conversations is how these highly educated, intelligent and motivated individuals can have such a passion for a career about which they know very little. As the inner workings of the entertainment industry have become the object of media scrutiny and fascination, careers in the industry have achieved an unusually high level of appeal and acceptance in the mainstream. The allure of Hollywood is sufficient to obscure any unglamorous specific questions such as, "What will I *do* in the industry?" or, "How does the industry actually work?" However, it is important—arguably of supreme importance—to have an understanding of the structure of the business, and the paths which can be followed toward career goals, before using up valuable personal contacts on a round of exploratory interviews.

The goal of your first work experience in entertainment should be to learn as much as possible, not make a lot of money or have a great Southern California lifestyle. Those will follow if you take the first step correctly. The business is complex, and different from other industries, so what you already know will probably be of little use. There is not much you can learn in school—even film school—which will prepare you properly to function in the work environment of the entertainment industry.

The entry level is a unique opportunity to learn, with few strings attached. Though you will have a large number of demands placed on you in the beginning, it is unlikely that you will have to produce any real results, such as forging a development deal or finding a hot script. This is a great chance to formulate as complete an understanding of the business as possible before your professional reputation is riding on every move you make.

While there are a few entry-level executive positions at studios and networks, in which people start at the decision-making level, the vast majority of successful people in the entertainment business began their careers as someone's assistant. They realized that they knew nothing, and sought a job where they could learn. Industry giants such as former Fox Chairman Barry Diller, record and movie mogul David Geffen and MCA President Sidney Sheinberg all started in educational entry-level training positions. In short, your wisest route to the top is to find the best learning job and mentor available, and absorb the experience like a sponge. It is your rite of passage.

You may feel a strong desire to be a producer, agent or writer immediately, but nobody will take you seriously unless you demonstrate some competence and familiarity with the way business is transacted in

Hollywood. The degree to which you master those skills and the speed with which you progress toward your goal, depends on your personal abilities and the quality of your education in the business. Think of it in terms of bridging the gap between what you know about the business from reading *Final Cut (NAL-Dutton, 1986)* and *Indecent Exposure (Dell, 1983)* , and what you can actually do. You may understand how power brokers work from afar, but can you pick up the phone and make something happen by yourself? That is the critical distance you can cover by breaking in at the entry level.

MYTHS AND REALITIES

"There are a million talented people out there. Nobody will ever hire me..."

I have heard this unfortunate prediction many times from bright and ambitious people who are hunting for jobs in Los Angeles. The good news is that it is not completely true. There is an oversupply of underqualified people in the business. Flakes abound, and the turnover in some companies is extraordinary as a result.

Why the high failure rate? Many people choose the wrong job based on a poor overview of the workings of the industry. They take jobs without much thought of where they might lead. Some career tracks will take you in concentric rings around your ultimate goal. Ask anyone who became a business affairs lawyer in the hopes of becoming a producer or creative executive and they will tell you about the agonizingly long transition period between career paths.

Some simply underestimate the long hours, low pay and pressure which are necessary evils of working in a busy entertainment office. Others fall victim to their own incompetence or lack of training in specific industry skills. In most jobs you have to be able to hit the ground running, so adaptability can be a good substitute for knowledge; but if you lack both, you may not last long.

A lack of emotional preparation for the job is the classic reason why many assistants bail out, or get forced out of jobs which they worked hard to find. After making honors in school, or working in a high position in another industry, you are now assigned menial tasks and given little respect. Or worse, you may be subjected to outright humiliation and ridicule because of your inexperience. It is a major comedown for many people, but it is an unfortunate reality of the industry. If you have reservations about your ability to withstand this shock to your ego, you may want to reassess your career plans. This notion gains increasing validity with age. I have seen many fine people in their thirties *say* in a job interview that they don't mind doing menial work, and in the beginning they don't, but after about four months of gofering they invariably blow a fuse and quit.

If you have intelligence, determination, organization and humility you stand a good chance of getting an entry-level learning job. Remember, if you are competent, you are already ahead of the pack. It may take a few months to find the right position, but one will open up just as soon as one of the above-mentioned flakes drops out.

"I'd love to work in movies, but don't you have to be a loud, amoral, tasteless sleazebag to be a success in the industry?"

I have been asked this question numerous times. People are afraid that if they don't match this personality type, they won't stand a chance. Though there is some truth to this generalization, it is largely a myth that everyone who succeeds in the movie business is a screaming maniac and a crook.

There are thousands of people working in the entertainment industry, so it is probable that you can find an employer with a personality compatible to your own. There are some examples of outrageous, even sociopathic behavior which are tolerated in the name of talent and ability, but having such a character type is not a prerequisite for success. Much of the entertainment business is based on trust and relationships, so honesty is valued above all else in many circles. Many of the industry's most powerful figures are in fact relatively quiet and gentle-mannered people. That doesn't mean they aren't tough and determined. They simply don't yell at headwaiters.

"I don't want to be too good an assistant. Then I won't move up."

The premise of this argument is that if you are a good assistant, you will be permanently relegated to servitude. This is rarely true. If you are good at being an assistant, you will show your superiors that you are capable of moving up. If you show that you can work hard and productively (there is a difference), then you are a prime candidate for advancement. However, if you don't perform well as an assistant, it is unlikely that anyone will trust you enough to offer you a chance to do more fulfilling work.

The cases where a "good" assistant does not get promoted are usually ones in which the protagonist is competent, yet lacks sufficient perspective and poise to make himself or herself visible as a future executive. Hence, the myth of the good assistant being forever trapped at the bottom.

"I have an MBA. I don't make coffee."

This is the battle cry of the over-educated, over-experienced job hunter in Hollywood. These words are usually uttered by the person who still possesses a shred of ego left over from the normal world. This person is holding out for an offer to be an executive with no direct experience. If you hold firmly to this type of conviction, you may be looking for work in the wrong industry. Many employers will make you serve coffee *because* you have an MBA, just to show you they think it's worthless.

Humility is the foundation of a successful entry-level work experience in entertainment, at least in the early stages. The amount of respect you command is proportional to your contribution to the organization. So, in the beginning, when you can add little to what is going on, you will probably be assigned the most mundane tasks, regardless of your background or age. Not to worry, though. The more you learn, the more you will be respected. As time goes on, you will have to make coffee less and less often. If you have an impossible ego, then you would do well to try to put it in neutral for the first year of work. If you are incapable of doing this, you may want to hold out for that executive position, but it can be an awfully long wait.

The reality of most entry-level jobs in entertainment, assistant or otherwise, is that they are stressful, demeaning, and low-paying, though enormously educational. Without the benefit of an institution offering formal training in assistantship, you will be expected to drop right in and start performing. This means having excellent office skills, and fluency in the peculiar language and customs of the business. In addition, you will have to be a story analyst, paralegal, essayist, researcher, chauffeur, valet, accountant, librarian, travel agent, cultural attache and babysitter. Ready to quit before you begin? Take heart! The pain and suffering is your tuition payment for the real-world course you are taking.

While some jobs are wildly stressful and demeaning (a friend of mine was instructed to take the producer's wife's poodle to a posh restaurant and feed it a bacon cheeseburger under the table), most are simply high-pressure experiences with long hours, difficult personalities and a small paycheck. If this seems like cruel and unusual punishment, perhaps looking at the world through your boss's eyes can give you some perspective on the situation. Your role is to help in the advancement of your boss's career, not the other way around. In your struggle to find work, it is easy to forget this essential priority.

No matter how successful your boss is, he or she will be caught up in improving two critical areas: management of time, and maintenance of professional relationships with colleagues in the business. You have influence over both areas. His professional relationships are in your hands as you prioritize reading, answer the phone, write letters and make appointments. Time management for your boss is partly dependent on the degree to which you can process and present to him the information overload which is prevalent in an entertainment office. Much of the day-to-day business involves staying in touch with people on the phone, synthesizing creative ideas and making personal decisions. The better you are at organizing your boss's work flow and schedule, the more he can accomplish, and the further he will advance.

Conversely, if you don't know what you're doing, you impede your boss's career. You are a tiresome bottleneck who is getting in the way of his productivity and enrichment. If this happens, you will feel the high-pressure element characteristic of many assistant jobs. You do not want to stay on this track for very long if you can avoid it. If you are lucky, you will be allowed the time to improve, but you might just as easily be let go for being a bottleneck. Your boss's time is too valuable to waste bringing you up to speed.

Many entertainment firms are poorly managed, so the need for good people in staff positions is even more critical than it is in other industries. Poor management is endemic to the entertainment industry. It's not that entertainment executives are genetically bad managers, it is simply a necessary by-product of the haphazard way business is transacted. Many structures and partnerships are short-lived. Production companies are established and disbanded in the same year. A new president takes over a studio and everyone leaves.

There is not much room for solid, effective management in this system. Given the nature of the problem, though, you can make yourself a useful counterbalance to the instability by mastering a few basics in running an office, to protect it from the storm. This book is a step-by-step guide to organizing and running a busy entertainment office through problem-solving procedures for managing your boss's time. It is unlikely that you alone will be able to institute every one of the ideas described in this book, since it is based on an office with an atypically large staff. However, if you can absorb the core ideas, you will have gone a long way toward differentiating yourself from the raw job applicants roaming around Hollywood.

This book should answer two persistent questions you will have at every point in your entry-level position: "What's going on?" and, "Where do I fit in?" This book aims to provide a constant overview of happenings and decisions. Much of the book is concerned with how a movie gets made from start to finish. That is a basic building block of your industry education. At each stage of development, pre-production and post-production, you will have a distinct role to play.

This book assumes the perspective of an assistant to a producer or studio production executive. However, virtually every detail of this book could be applied to an agent's assistant. For the sake of continuity, however, the ubiquitous "boss" in this book will be a female producer.

Chapter 1 gives a broad overview of the entertainment industry. It identifies who does what, and interprets some of the corporate structures that make up the business. Chapter 2 explores what it takes get the actual job. Chapter 3 lays out the basic office skills and tasks. Chapter 4 teaches the process of handling scripts and other written material. Chapters 5 and 6 describe the script development process and production. Chapters 7 and 8 cover travel and information gathering. Chapter 9 ties it all together and outlines the basic work routine and some issues surrounding it. Chapter 10 discusses some common problems facing assistants who are preparing to advance.

The Appendix is a factual supplement to the book. It contains a glossary of entertainment industry terms, samples of typical legal agreements and deal memos, as well as samples of story coverage and reader's notes. Some useful details of film production are included, plus some essential phone numbers that every assistant should know.

This book is about achieving your personal goals in the first step of a career in the entertainment business through making the most of a learning experience. It is more an approach to learning and preparedness than a simple formula on how to succeed. Even if you are not directly interested in working in an office, its central themes of excellence, responsibility, communication and attention to detail can readily be applied to any Hollywood job. However, this book is not a substitute for imagination and creativity, the two skills which you must cultivate if you want to move up.

Chapter 1
An Overview of the Industry

1.0 THE PRODUCT FLOW

The entertainment industry produces films and television programs and distributes them to a series of audiences around the world. Figure 1.1 diagrams this essential industry pattern of production and distribution. The chart shows the chain of relationships and exchanges necessary to produce film and television programs, collectively known as *product,* and bring them to an audience. Agreements, services and performances resulting in finished product flow from the creative community through distributors to the audience. This is shown by the downward arrows on the left side of the chart. In payment for these services, performances and finished films, money flows upwards from the audiences, through distributors, producers and back to the creative community. The arrows on the right side of the chart show this flow of money.

Figure 1-1 Flow of product, services and money in the entertainment industry

1

Virtually every job in the industry relates in some way to the creation of product, or the distribution of product to audiences. Though people in the business like to describe their jobs as unique and without parallel, you should be able to fit them into one of these categories. As you search for a job, you can position yourself on the product flow diagram.

1.1   AUDIENCES AND MARKETS—THE DEMAND FOR PRODUCT

The entertainment industry begins with the audience. All of us watch films and television and partake in the mass culture of Hollywood. We go to the movies, rent videos, watch television and buy movie merchandise. Audiences around the world are clamoring for entertainment product. For the most part, that means American movies, television programs and derivative merchandise.

Though in some sense there is just one huge audience composed of everyone who goes to the movies or watches television, the industry segments this audience by medium and venue. Each venue represents a different distribution challenge and economic prize.

Film—Primary Markets

DOMESTIC

The American moviegoing audience has always been the most important market for a feature film. This audience is willing to pay more money to see an entertainment product than any other audience. Despite the growth of home video, the *Domestic Box Office* is still one of the greatest sources of revenue and awareness for a feature film, and as such it is widely watched by people in the industry. Americans spend over $4 billion a year at the box office.

Movie theater chains, known as *exhibitors*, rent feature films from the studios. The rental agreements typically allow for the studio to take a large percentage of the theater's gross revenues, sometimes up to ninety percent, in the first week or two of a film's release. After that, the exhibitor receives an incrementally larger share of the take, but the attendance in the later weeks usually falls off, so the theater owner gets a larger share of a smaller pie. The division of proceeds between exhibitors and studios has been a subject of acrimonious dispute for decades. However, the studios control the process. The studio pays for film production and release costs, so it takes the greater risk in the venture. The exhibitor bears substantially less risk, and as a result earns less revenue.

Exhibitors have evolved over the years. Originally, virtually all movie theaters were owned by the studios, which could dictate the films a theater would show. This *Studio System* was broken apart by an anti-trust suit in 1948, and the studios agreed to sell off their movie theaters. However, the power imbalance has remained, even though exhibitors have consolidated into powerful chains. Some theaters are still independent, but the chains and their multiplex theaters dominate the exhibition business.

FOREIGN

The international audience for American films has grown substantially in recent years. The *Foreign Box Office* revenues of a feature film now account for an important share of total revenues for a film. For example, HOME ALONE grossed over $240 million domestically, but its *worldwide gross* was over $500 million. The international market in aggregate is about as big as the domestic market. Some of the major studios operate abroad on their own. Others release their films in foreign countries through joint ventures such as United International Pictures. For small countries, the studios often rely on local distributors who book the films with exhibitors. International film releasing has always presented American studios with problems of currency fluctuation, piracy and accountability.

HOME VIDEO

Feature films produced directly for home video are a recent but growing phenomenon. The home video market is so large now that a film which can be made cheaply enough will earn a profit even if distributed only in cassette form through video retailers. The greatest numbers of made-for-video movies are in the action and horror genres. For this type of film, there is a loyal audience of measurable size that wants to rent a new title every week, and theatrical releases cannot keep pace with this demand. The tradeoff, however, is in quality. Most made-for-video films have budgets of less than $2 million, an amount that delivers little production value.

Television—Primary Markets

NETWORKS

The three principal networks—ABC, CBS and NBC—command the largest television audience, and despite recent gains by cable, the networks still maintain an enormous lead in audience size and consistency. Though the total network audience has fallen from ninety percent of the country to just above sixty percent, the next largest audience is substantially smaller. The networks are still the only service that can offer high-production-value entertainment product to their audience for free.

A television network either produces its own programming through its in-house production arm (such as NBC Productions), or licenses the rights to programs made by outside studios and producers. The network then broadcasts to a national audience, earning a profit on advertising revenues in excess of program costs. A Federal law limits the amount of programming the networks can produce by themselves, and bars them from participating in the aftermarket profits of programs it broadcasts. (This is the frequently discussed *Financial Interest And Syndication Rule*, or *FinSyn* controversy.) As a result, the networks do not own the copyright to the programs they air in prime time. They merely pay a *license fee* for the exclusive right to broadcast a program a certain number of times (usually twice) over a period of years (usually four).

The license fee usually equals about eighty percent of the production cost of the program. The balance of production costs, known as the *deficit*, is paid by the studios or production companies in return for ownership of the copyright on the program. Since the networks pay such a large portion of the costs of programming, they have a great say about its content. The network controls the selection of subjects and the development of stories. Most importantly, the network chooses which programs it will broadcast and which it will not.

Networks broadcast their programming over two types of television stations. Each network owns and operates seven stations in major markets such as New York and Los Angeles. These are the *O&O's* (for "owned and operated"), the flagship stations of each network. The network broadcasts to the rest of the country through *affiliate stations*, which are independently owned but which carry network programs. The networks pay their affiliates a nominal sum in exchange for carrying network programs. However, most affiliate income derives from a number of commercial slots in each program that the network allows the affiliate to fill with local advertising. Each network has about two hundred affiliates.

The *Fox Network* is comprised of the old Metromedia television stations, which are Fox's O&O's, and more than a hundred affiliated *UHF* (Ultra-High Frequency) stations around the country. The Fox network reaches about eighty-nine percent of the country on three or four nights a week, compared to virtual one hundred percent, seven-day, multiple-timeslot penetration by the three major networks.

FIRST RUN SYNDICATION

A television program in *First-Run Syndication* is financed and broadcast by a group of *independent stations* instead of a network. Independent television stations are those broadcast stations that are not affiliated with the three networks or with Fox. *Charles in Charge* and *The Arsenio Hall Show* are both produced for first-run syndication. In the case of Arsenio, the Paramount syndication department—the *syndicator*—arranged for independent stations in about ninety percent of the country to license and broadcast the show. In effect, each syndicated show creates its own ad-hoc network. The independent station benefits, as it gets access to new programming with which it can air in competition with the network affiliates. The syndicator benefits because it is able to produce programming without network interference. A syndicator must get a large number of stations—about ninety percent of the country—to commit to a program for it to be financially viable.

CABLE

Cable Television in the United States is made up of a large number of local cable systems, each of which serves a local community. *Operating companies* manage the system, bill subscribers, and maintain the physical lines connected to people's homes. Local government grants an operating company a monopoly to provide television over cable to subscribers in the area. The operating company then installs the cable and sells subscriptions. The government now regulates the rates that cable operators charge to customers. Operating companies that control more than one system are known as *multiple systems operators*, or *MSOs*.

The operators supply programming to their subscribers by purchasing access to satellite broadcasts from the various *cable programming services* such as The Disney Channel, CNN (Cable News Network) or HBO (Home Box Office.) Most cable operators also devote one channel to whatever programming the local people in the system want to produce. This is known as *public access*.

Cable programming services are either *pay services* or part of the *basic cable* package carried by the system operator. A cable subscriber has the option to subscribe to a pay service such as HBO for an additional charge over the system operator's base rate. Pay services finance their programming through subscriber payments. Basic cable services such as Turner Network Television do not cost the subscriber anything beyond the base rate. To finance their programing, basic cable services sell advertising time on their service.

Cable programming services offer both original and old programming for delivery over cable systems. Services such as Turner Network Television, The USA Network and HBO function as miniature movie studios, producing original feature-length movies exclusively for the cable audience. The cable programming services maintain the distribution rights to most made-for-cable films. In contrast, the television networks generally do not own the distribution rights to the films they broadcast, unless the program is produced by the network's in-house production arm.

PAY PER VIEW

Pay Per View, a system of broadcasting where individual people pay a fee to watch a show, is a burgeoning new primary market for programming. Pay Per View is still in its infancy, though it has tremendous potential as technology makes it more feasible on a large scale. Currently, Pay Per View is used mostly for special sporting events. In the future, however, as satellite dishes and two-way information systems become part of the home entertainment center, Pay Per View has the potential to replace home video as a way for people to watch movies at home. It is probable that when this advance occurs, feature films will be produced specially for a Pay Per View debut.

Aftermarkets

After a film or television program has been through its primary audience, it still has tremendous revenue potential for the distributor. Increasingly, the release of a film to the primary audience is merely a prelude to the lucrative series of *aftermarket* releases.

HOME VIDEO

Home video now accounts for a greater portion of a movie's gross revenues than its theatrical release. Starting out as a highly fragmented mosaic of mom, and-pop stores in the early eighties, the home video business is now controlled by several large distributors and chains, or retail stores such as Blockbuster Video.

The home video market has two components, rental and *sell-through*, which refers to tapes that are sold, rather than rented, to the retail customer. Home video rental and sell-through both create important sources of income for the studios. The studios sell many rental copies of cassettes to stores. In addition, a large number of consumers will buy their own personal copy of the film. In a major release such as BATMAN or E.T., the studio can sell millions of cassettes for both rental and sell-through.

The international home video market has also taken off recently as videocassette recorders spread to foreign countries. Home video is a lucrative business in some countries where broadcasting is still regulated by the government and television programming is quite dull. The audiences in those countries have a great appetite for quality movies on tape.

TELEVISION SYNDICATION

Independent television stations differentiate themselves by *counter-programming*, the practice of competing by broadcasting programs that attract a different audience from that drawn by network affiliates. For example, an independent station might broadcast a famous old movie in a timeslot where the networks are broadcasting sports or news. The audience for independent station counter-programming creates a market for old movies and series. This is the television syndication market, an important source of revenue for the studios.

The movie studios market their old movies to independent stations in packages. If you look through *Electronic Media* magazine, you will see studio advertisements for film packages aimed at program directors of independent stations. To create its package, the studio takes two or so hit films and bundles them with a dozen or so average films and some made-for-television movies.

When a studio syndicates a television series, it licenses the broadcast rights to a number of episodes at a time. For example, the series *M*A*S*H* has over two hundred episodes. An independent station can license several volumes of *M*A*S*H* episodes. Each volume has enough episodes to run five days a week for a certain number of weeks. A syndicated show that runs five days a week at the same time of day is called a *strip*. Stripping allows the independent station the ability to promote a convenient and predictable counterprogramming schedule. On Channel 38 in Boston, for example, viewers know they can see *Hogan's Heroes* at 10:30 and *M*A*S*H* at 11:00 every weekday night.

The syndication market for successful television series is enormously lucrative. A huge hit series such as *M*A*S*H*, which can run in syndication for years, will bring in tens of millions to the studio that produced it. Even a more average syndication success will bring a handsome profit to the studio. The key to syndication is to produce enough episodes to be able to sell a strip to stations. The magic number is about one hundred episodes, or five network seasons of twenty-two episodes each, though some shows are syndicated with fewer episodes.

The potential profits of syndication are what induce the production companies or studios to pay the production deficit on a network series. (Remember that the network pays about eighty percent of the production costs and the production company or studio pays the balance.) Each season, if the network renews the series and orders another twenty-two episodes, the studio gets closer to its magic hundred-episode syndication mark, where it will be able to recoup its deficit investment. When the exclusive network license agreement expires, the show is said to be *off-network*, and the studio is free to license it to independent stations. Unfortunately, the network often cancels series before they reach the magic number, and the studio loses its investment. An hour drama series that runs for three seasons before being cancelled could cost the studio $30 million, which it will have to write off completely.

Cable programming services also license old movies and television programs. Pay cable services license recent movies for high prices as part of their differentiated strategy. Basic cable services license older movies and television shows in a comparable manner to independent stations. You can watch *Spenser: For Hire* on Lifetime Television, for example.

Not all license fees for syndicated programming are paid in cash. In many instances the stations *barter* for the shows. In exchange for the licensing agreement, the stations give the studio a number of free advertising slots. The studios either resell the commercial spots to advertisers, or use them to advertise upcoming feature releases. You might see Paramount feature films being advertised during reruns of *Cheers*, which is a Paramount series. Both parties benefit from the conservation of cash. The barter market has had its ups and downs as the market for syndicated programs becomes alternately glutted or starved of off-network shows.

FOREIGN TELEVISION

Television stations around the world license American programming. You can watch *Starsky and Hutch* in France or *Dallas* in Romania. The foreign market for television shows is growing, especially as many European countries deregulate their television industries. *Satellite broadcasting* in foreign countries, where viewers receive programs with satellite dishes in their own homes, has also added to the international demand for films and television programs. Foreign licensing is a major source of revenue for television movies and hour-long action and drama series and, to a lesser extent comedy series, since comedies often do not translate well into foreign languages.

A *co-production* is a television program financed jointly by an American network and a foreign network or programming service. Co-productions arise when programming executives from two countries can agree that an idea appeals to both audiences. The advantage of co-productions is that they can raise more production funding than the regular network and studio process and can yield a higher-quality program.

INSTITUTIONAL

Educational institutions, the military, airlines and prisons all rent movies. The institutional market for films and television shows is small but significant. Since the film asset is depreciated as quickly as the law will allow, the revenue from institutional sources is virtually pure profit.

MERCHANDISING AND DERIVATIVE PRODUCTS

The studio retains the merchandising rights to a film concept in almost every case, though sometimes the rights agreement for a film will provide for profit-sharing between the studio and the rights holder. In any event, the market for merchandise and derivative products can be enormous. The merchandising frenzy surrounding BATMAN and *The Simpsons* is proof of this market's potential. Warner Bros. sold millions of BATMAN T-shirts and other paraphernalia and saw a huge profit. *The Simpsons* craze was described by toy companies as the greatest merchandising event in decades!

Besides merchandise, the studios also create derivative products based on films and television shows. GHOSTBUSTERS was a film, then a Saturday morning animated show. TEENAGE MUTANT NINJA TURTLES was a cartoon first, then a film. The ADDAMS FAMILY was a series of *New Yorker* magazine cartoons, then a television show, and now a feature film. Studios also arrange for publication of *novelizations*, or book versions of well-known films. Disney publishes comic books based on its film characters. Disney also derives much of its theme park success from the synergy between its film characters and attractions at the theme parks based on those characters.

Summary: Release Windows

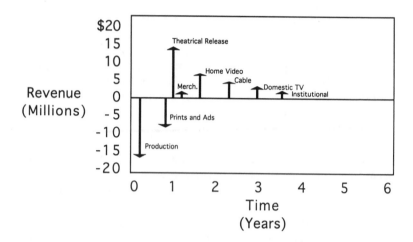

Figure 1.2   Motion Picture Cash Flow: The expenditure and revenue for a feature film.

Distributors sell access to product, exploiting the markets in order of size. The time a film spends in a specific market is called a *release window*. The film release depicted in figure 1.2 has a theatrical release, followed by a home video window starting late in the first year after the release date. The film's cable window occurs a year and a half after release. The television window begins in the second year, and so on.

Release windows must be carefully planned, because the successive releases of a film generate incrementally less revenue. As a result, the studio wants to exploit the most lucrative windows for as long as it can. Only after one market has been exploited will the studio proceed to the next, less attractive window. A studio would not put a film on television, for example, before its home video release. To do so would be to cannibalize the video sales, and the film would make less money overall.

It is often difficult to determine where the primary market ends and the aftermarket begins. One market often drives another. For example, the viability of network television depends on the health of syndication and foreign markets. If there were no foreign market for American programs, the American networks would probably not be able to bear the cost of producing the current volume of new programming. Distributors have to manage these markets in a process that presents many business challenges, especially as the market for entertainment grows global and the preeminence of the American market declines.

1.2   STUDIOS AND NETWORKS—FEEDING THE DEMAND

The enormous world market for entertainment product has created a vast and complex system of production and distribution. Three core groups of organizations, studios, networks and independents, dominate the system. However, many other players participate in the production and distribution business at various levels.

Film—Studios

Film studios exist to feed the product pipeline created by the world markets for feature films. Seven firms, Universal, Warner Bros., Sony Pictures Entertainment (made up of Columbia Pictures and TriStar), Paramount, Twentieth Century Fox, Disney and MGM-UA, dominate the production and distribution business. Collectively, they are known as the *major studios*, or *the majors*. The employees of a studio and their business dealings all revolve around the production, acquisition or distribution of product. Distribution is the studio's raison d'être.

PRODUCTION DEPARTMENT

Since production is the key to distribution, the studio employs a range of *production executives* to oversee the production of each year's releases. Production executives are layered in a Byzantine hierarchy, and the titles are too numerous to examine in detail here. However, several generic positions dominate the production side of the studio.

The *Head of Production*, or *President of Production*, is the person at the top of the production hierarchy who has the right to make the final decision to commit to financing a film, a power known as the authority to *greenlight* a film. The head of production is involved in all "big deals" the studio is making, such as producer deals, large literary acquisitions, or star casting. The head of production oversees all productions through his or her staff of production executives. The head of production is judged on the quality and commercial success of films made during his or her tenure in the position. At many studios the head of production has to make the financing decision together with the *Studio Chairman*, who is ultimately responsible to the shareholders for the financial performance of the studio as a corporation. (The highest ranking production executive is sometimes called *Chairman of the Film Group*, but he is not the chairman of the board of the corporation.)

The *Executive Vice President of Production* is the next highest position after Head of Production. This person has most of the same authority as the head of production, except that he cannot greenlight productions on his own. Executive vice presidents of production initiate big deals and oversee large projects solo. At some studios, these very senior executives run their productions like personal fiefdoms, with minimal intervention from the head of production.

At the next level down the power hierarchy, *Senior Vice Presidents of Production* and *Vice Presidents of Production* oversee the development and production of films. They report to the head of production and executive vice president(s) of production. The power of Vice Presidents varies greatly depending on the studio and the individual executive's tenure and reputation.

Creative Executives are the junior executives who help vice presidents of production supervise development and production. Typically, a feature film project at a studio will have two supervising executives, one senior and the other junior. Junior executives read scripts, write story notes, and generate cast lists and director lists.

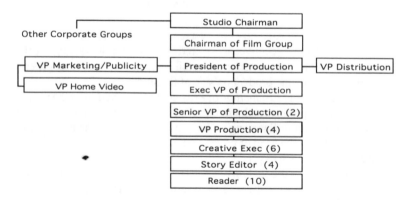

Figure 1.3   Chart of Organization for a generic studio production department

ACQUISITION, DISTRIBUTION AND OTHER DEPARTMENTS

The *Distribution Department* is in charge of releasing films in theaters. Film releasing is a complex and detailed process. For a studio to enjoy a successful run, it must release trailers months in advance, coordinate advertising at the national and local level, book the film in individual theaters and in chains, and deliver a perfect copy of the film to hundreds of theaters around the country by opening day. (Seasoned distribution executives know the seating capacity of hundreds of local theaters around the country as well as the names of the theater's managers.) As the first several weeks of a film's release go by, the distribution department decides whether to release the film in more theaters for greater revenue, or pull it back and release another film sooner than planned.

To feed the domestic theatrical product pipeline, the studio needs to release at least a dozen or so films every year. However, the unpredictable nature of film production makes it difficult for the studio to supply itself with a reliable source of releases through its own production. In one year the studio might finish twenty films, but in another year the studio will only complete six. To make up the difference, the studio acquires finished films for distribution. These films include foreign films and independently produced films. The advantage of acquisition for the studio is that they get finished films for a predetermined amount of money. Another financing entity has borne the risk of cost overruns. In many cases the studio can also decide whether it wants to acquire the film after it is finished. In a studio production, the decision to release the film is made after the company has sunk millions into the project. Acquisitions remove some of this risk.

Each studio has executives who oversee the acquisition process. These *acquisition executives* scout the world of independents and foreign filmmakers for finished and partially finished films that the studio can *pick up* for release. Many of the studio's production executives work part of the time in acquisition.

No two acquisition deals are alike, though they follow a set of generic terms. The studio pays more or less money for the film based on the film's level of completion and the territories in which it can release the film. The studio may or may not pay for *prints* (the copies of the film shipped to theaters) and *advertising*. *P&A* is the abbreviation used to describe the financing commitment of paying for *prints and advertising* in a film's release. A studio might buy the right to release a film in the US, UK and Japan, including P&A. Another distributor has paid for the right to release the film everywhere else in the world.

The film being acquired might be completely finished, or halfway through production and running out of money. In that case the studio would pay completion funds in exchange for distribution rights.

In a *negative pickup* deal, the studio makes a guarantee to an independent company that it will release the film in exchange for a set amount of money. This studio guarantee enables the independent to arrange financing for production and do the picture non-union.

The *Publicity, Advertising* and *Marketing* Departments work jointly with the distribution department in releasing films. The Publicity Department makes sure that the film and its stars get noticed by the entertainment press. They book the stars on talk shows and coordinate the awkward process of assuring the availability of stars in the pre-release promotion of a film. The advertising department creates the trailers, posters (called *one-sheets*) and logo for films. The Marketing and Advertising Departments have the critical responsibility of positioning a film for the audience. They decide, for example whether a film will be billed as a comedy or a romantic comedy. This designation will affect the success of the release. There are many examples of excellent films that were poorly promoted and flopped at the box office.

Distribution, marketing, and advertising do not work completely alone. Advertising and publicity also work extensively with outside firms to provide specialized services in graphic design and copywriting. Ideally, they work cooperatively with the production department and the studio's senior management. In fact, the departments can clash over control of projects. At issue is the "knowledge" of what the audience really wants. This is the Holy Grail of Hollywood that nobody can pinpoint exactly, but which everyone claims to have.

The studio has a department to match each aftermarket. The studio has vice presidents for home video, cable, domestic television (movie) sales, foreign distribution, and institutional distribution. Each vice president reports to the president of the studio. Their job is to sell the studio's product in their particular market to the greatest extent possible without hurting any other departments. That is, the distribution executives have to manage the release windows of Figure 1.2 carefully so that the studio realizes the maximum potential revenue from one market before it releases the product in a less profitable one.

The *Physical Production Department* is responsible for the actual, practical production of the studio's films. While each movie has its own producer who oversees the minutiae of the day-to-day production, the studio employs executives who know the ins and outs of physical production to monitor projects that are being filmed. The studio wants an overseer to watch how its money is being spent by producers. Because films are produced around the world, the studio has an even more pressing need for a knowledgeable set of eyes and ears on locations. At studios in Los Angeles that have back lots and sound stages, the Physical Production Department also manages the physical assets of the studio lot.

Film—Independents

Any production and releasing entity that is not a major studio is defined as an *independent*. Some independents characterize studios as narrow-minded, risk-averse, big corporations that only want to make sequels and movies which appeal to people's base instincts. Independents, on the other hand, supposedly value the filmmaker as an artist and are not fettered by the petty corporate constraints of the studio mentality. Such is not always the case. "Independent" is a much-abused term. The independents run the gamut from successful, well-funded mini-studios such as Morgan Creek or Imagine Films, to fly-by-night hucksters who scrape by on scams and hope.

A number of promising independents went bankrupt in the 1980s. Started by talented producers and financed by Wall Street, the defunct independents attempted to duplicate the business strategy of the majors. They produced big-budget films and distributed them in wide release. The problem was that one flop will kill a small independent attempting this strategy. The graveyard of independents is full of companies that ran out of cash to produce new films. Unlike the majors, the independents did not have the cash reserves to survive a failure, nor did they have the libraries of old titles that would provide the company with a revenue stream in hard times. Even the most successful independent of them all, Orion Pictures, which functioned at almost the full level of a major, went bankrupt in 1991.

Two independents, New Line Cinema and Miramax Films, have succeeded as mini-studios by concentrating on niche productions and controlling costs. Avoiding blockbuster thousand screen releases and excessive production budgets, these firms earn good returns on modest releases. They rarely score a megahit, but they never crash with a multi-million dollar flop.

One faction of independents that survived the 1980s engages in *rent-a-studio*, an effective strategy for production and releasing. A major independent such as Morgan Creek will finance the production of a big-budget film. They will then select a studio to release the film for them. With rent-a-studio, the independent concentrates its money and attention on producing films and avoids the large investment inherent in creating a distribution department. Unlike the independent, the studio knows the distribution business and has the people and the resources to release a film successfully. The key to being able to work in the rent-a-studio mode, however, is cash.

Most independents lack cash. After grandiose intentions have faded from the pages of the trade press, many independents hit the wall because of a fundamental law of film production: A film requires a mountain of cash in advance. In some exceptionally rare productions, everyone works for free, or for a share of film's profits. All others pay cash. For most, this means preselling the rights to distribute the film to the various markets outlined in Section 1.1. Foreign release rights are worth so much, American home video is worth something else, foreign television rights have a value, and so on. Through pre-sales, the independent can cover its production budget and earn a producer's fee or even some profits, provided there are no cost overruns.

Television—Networks

The three networks, the Fox network, independent stations, and cable all vie for a piece of the primetime television audience. Advertisers pay for access according to audience size, so the network that can deliver the largest audience to advertisers generates the most revenue. The network hierarchy functions to create the largest audience possible.

The *Entertainment Division* is the network department responsible for primetime programming. While the network as a corporation has interests in news, sports and radio, only the Entertainment Division is really considered part of the Hollywood establishment. From the perspective of the entertainment industry, the *President of the Entertainment Division*, or *Head of Programming*, is the most important person at the network. He or she makes every important programming decision. It is a position of tremendous power and influence.

Several *Senior Vice Presidents of Programming* aid the head of programming in running the network. The head of programming and the vice presidents oversee the whole process of development, pilot production and scheduling. This top management group often functions as a tightly knit team.

The *Vice President of Current Programming* supervises the scripting and production of all ongoing series. The current programming department reviews the scripts of every series before each episode is produced. The current programming department then approves the final cut of each episode before it goes on the air. Some producers have less accountability to detailed oversight if they have an established track record.

A *Vice President of Drama* and a *Vice President of Comedy* each oversee the development and production of pilots for new series in their respective areas. These development vice presidents maintain relationships with producers, writers and stars to bring the right shows to the network.

The *Vice President for Motion Pictures* oversees the development and production of all *made-for-television movies* (also known as *movies of the week*, or *MOWs*) and *mini-series*. Some networks also employ a separate *Vice President for Mini-series* who reports to the vice president of motion pictures.

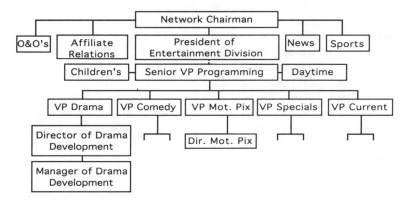

Figure 1.4   Network Primetime Organization Chart

Below the vice president level is the position of *Director*. Each department in the network's entertainment division has several directors working under the vice presidents. Directors of motion pictures, for example, have personal responsibility for a certain number of movie projects. They follow the projects from the initial presentation of the idea through script development, casting and production. Some departments employ a third level of executive, the *manager*. Managers help the directors and vice presidents supervise the development and production process.

Each network has an *in-house production* subsidiary that functions like an outside studio, except that it is owned by the same parent corporation as the entertainment division. Many industry newcomers miss the distinction between the entertainment division and the in-house production company. NBC *Entertainment* makes the programming decisions for the network. NBC *Productions* is a subsidiary company that produces some programs on the NBC schedule. NBC owns the copyright to an NBC Productions program, whereas it would not own the copyright to a program licensed from an outside studio. Both NBC Entertainment and NBC Productions are wholly owned by The National Broadcasting Company, which is owned by General Electric. Since the Federal Government regulates the amount of programming the network can produce for itself, the in-house production companies have a limited, if solid position.

The network *Publicity Department* promotes the primetime lineup through advertising and on-air promotional spots that they create. The publicity department also coordinates the promotional appearances by stars of network programs on talk shows. The publicity department of a network dances between the needs of the entertainment division, the studios, the producers, the stars and their management.

The needs of the affiliate stations are seen to by the *Head of Affiliate Relations*. This executive has the demanding job of pleasing over two hundred station managers year-round. At issue are financial affairs concerning compensation and allotments of advertising spots, as well as program subject matter. (The affiliate station has the option to *preempt* a network program and broadcast something else if it considers the program inappropriate for its audience.)

Television—Studios

The television studios are in the business of producing programs that they can then distribute. The studios function in three areas: network production, first run syndication and aftermarkets. The dominant television studios are the television divisions of the major movie studios, plus large distribution companies such as Viacom.

Television studios manage the process of development and production through an executive hierarchy that mirrors that of the networks. Each studio has executives in charge of current programming, movies, and comedy and drama development. The studios also mount their own promotional efforts on behalf of their programs. The studios maintain a stable of producers who are contractually committed to let the studio distribute their shows. However, while the studio directly oversees creation of feature films, in network television the studio has a limited creative role. The producer and network actually create the programs.

Television studios serve the first-run syndication market directly. They develop their own concepts for syndicated shows and open their doors to ideas from independent producers. The studio syndicators then take their ideas to the station buyers.

The studio has several sales groups to exploit programming which has run through its broadcast license and can be licensed to broadcasters worldwide. One concentrates on selling to domestic independent stations. Another sells to stations abroad. A third sells to basic cable. The studio tries to package its less successful series with hits to force stations to pay for a series that otherwise would not receive any attention. This practice is known as the "locomotive and freight cars" approach to sales. The hit show is the locomotive that pulls a string of shows (the freight cars) into distribution.

The market for television programs is highly susceptible to the law of supply and demand. Only a handful of hit series will be available in some years, and the studios will be able to auction them among competing stations serving the same market. At other times, the market for series will be saturated, and the studio will have a hard time selling them at all. There are a finite number of independent stations creating demand for programs, but the supply of television programs is variable, so the market alternately favors one party or the other. Equilibrium does not last for long. It depends on the network programming cycle. If a large number of network series have been running for five seasons, then they will come off the network shortly and cause the syndication market to be saturated.

Television Independents

Many companies compete in the production and distribution of television programming without studio backing. Though the major studios dominate the series business because of the financial risks of deficiting a series, dozens of small companies participate in the television movie market. The deficit investment for a movie is finite and small, so independent producers can pay their own deficits and then sell distribution rights one piece at a time. A few rich independents attempt to deficit series, but it is a rare and risky enterprise for an independent.

Major *station groups* such as Westinghouse's Group W Stations maintain independent production companies in Hollywood. A station group is a collection of independent television stations in different markets owned by the same corporate parent. Station groups often make buying decisions in concert to bring about economies in program purchasing. Station group production companies participate in both the first-run syndication and prime-time markets. The station groups want to secure a cheaper, controlled source of programming for themselves. Instead of subjecting themselves to the market forces and pressure sales tactics of the major distributors, the station groups enter the production business themselves and build their own supply of programs. Some station groups have even produced feature films.

A number of foreign television production companies and networks function as independent producers in the American market. Like the domestic station groups, the foreign firms want to secure a reliable source of programming at a price which is controllable. The foreign firms enter into co-production agreements, or simply deficit-finance wholly American productions in exchange for pre-sale to their territories. Britain's Granada Television, a studio and network, and Italy's RAI Television Network are both examples of foreign firms working in the American production business.

Corporate Sponsors

Several large corporate advertisers develop and produce their own programs. Hallmark Hall of Fame, Chrysler Showcase, AT&T Presents, General Motors Mark of Excellence Presentations, and Procter and Gamble Productions all sponsor their own movies and specials. In a typical corporate sponsorship deal, the sponsor pays for the development of the script, the costs of production, the production of commercials to be run with the program, and the airtime on the network. A sponsored show is an enormous expenditure, but direct sponsorship allows the advertiser complete control over the content of the program and exclusive advertising during the airing of the show. Given the variation in programming quality and audience attention spans, corporate sponsorship can give the advertiser greater impact for the money.

Cable Programming Services

The cable companies have divisions that function as miniature movie studios producing feature-length movies for their programming services. HBO, Showtime, TNT, The USA Network, The Disney Channel and Lifetime Television all produce original programming. They have heads of production, vice presidents of production and development executives. They take movies from concept through production, supervising the process the whole way.

Cable programming services produce their own programming as a supplement to what they can buy on the market. With their own programs, the cable companies are not vulnerable to the studio's shifting cable release windows. The cable company can control when they will have access to high-quality material, and they can gear their productions to the tastes of their particular audiences. Economically, the costs of producing a low- to medium-budget feature film are comparable to licensing a major film from a studio. If the cable company owns the program, which it often insists on doing, the cable company can give itself a limitless license agreement, while the studio license allows for only a fixed number of runs.

Cable companies that produce their own programs build a library, which they exploit in distribution to all the worldwide markets. Some higher budget cable movies are released as feature films abroad. The cable services also have home-video labels and domestic television sales departments. Cable companies also participate to a lesser degree in the financing of full-blown feature films, for which they have pre-bought the cable rights.

The Shifting Center

The United States has dominated the entertainment industry for decades, and it still does, with amazing strength and staying power. However, the rise of international markets has begun to change the way Hollywood works.

As production costs soar, the studios look to foreign markets to enhance domestic box office performance. As long as those foreign markets were tiny compared to the American market, the American moviemakers could ignore the needs and tastes of the foreign audience. Today, with up to half of a film's theatrical revenue coming from foreign release, the studios can no longer completely ignore their likes and dislikes.

The recognition of different preferences in foreign countries has had an impact on casting and subject matter. Certain stars now have global standing. Jack Nicholson or Arnold Schwarzenegger are bankable anywhere on earth. Other stars have followings in certain countries, but not others. Witness Mickey Rourke's superstardom in France. Each national audience has a distinct preference for the kinds of movies it likes to see. Japanese audiences tend to like male-oriented action and fantasy adventure films, for example. The problem is that it is difficult to make a film which is equally appealing to every major audience on earth. A studio that tries to please everyone is likely to produce a watered-down film that pleases no one.

In television, the demands of foreign audiences are equally diffi-

21

cult for American studios to address. Since the American network pays most of the production budget, they can insist on control of the content. The foreign buyers have to accept whatever the American network wants. Even in co-productions, the foreign partners have a severely limited voice regarding content. Attempts to create an international television series have failed due to differences in tastes and buying cycles. In the future, however, cost pressures will force studios to continue to explore the possibilities for dividing productions between national partners.

1.3 PRODUCERS—MAKING THE PRODUCT

It seems as if everyone you meet in Los Angeles is a producer. What is a producer, anyway? Producer is a much-used, little-understood word which has many meanings at once. While the word usually identifies a single person, "producer" can also refer to the studios that create the product. (In that sense, the Wall Street Journal refers to steel companies as "steel producers") To simplify matters, the following general working definition should suit our needs: The producer is the person who *initiates and facilitates the making of an entertainment product.*

Given the variety of producer roles and titles, it is hard to pinpoint exactly what the producer does. But that doesn't matter. A good producer does many things and handles each film differently. However, to recognize a real producer when you see one in action, you should be able to discern some of the following roles.

Creator—A true producer is a creative person. He or she constantly reads scripts, books, plays and newspapers looking for special ideas and stories. He or she is open to ideas and knows how to cultivate creativity in people. The producer is often the leading coach for a writer who is having trouble getting a story down on paper.

Synthesizer—The producer knows how to put together pieces of an idea and arrive at a whole that is greater than the sum of its parts. For example, a producer might take two mediocre scripts and a live performance act he has seen and combine them into one terrific concept for a film. Each component on its own was a loser, but the producer had the imagination to see what the synthesis of the parts would create.

Packager—The producer seeks to create a package out of different talent elements. Given a decent script, the producer looks for a star and director that will make the project appetizing to a studio.

Boss—Hard decisions float up to the producer. If a difficult creative issue has to be settled, or if someone has to be fired, the producer will usually have a major say in the matter. The producer is also an adjudicator of disputes between people in a production. If the star threatens to walk off the set unless the director is replaced, it is the producer who steps in to resolve the potentially disastrous conflict without causing anyone to lose face.

Production Overseer—Regardless of hired line producers, the producer presides over the production. The director controls the moment to moment events on the set, but the producer is responsible to the studio or network for the final product and costs. The producer tracks the progress of the film shoot every day and watches the *dailies*, which are the scenes that have been filmed the previous day. Production is, after all, where the word "producer" comes from.

Films and television programs contain a lengthy list of producers in the credits. Who are all those people, and what do they do? The industry has experienced a proliferation of producers lately. Let's examine what each type of producing title means in film and television.

The title of *Producer* in a feature film designates the prime mover of the operation. The producer of a feature is the person who put the whole deal together, optioned the script, supervised the development process, got the studio to commit, found a star and director and then supervised production. Feature film producers are usually paid a producing fee as well as some sort of profit participation based on the film's financial success.

The title of *Producer* in a television movie usually designates an experienced physical production person who is hired for a fee to oversee the actual production of the movie. This person is also called a *line producer*. In television series, there are so many different types of producers and credit scenarios that they defy easy explanation.

The equivalent of the film producer's title in television is the *Executive Producer*. The executive producer in a television production is the person who sells the idea to the network, oversees the development of the script, negotiates financing with the studio, and oversees production. On a feature film, the executive producer title is a bit more nebulous. Generally, a feature film's executive producer is someone who was important to the genesis of a film, such as a financier, but who did not have a hands-on role in creating the film. The executive producer title in features can have many other meanings, though.

The titles *Co-Producer* and *Co-Executive Producer* usually refer to an individual who made a significant contribution to the film, but for contractual reasons cannot be called a full producer. Many line producers in television insist on retaining *sole producer credit* in the production. That means that no other person can be called producer. Or the executive producer on the project feels that she deserves sole producing credit, because it was her effort that got the whole thing going. As a result, other people who work on the production must receive credits other than "producer."

Associate Producer is a title that has at least three meanings. In most cases, the associate producer is a junior member of the producing team. If a producer develops many projects, she may designate a younger staff member to run a particular project and call this person the associate producer. In physical production, the associate producer is the line producer's second in command. The precise role of the associate producer in physical production depends partly on the budget. If there is enough money to hire a production manager and production coordinator, then the associate producer's role is more narrowly defined than if there is just one producer running the entire production. The title of associate producer is also frequently conferred on financiers who back a movie.

An *Independent Producer* is a producer who functions autonomously, without reliance on a studio. Though many people describe themselves as independent producers, very few exist. The purely independent producer pays for all script development and production costs without studio support and may even arrange for domestic releasing and foreign sales. Most so-called independents are just producers without a firm studio affiliation, though any projects they produce are made with studio funds.

The challenge you face is to differentiate between real producers and phonies. Even to the untrained eye, it is apparent that there are more people claiming to be producers than there is product to be produced. First, remember that anyone—maybe even you—can get an office, phone and business card and call himself a producer. There are thousands of people like this in Los Angeles. Often, they are desperate and corrupt. They will lie and tell you that they have a deal somewhere, or that a major star has committed to a project. They are to be strenuously avoided. How can you tell if someone is for real, particularly if they are offering you a low-paying job? You have to check these people out. Look them up in a reference book such as the *Film Producers, Studios, Agents, and Casting Directors Guide (Lone Eagle Publishing)* and cross index any productions listed there with other directories such as *Leonard Maltin's Movie and Video Guide (Signet)*. Or simply ask around. The community is small enough to know who is real.

What's trickier, though, is that some people with legitimate producer titles contributed nothing to projects they cite as their "productions."

A person who makes a contribution to a film production might negotiate for a producer title and compensation, even though he or she has no knowledge of producing and has never set foot on the set. For example, in exchange for delivering the talent, a personal manager might extract a producing credit and a fee in addition to their management commission. Book authors and attorneys who represent true story rights also cash in on their control of the property to get producer titles.

Producing credits are also doled out to peripheral people who find scripts and deliver them to legitimate producers. The legitimate producer makes the studio deal and makes the movie happen, but the original person, who may contribute nothing else to the project, is called some sort of producer.

How can you tell if someone is a real producer if they have credits on real films? Personal references are the only way to ascertain the role someone played on a production, but as a newcomer, you will not have the kind of connections it takes to check someone out properly. So, in a way you are out of luck. It would not be appropriate to ask a potential employer for references in a job interview. Your instincts, too, may fail you in trying to get a reading on a producer's legitimacy. The phoniest producers are usually superb con artists, for that is how they survive. Even if you have good antennae for manure, you may still get taken in.

Producer Deals—Film

The movie studios forge alliances with film producers to guarantee themselves a steady supply of product. Some alliances are formal contracts. Others are simply long-lived relationships. The terms of these alliances depend on the stature of the producer.

In a *housekeeping deal*, the studio provides the producer an office, a telephone and sometimes a secretary. In return, the producer gives the studio *first look* at any projects she develops. If the studio passes, the producer is free to take the project elsewhere. When the producer makes a film, the studio charges the production for the costs of maintaining the housekeeping deal and recoups its investment.

Next comes the formal *first-look deal*, which is more substantial than a simple housekeeping deal. First-look deals provide for secretaries and sometimes even a development executive to work with the producer. Many film stars and directors have first look deals with studios. The studio tries to retain the loyalty of stars by allowing them to produce films of particular interest to them. First-look deals vary in complexity and expense. At the high end, the studio will pay for a large staff of assistants and executives and will offer the producer a discretionary fund to spend on options and script development.

At the top of the scheme are the *mega-deals*, which the studio offers to its best producers. Mega-deals typically involve broad promises of production commitment and autonomy for the producer. The Simpson-Bruckheimer deal at Paramount in 1989 and the pre-Columbia Guber-Peters deal at Warner Bros. are good examples of mega-deals. Paramount guaranteed Don Simpson and Jerry Bruckheimer several movies and/or a multi-million-dollar production fund, with total discretion and limited interference from the studio.

In most feature film producer deals, the producer's first-look is exc*lusive* to the studio in film only. The producer can take a television project anywhere she wants. However, in some cases the producer is exclusive in both film and television. This is known as an *overall deal*.

Producer Deals—Television

The producer deal in television is derived from the three-way partnership between the producer, studio and network. The economics of syndication reward the studio for retaining a stable of producers in order to secure an exclusive hold on their creative output. Television producer deals are structurally similar to film deals, with housekeeping arrangements, first-look deals and mega-deals. The deals can be either exclusive for television or overall deals.

A television writer-producer who is trusted by the network to produce a series is known as a *showrunner*. There are a finite number of showrunners, and it is extremely difficult for non-showrunners to produce series for the networks. As a result, the studios have to capture showrunners in exclusive contracts in order to stay in the series business. The producing deals for showrunners at studios can be very financially rewarding, with annual fees routinely reaching the million dollar mark. All the studio is buying is the possibility that the producer will sell an idea to the network, and there is no guarantee that this will happen.

Producers of television movies and miniseries receive more modest deals at the studios than series producers because the aftermarket for longform programs is limited. Depending on their volume of production, however, longform producers can sustain fairly large production organizations at the studios.

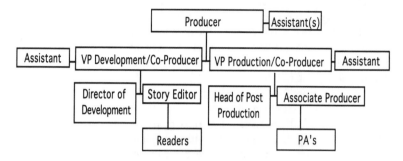

Figure 1.5   Organization Chart of a large Production Company

Figure 1.5 shows the structure of a typical large production company. The company is split between development and production functions. Each department head manages a small staff that supports the activities of the producer. The *Vice President of Development* is responsible for finding new material, which can come through the *Story Editor*, and supervising ongoing development, which is handled jointly with the *Director of Development*. The production department shepherds each movie through budgeting, shooting and post-production. Some companies also have an *Office Manager* who administers the whole organization.

1.4   AGENCIES—REPRESENTING THE CREATIVE TALENT

Much of the recent hype about talent agencies has obscured what these companies actually do. A talent agency is essentially an employment agency for actors, directors and writers. *SPY Magazine* articles and glamour aside, a talent agency is in the business of securing employment for its clients. For every dollar earned by a client, the agency receives a commission. It's as simple as that.

The word *agent* describes someone who acts in business on behalf of another. The economic interests of the agent and the client are linked, so the agent has an incentive to represent the interests of the client as aggressively as possible. For this reason, agents have taken the initiative in recent years in forming revolutionary deals for their clients, ranging from lucrative gross revenue participation to representation in international corporate acquisitions such as the Sony-Columbia deal.

The recent public attention focused on talent agents has emphasized their growing power in the industry and their great financial success. Why are they so successful? In some senses, the agencies stepped into the power vacuum that was created by the demise of the studio system. Astute agents realized that the key ingredient to successful product was the talent. By restricting access to talent, the agencies could increase the power and the income of their star clients.

At a more fundamental level, however, the agencies are run more like normal businesses than other entertainment companies. The agency can measure individual performance against goals, share information effectively, and set targets for people much like a regular industrial company. As a result, the agencies can pursue clear-cut business strategies and reap financial rewards. By comparisons, the studios are haphazard business entities.

When an agent books a client for an assignment, the agent invoices the customer for the client's services. The agency then deducts a commission and forwards the remaining money to the client. When an agency controls the key talent elements in a deal, for example the writer, director and star actor, then the agency charges a *packaging commission* to the customer. From the agent's perspective, the agency has constructed a "package" of talent, saving the studio the time and energy it would take to do the same. From the studio perspective, the package is like blackmail. Either they buy it or they lose the access to all the talent elements. Since the packaging commission is often a percentage of the total budget of a production, packaging deals can be extraordinarily lucrative for the agency.

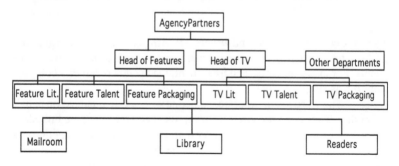

Figure 1.6   Agency Organization Structure

There are three basic types of agent: *Literary agents* specialize in representing writers and authors; *Talent agents* represent directors and actors; *Packaging agents* specialize in arranging packages based on current projects. Packaging agents tend to be the synthesizers and integrators.

Though highly simplified, Figure 1.6 shows an agency structure, split between film and television, with a full complement of literary, talent, and packaging agents in each department. The department heads might be partners in the agency, as well as specialists in an area such as feature film talent. Some high level agents do a little of everything, since their primary business is the manipulation of power and influence.

Agent jobs are specialized within the agency. At the lower level are *covering agents*, who represent few clients of their own. Instead, they canvass a specific sector of the industry relentlessly in search of work opportunities for their agency's clients. Any dealings with a producer or studio should flow through the covering agent, though some executives insist on dealing only with the top agents directly. Virtually all agents have some coverage assignment, but the senior agents tend to emphasize their own clients' needs—they are the *principal agent* for that client.

Agents work under a great deal of pressure. An agent must find talented, fresh new clients to sign. Then, he must book these clients to assure that they will be happy and make an income. If he does not devote enough time to booking a client, the client may leave the agency. As the client becomes more popular, he may feel the need to find a higher level agent, so the agent faces the pressure of growing with his clients or losing them. It is a delicate balancing act that places a great deal of stress on the individual.

Three large agencies dominate the industry. They are Creative Artists Agency (CAA), International Creative Management (ICM), and The William Morris Agency. Through their large size and influential client lists they can offer better representation to talent and more big-name package deals to producers than smaller agencies. These three agencies dominate the packaging business because they control so many of the key elements of a package deal.

After the big three, a number of smaller but powerful agencies predominate. Metropolitan, Agency for the Performing Arts (APA) and United Talent, among others, are all smaller than the big three but each represents impressive star talent and plays a major role in shaping deals in the industry. These agencies often hold one piece of a package, such as a big name director or actor. By cooperating with the larger agencies or with each other, the smaller agencies can combine their clients for a package and split the fee.

Some agencies only represent writers. These are known as *literary agencies*. Most literary agencies are small, with a handful of agents and a client list of perhaps a hundred or so writers. Literary agencies often succeed where larger agencies fail because they are focused exclusively on the needs of the writer.

Theatrical agencies only represent actors. The client mix for a theatrical agency might include a large number of commercial actors, character actors and perhaps a few star-level actors. Like the literary agency, the theatrical agency succeeds because it is more focused on the needs of the individual actor than the larger agencies. Theatrical agencies often build their clients by promoting them through commercials, bit parts and finally into larger roles. Child stars often come from theatrical agencies. The problem for a theatrical agency, however, is that once an actor reaches a certain level, there is a great temptation for him to defect to a large agency that can package him with other talent.

Book agencies represent authors of books. The publishing industry refers to book agencies as "literary agencies," but since that expression has a specific meaning in the entertainment business, we use the term "book agency" to distinguish them from agencies that represent screenwriters. Almost all significant book agencies are small companies based in New York. Some are as small as one person alone in an office, but such appearances can be deceiving. A few of these tiny companies represent some of the greatest living and dead authors in the world. Yes, dead. Book agents can continue to make money for the estate of deceased authors by selling rights to their works.

Book agencies make money by selling various publishing rights to their clients' works. For example, a book agent might sell the hardcover rights to a book to one publisher, paperback rights to another, and German translation rights to a third. The author's contract with the book agent usually allows for them to represent film rights to their work as well. Since a film will invariably increase sales of a book, the book agents aggressively try to sell film rights. The larger book agencies have a person who specializes in film rights sales.

Other agencies concentrate on technical specialties or specific performance categories. There are agencies for cinematographers, animation writers, composers, comedians and art directors. Like the literary agencies, these specialized firms know the market for the clients' services, and they know how to keep a particular set of clients happy.

Any small agency is known as a *boutique agency*. Most boutiques

are owned by former agents from the large agencies who struck out on their own. Some boutiques represent big-name talent. There is little correlation between the size of the agency and the prestige of its clientele, or the range of services it offers. Some boutiques represent actors, authors, performers, screenwriters and directors. The key success factor is the reputation of the principal agent. The success of the boutiques underscores the fact that representation is a personal business and size is often a disadvantage. Loyalty, too, plays a great role in keeping the big agencies from destroying the boutiques. Many actors and directors are happy with the handling they have received from the agents who signed them when they were young and built their careers.

Small agencies have adapted to the concentration of power in the large agencies by forming various permanent and temporary alliances. Many influential book agencies, for example have forged reciprocal agreements with large packaging agencies to sell the film rights to their books. For example, a book agent in New York may appoint the literary department of CAA to sell the film rights to a bestseller. That way, the New York book agent is guaranteed a good deal, better perhaps than she could have gotten on her own, and CAA is guaranteed a hot book around which to create a package. The incentive for the large agency is to be involved in the formation of a film project at an early stage. That way, the agency can demand a package commission because they "created the project."

Personal management firms play a related, though different, role in the representation process than talent agencies. Many artists hire personal managers in addition to agents to further their careers. Part of the manager's job is to take care of the business details of the client's life. This can include money management and other practical necessities which the client may not have the time or the inclination to understand. The manager is also usually a long-term strategist and advisor to the client. Manager-client relationships tend to be more personal and permanent than agent-client relationships. Indeed, it is often the manager who selects and hires the agent. When potential projects are sent to the client, it is often the manager who plays the key role in making the decision.

Law firms play also an increasingly important role in the representation of talent. This trend stems from several important developments in the industry. First, lawyers have taken over many vital functions at the studios, and lawyers tend to deal best with their own kind. Second, the deals are becoming more complex, so lawyers are better able to negotiate them than agents who are not lawyers.

Lawyers can also be cheaper than agents since they bill by the hour instead of taking a commission on the whole talent fee. Even if a lawyer takes a percentage of the fee like an agent, the percentage might be lower than an agent's. Typically, a lawyer will take five per cent versus an agent's ten per cent or a manager's fifteen per cent.

Business Affairs and Legal

Business Affairs refers to lawyers who work for the networks, studios, and producers. The Business Affairs department negotiates the contracts between each element of the entertainment industry in the chain of production from origination of the idea to the final audience. Every major entertainment industry firm has a business affairs department staffed with lawyers and paralegals. Their responsibility is to assure that the deals made by the company are in the best interests of the company. Then Business Affairs sees to it that the agreements are properly enforced.

Business Affairs attorneys will typically oversee negotiations between producers and agents in the hiring of talent or the acquisition of literary properties. They make the deals between the studio and producers. In many cases they also negotiate distribution contracts.

Business Affairs attorneys enjoy varying degrees of discretion in their negotiations. Sometimes, the studio will allow them a lot of latitude to make a deal as they see fit. Other times, Business Affairs will enter a negotiation which has already begun and redraw the terms to fit with studio's agenda. Conflicts arise at times like these because producers and executives often make promises they can't keep.

Chapter 2
Getting the Job

2.0   PAIN AND SUFFERING

"Getting your first job in the business may be the hardest thing you do. It is horrible, and frustrating and full of rejection... It creates vast reservoirs of insecurity."—**Chip Diggins, Vice President, Production, Hollywood Pictures**

If you are like most people, you will suffer through an agonizing search before getting your all-important first job in the movie business. Not all job seekers suffer equally, however. The least prepared people suffer most. The solution is to prepare yourself thoroughly for your job search before you begin it. That is what this chapter is about. The better you know the business, yourself, and the paths you can follow, the less pain and suffering you will have to endure.

2.1   PATHWAYS

Everyone has an ultimate destination in the business. They want to be in the director's chair, the agent's office, or the producer's Winnebago. If you do not have an objective in mind, you will after you have conducted a self-assessment and a round of informational interviews, which are described below. However, you may still have trouble answering the question, "How will I achieve my goal?"

The entry-level job is merely the first step on a path which you should think through in advance. If you haven't thought through a career path in advance, you run the risk of wandering blindly. Of course, your planned career path will change many times even before you arrive at your first job. However, you should always have a path in mind. The entertainment industry is complex and frenetic. If you are not organized about what you want to accomplish, it is easy to get lost in the confusion of the business and waste time.

The Two Essential Tracks

There are many paths to success in the entertainment industry. No two people have the same story of how they got to their current position. As you listen to people's anecdotes of their career paths, though, you will discern two broad patterns—the *Production Track* and the *Development Track*. The production and development tracks encompass hundreds of separate career paths. You can place almost anyone you meet in one track or the other.

The production track trains people in the craft of physical movie production. People on the production track learn about every aspect of physical production, from set construction to sound mixing. If you want to be a cinematographer, editor, production manager, line producer or even a director, then the production track is probably for you.

The typical entry point for a person on the production track is a *Production Assistant,* or *PA* position. A PA's responsibilities might include running errands on the set, taking film to the lab, cordoning off parking spaces, and a host of other glamorous tasks. In a PA position, one learns the nuts and bolts of physical production by observing the filming of a movie. In addition, the PA quickly learns the protocol and language of the set.

People who know which technical specialty they want to perform can go directly into specialized entry-level positions. For example, one can be a camera PA, or a costume assistant. The initial responsibilities are similar to a general PA's, however. People who want to be producers or production managers tend to do general PA work in the beginning.

Aside from such critical tasks as fetching bottled mineral water for the director, PAs serve as a sort of cannon fodder for a production. In the hierarchy of egos, they are the ones who will do anything, perform any task deemed unworthy by people further up the food chain. In one sense, PA's exist so that everyone else can say, "Thank God I'm not a PA anymore."

A PA position can be a superb learning experience, especially on a low-budget or non-union production. The fewer professional people there are on a set, the greater the responsibilities of the PA. On a low-budget shoot, a PA might get to help light a scene, decorate a set, hold a microphone boom, or pull focus on the camera. All of this contributes to a growing knowledge of the complete production process.

The production track consists of a long succession of short-term freelance jobs. As such, it presents frequent opportunities for promotion. As they come off one shoot and apply for new jobs, PAs can ask for increased responsibility and pay. As they figure out what they really want to do, PAs begin to focus on one specific area in which to build a set of skills and a reputation. Substandard performance is not tolerated, so production track people tend to be very serious about their specialties. One does not dabble in cinematography, for example. The end result is a fairly strict system of separate career tracks which are difficult to escape. The person who chooses to concentrate on cinematography after a period as a PA would have trouble switching to another production specialty, or the development track, without sacrificing prestige and salary. Union affiliations make such transitions even more difficult.

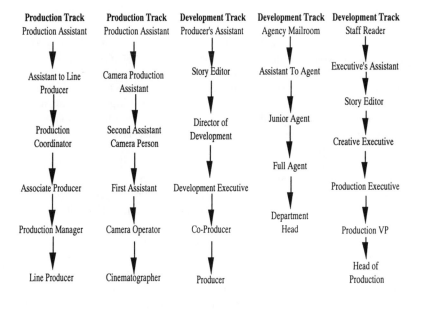

Figure Figure 2.1   Five typical career paths

Figure 2.1 shows simplified pathways for some of the major careers. Everyone's individual path will look slightly different, but most people follow the type of progression shown in the chart. In reality, people switch around, so their paths are never quite so linear. The time frame for each path differs as well. The time elapsed between the mailroom and the position of full agent might be as little as a year, though two or three years is the norm. The process of becoming a producer can take five years, and often takes more.

The development track covers every aspect of getting a film ready for production. This includes story development, talent representation, and deal-making. The development track is considered the power track in the entertainment industry. Most major producers, agents and studio executives have emerged from a career in the development track, because the deal is more integral to getting a film produced than the craft of production. That does not make the development track better than the production track. It simply caters to a different set of needs. The important thing is to find a track that is right for you.

Development teaches you story selection, screenwriting supervision, deal-making, and the art of politics. One can argue for or against the preeminent role of development in the industry, but it is a fact of life nonetheless. The process of writing a script, selling it to a studio, hiring a director and casting can take years of intense maneuvering. A huge apparatus supports the process, and for better or worse, it remains the seat of power in the industry. After all the politics and heartbreak have taken place, the production people are hired to shoot the movie.

Since the development track is more diverse than the production track, there are more distinct entry-level opportunities than there are in production. Each entry-level position teaches a similar range of knowledge, but the various jobs demand different backgrounds and personalities. The one you choose will depend on who you are.

Working for a busy producer or production executive will give you a broad exposure to development, casting, directors and production. In addition to personal care and maintenance of the producer, these jobs emphasize development work, which requires a lot of reading, writing, and discussion of ideas. A typical assistant in this category might work sixty to seventy hours per week. A stint as an assistant to a producer will prepare you to become a story editor or creative executive. Most of this book deals with working as an assistant to a producer or executive, so I will not go into too much detail at this point.

Agencies offer entry-level positions to people who want to become agents or who just want gain basic industry knowledge. People who really want to make movies usually leave agencies because agent work, though exciting, misses the actual production of the film. However, agencies provide excellent entry-level experience and teach a broad range of industry skills. And if you can survive the rigorous agency training, you will be regarded as a competent person.

For people who are serious about becoming agents, most agencies hire only at mailroom level. Even if you have a graduate degree, you will probably find yourself in the mailroom. Besides being a calculated humiliation to force you into agency culture, the mailroom is supposed to instill a deep understanding of the workings of the agency beginning at the lowest level. After all, the essential ingredient of success for an agent, knowing who's who in town, begins by typing labels in the mailroom. You will also photocopy extensively, read an enormous number of scripts, and drive around town delivering packages to clients in *dispatch*.

Smaller agencies don't insist on hiring into the mailroom, and some larger agencies hire people directly as assistants to agents. However, the people who are hired directly as assistants without the ritual mailroom assignment may not be on the *agent track*. These *agent trainees* on the track are the priority candidates for promotion. In most cases, once you are hired at an agency, you become part of a pecking order, and promotion is normally based on seniority. Some agencies make no promises about promotion, and will promote newer assistants over more senior people.

After the mailroom experience, you get promoted to be an assistant to an agent. This is known as *getting on a desk*. Your performance as an assistant will determine if and when you will be made into an agent. As an agent's assistant, you learn the mechanics of dealmaking by helping your boss do his job. Duties include correspondence, reading, overseeing client's booking calendars and tracking deal progression.

An agent's assistant might work seventy-five to one hundred hours per week. Unless you have a burning desire to be an agent, you might not feel the sacrifice is justified. Some agents will only hire assistants who want to be agents because only someone who is passionate about becoming an agent will make the effort to do the job properly.

Some people get their start working as assistant to a director or star. Many directors and stars have their own first-look production companies at the studios. They employ assistants and even development executives, depending on the magnitude of their deal. Working for a director or star presents a mixed opportunity as an entry-level job. One advantage of working closely with important people is that you develop a relationship with them, and you will be able to use that access later on in your career. As an assistant to a star or director, you will probably have more close contact with top agents and executives than you would working for a producer or executive. Unfortunately, directors and stars normally work on a narrower range of projects than a producer or executive, so you shortchange yourself in terms of overall education. Then if the star or director gets a job, they may disappear for months, and all activity will cease.

Relegation to purely personal servitude is another risk of working for a star or director. Karina Downs, a college graduate who now works as an assistant to a studio production executive, had an experience early in her career which we can all hope to avoid.

> "I was somebody's personal assistant... working in her house. This woman was renovating her house in Beverly Hills. She bought this house for zillions of dollars and they're renovating it for another zillion dollars. I had to sit in this place in hundred degree weather with no air conditioning and she's a chain smoker and I'm very allergic. And she's blowing smoke in my face all the time. I had to get her dog cleaned... I had to buy Baccarat crystal."

Most of us have done personal assisting because it was part of a larger learning experience. However, Karina learned nothing working for this woman, so she eventually quit.

A full-time *script reader*, or *staff reader* position is another entry level job on the development track. Producers, studios, networks and agencies all employ a staff of script readers. Reading jobs provide extensive experience in story analysis and the writing of coverage. Many production executives and producers started out as readers. However, a reading job offers limited learning about the production of films. The people who have risen out of reading jobs have usually had to learn about the rest of the business independently.

Whatever track you choose, it always pays to cultivate an understanding of the track you are *not* pursuing. If you plan to become a studio executive, then a working knowledge of physical production will help you as you progress. Having a sensitivity to the realities of production will help you in budgeting and the hiring of directors, for example. Conversely, an understanding of development will help on the production track. Knowing the politics behind a production rewrite, for example, will be of great use to you in a production career. If your chosen track is your major, then you owe it to yourself to minor in the alternate track and develop a workable dual knowledge. Almost every major figure in the industry has wisdom in the domains of both development and production.

Entry Points and Flexible Paths

You may be worried that you will choose the wrong first job and jeopardize your future prospects. The concern over point of entry is justified, because the first job is a unique moment, a chance to prove yourself. However, the exact position is far less important than the quality of the experience. For example, if you want to work in feature films but you can only find work in an agency mailroom, that in itself is not a problem. If the learning opportunity is good at the agency, take it. A good learning experience will prepare you to move into the area you want to explore. Taking the wrong job in the right field can be a costly mistake.

To further alleviate anxiety about picking the wrong starting place, let's examine the difference between flexible and inflexible positions. Most of the entry-level jobs described above are flexible. You can always shift over to another sphere of the industry during the initial period. Many people decide that they want to become development assistants even though they started in production. Numerous agent trainees decide they want to work in production or development instead of pursuing the agency track.

An inflexible position, on the other hand, is a job from which it is difficult to switch to another path. Assistant positions in business affairs, finance, accounting, or general corporate staff tend to be inflexible, as are entry-level jobs in marketing and publicity. Of course, anyone can attempt to change jobs, but the consequences can be daunting if you are on an inflexible track.

Flexible tracks tend to have readily transferable skills. If you have been trained as an assistant to an agent, you can use most of the same knowledge in working for a studio executive. If you have worked as an assistant to a publicity executive, you will have very specialized knowledge, which would not be of much use to a production executive. As a result, you would probably have to take a pay cut in order to make the change.

A flexible career path will allow you to learn as much as you can, and refine your ultimate goal as you progress. However, all career paths become less and less flexible as time goes on. Once you have achieved competence in one area and are getting paid well for it, you may be reluctant to start over as an assistant in another area, even if you don't enjoy what you are doing.

Mentors

Because it is easier to see other people's paths than your own, the overriding goal of your job search should be to find a *mentor* in the business. The word means "trusted counselor, tutor and coach." Mentors are usually older people who have a successful career in the industry. They take an interest in you, teach you the business, and and guide you along your personal pathway. Not everyone is lucky enough to find a mentor, but most successful people can identify a person who had a significant impact on their early development in the business. Your mentor need not be your boss. He or she can be someone you met in an informational interview, or a contact you made in your job. What you will find is that many older people enjoy sharing their knowledge with young people who take an interest.

2.2   SELF-ASSESSMENT

Self-assessment is the process of examining your own needs and abilities in order to find a career path that fits you well. Self-assessment requires a hard look at yourself and an honest evaluation of your strengths and weaknesses. It is one of the most difficult things to do, but also one of the most important.

The objective of self assessment is to be able to answer the persistent question, "Where do you want to be in five years?" honestly, even though you know your answer will change over time. You must be able to articulate a specific goal for yourself in the industry. If you are not comfortable with a goal for yourself, then you have not been introspective enough. A self-assessment exercise, as discussed below, will help you discover the career path that's right for you. That path may be different from what you expect it to be.

Self Assessment Questions

Try to answer the following questions in an attempt to establish your goal in the industry, and the suitability of that goal, given who you are as a person:

1) *How would you evaluate your personality?*
Do you get angry easily? Are you patient? Do you always need to

have the last word in an argument? How well do you handle stress? Different career paths reward different personality types. If you are extroverted, aggressive, enjoy politics and manipulation, you would make a good agent or producer. If you are more introverted and derive satisfaction from the creative process, you might be better suited to story development or production.

If you have trouble gauging your own personality, ask your friends for help. Ask them to rate your aggressiveness, desire to sell, comfort with people, and ability to speak in public. If they are good friends, they will be honest with you. If their assessment of you is different from your own, examine the discrepancies. The distance between your self-image and the way others see you will indicate how close you are to finding an appropriate career path.

2) *Do you have immediate goals in your personal life, or family responsibilities?*

Entry-level jobs in entertainment generally do not pay well, and they demand extreme commitments of time and emotional energy. A serious conflict between your personal life and your career path could do significant damage to one or both of them. Cathy Stone, a successful agent, asks potential assistants probing questions about their lifestyle goals. "They have to work like I work," says Stone. "I work like an animal. If they have family or other responsibilities, I try to be up front about how this job will affect them."

If you have serious goals in your personal life, and you cannot compromise them at all, you have two options. You can look for the entry-level jobs which do not make extreme demands on your time. If you take such a job, you will pay a price of diminished education. A reading job or a position with a star or director might offer reasonable hours. Agency jobs would be out of the question.

3) *What are your income and lifestyle needs?*

Most assistants gear their lifestyle to accommodate a low income level for a period of several years. If your needs are too great, it may be impossible to get the necessary entry-level experience. For example, a recent MBA had to decline a good entry-level job offer because the $20,000 salary would not cover her $60,000 in student loans. Most assistants make a sacrifice in lifestyle early on because they believe that for most people in the business, the money comes eventually.

4) *What is your educational background?*

Your area of study can enhance your suitability for certain paths and specific jobs. If you were a literature major, for example, you will have an advantage in some development circles. If you went to film school, you will have a set of technical skills which will help you work in production. Film school can teach you the rudimentary aesthetic sensibilities needed to become a producer. However, finding a perfect match between education and career is not always necessary. Passion and an interest in learning are much more important than a specialized background.

Examine the experience you had in school, as well as the courses you took. Did your education teach you anything about what you do or do not like? If you hated being a literature major, then working in development might be a mistake.

5) *What is attracting you to the entertainment industry?*

Are you fascinated by business and moneymaking, or is it the the allure of Hollywood glamour which is drawing you to the West Coast? Do you have a love of storytelling? A passion for making things? A love of power? A cerebral interest in academic theories of visual expression? Get at the core of your interest in the business. This is a much deeper question than, "*What* do you want to do?" This is, "*Why* do you want to do it?"

We all tend to gravitate toward what we enjoy, and we also perform better at tasks we like. Picking a career path which seems like "the thing to do," as opposed to one which "feels right," can be a catastrophic mistake. People who succeed as development executives are people who love to work with stories and writers. If you don't like stories, you will never be as good at development as someone who does. To discover which career path will feel right, you will have to examine your attitudes about the movies.

Beware of motivations which are unrealistic or egotistical. Is your passion for working in the industry really a desire to "cure" Hollywood of its aesthetic malaise? If that is your true ambition, maybe you should think twice before delving into the world of commercial filmmaking. If you share such a grandiose personal vision with people, they might dismiss you as an intellectual who has contempt for commercial film.

6) *What do you do well?*

Make a list of activities you perform well, ranked by ability. Then make a list of activities you enjoy doing, ranked in order of preference. Think hard, and include sports and hobbies. Small activities which you might not consider important could be relevant. Do the two lists look alike? If not, why?

7) *How are your basic skills?*

Can you read and write swiftly? Can you type and use a word processor? Do you drive? Do you speak well on the phone, even with strangers? If your answer to any of these was "no" or "sort of," then you need to address your weaknesses in these basic skills before you can hope to perform an assistant's job.

8) *How would you react to the following typical entry-level work situations?*

a) It's your sister's birthday and you promised to take her out to dinner. You haven't seen her in a year and she's only in town for one more day. At seven P.M. your boss hands you two scripts and explains that he needs coverage on both of them by nine the next morning. What do you say?

b) You've been sitting for twelve hours in a windowless, fluorescent-lit space with a humming computer and a phone that rings every thirty seconds. You didn't get to take lunch. You are in a vile mood. An executive starts to give you a hard time about something that was not your fault. He's really just using you as a scapegoat. He criticizes you and threatens to get you in trouble. Would you talk back?

c) You read a script and like it. You describe the story to your boss and state that you think it would make a fine movie. He cracks up laughing and tells you it's the worst idea he's ever heard. How would you respond?

d) You take lunch orders for a meeting of six executives. The restaurant gets the order wrong and, in front of six people, you are subjected to a humiliating tirade concerning your lack of brains. Would you say anything?

There are no right or wrong responses to these scenarios, but your responses can identify your suitability for certain kinds of entry-level work. In Question A, if you would have refused to read the scripts for your boss, then you would not want to take an intense job, such as an agency position. Most assistants would not have made plans on a work night in the first place. However, you have a right as a person to maintain some personal life, and no reasonable boss will deny you that. Questions B, C and D deal with patience and self-control. The entry level allows little room for egos. If you felt a forceful urge to strike back in these three questions, you should assess your reserves of inner strength. The compulsion to talk back will harm you. Nobody likes a complete doormat, either. The question is, do you have the self-control to pick your battles carefully?

9) *Do you have a desire to learn?*
You may understand that you need to learn about the industry before you can excel in it, but do you have a passion for learning? Will your desire to learn make you enjoy working long hours?

How did you fare on these questions? If the whole experience makes you a little uncomfortable, that's good. It pays to dig deeply into what is drawing you to the movie business and explore what it is that you do well and enjoy.

There is no organized way to interpret the answers to these questions. Inconsistencies, though, will indicate areas where you have to be more introspective. For example, if you value your personal life and require a certain income, yet you also identify yourself with the professional profile of an agent, then you must acknowledge that you will have to make a tradeoff in the short term. You cannot have a personal life and a good income and be an agent trainee. Can you put off your needs for two or three years until you reach a position where your goals are attainable? If you can't wait, is there some other job you might want to do?

2.3   INFORMATIONAL INTERVIEWS

Now that you possess a career goal and a probable path, you can venture out into the world and seek advice from established people in a round of *informational interviews*. Your objectives in an informational interview are to learn more about the industry and your chosen path, make a good impression on the person who meets with you and, with luck, gain further introductions, or even job leads. An informational interview is not a job interview. It is inappropriate to ask for a job when you have come into someone's office on the pretext of seeking advice.

List every single contact you have in the industry as a first step. Be exhaustive. Include family friends, college alumni, friends and relatives. You don't have to know someone personally to put them on your list. Some colleges, for example, have alumni who offer to speak to any student who writes to them. (More on letter writing in Section 2.4.)

Some people prospect for job interviews through mass mailings and *cold calls*. (A cold call is a phone call to a person you have never met.)

In the majority of cases, cold calling is a waste of time because your calls will seldom be returned and you will have to describe your credentials over the phone. Mass mailings can work, but not with form letters. Executives generally don't interview strangers unless the candidate has written an extraordinary letter. You will have to take the time write a customized letter to each executive, which defeats the idea of a mass mailing.

Rank the list starting with the people who have the least stature in the industry. You will begin with the most junior people and work your way up. Save the big guns for when you have a better idea of what you want to do. Your presentation will also improve as you practice in meetings with less influential people. When you finally meet with an important person, you will want to make the best impression possible.

The informational interview process can take a long time. By the time phone calls are returned and meetings scheduled, a month or two can go by. As each interviewer refers you to more industry people, another month passes. Once an initial contact is made, you should get in to see almost everyone, but you have to be patient.

In the informational interview itself, you want to listen and learn, and make a good impression so you will be referred to a job interview. Ask the interviewer how he got his current job, and listen carefully to his story. Does his career path match what you would have expected based on his background and goals? You can learn a lot about the flexible nature of career paths by talking to people.

Most people will want to help you, but you have to tell them how. This is where the goal derived from the self-assessment process becomes vital. If an interviewer asks you what you want to do in the industry and you answer "I don't know," you are letting him down. He wants to help you, but by being vague, you are denying him the chance. If you disappoint someone, he will write you off.

If you make a positive impression and put forth a plausible goal for yourself, your interviewer may refer you to someone else. Your contact list grows, and you enter a phase of interviewing which can lead to a job offer. If you feel that you've made a good impression, ask the interviewer if she can recommend you to anyone. It never hurts to ask.

After you have completed the initial round of informational interviews with lower-level people, you can undertake a second self-assessment and refine your goal. Does your original goal still seem attainable and suitable for you? Have the people you met seem like the kind you would want to work with? If not, what is it that bothers you? One friend of mine met with a powerful talent agent and commented afterward, "He was very intelligent and smooth-talking. Kind of like, you know, Satan." This person decided not to become an agent.

You are now ready for your second round of informational interviews. You have sharpened your interviewing skills and discussed the industry enough to refine your goals. It is time to impress an industry player. When you meet with an important person in an informational interview, you will only have about fifteen minutes in which to learn something from them, make a good impression, and try for a referral. You have to know your material to accomplish such a challenging task, which is why I recommend waiting to see these people.

The value of meeting with an important person is that they can make things happen for you. They can pick up the phone and get you an appointment with another important person. Something which would take months of effort by you takes them thirty seconds. And, since major figures in the industry deal in hyperbole and "hot" properties, you can, for a brief instant, become a prized commodity.

Your informational interviewers wil lead you to a job opening if you follow up with them. They will not help you unless you take the initiative and communicate with them, but you have to judge the appropriate level of follow-up. There is an art to checking in with people. You don't want to be a *nudge,* or put pressure on anyone. Begin with a letter thanking them for their time and continue with the occasional phone call to touch base.

The intensity of follow-up will depend on your relationship with the interviewer. If he or she is about the same age as you, and you have a good rapport, you can call them frequently and ask their advice on different situations. A major person in the industry must be handled with great care. If you bug the people in his office, you can become a non-person. However, if you call in once a month and treat everyone you speak to politely and never ask for anything point-blank, you might see some results.

The people you meet in informational interviews are your first set of industry contacts. By definition, they will be your oldest friends in the business, and the informational interview is the first step in a long relationship. With this long view in mind, you should treat your relationships with these people sensitively.

2.4   RESUMÉS AND COVER LETTERS

A typical studio executive might receive thirty cover letters and resumés a month. Of these candidates, he will meet with perhaps only one person, if any. To get a good informational interview, you have to be the one person in thirty. When a real job opening is publicized, you have to be the one chosen out of hundreds of letters.

Dozens of books can instruct you on the best way to prepare a resumé and cover letter. These books give you the standard formats and protocols to use in letters and resumés. That is your starting point, but you will have to do a lot better than the "ideal" described in the books. If you emulate the model letters and resumés described in the books too closely, you will blend in with the crowd and get overlooked. "I'm suspect of anything [in a letter] that looks too conformist," says Chip Diggins. "I want the person who walks into my office to offer something that no other person will offer, because that's what it's going to take to get movies made."

To be the one person who gets invited to an interview, you have to craft a letter which stands out without being obnoxious. Try to express something unique about yourself. Diggins looks for "...something that interests me, and nothing that turns me off...There's someone I'm going to meet who just directed a Strindberg play. That interests me."

What's a turnoff to Diggins? The expression "I will call to arrange a meeting" is especially irksome. "I have no problem with arrogant people. I just don't want them to be arrogant about my time." Most corporate letter-writing books encourage you to be positive and confident enough to expect a meeting to be arranged. That does not fly in the entertainment business. Diggins much prefers for a person writing to him to say something like "I understand that you may not have the time, but I just wanted you to have this resumé in front of you." Humility is the key.

Michael Barnathan, Senior Vice President of Production at Largo Entertainment, looks for passion in a letter.

> "I think passion is important. If you can convey passion in a letter, it reminds me of myself when I was looking for a job, which at the time seemed terribly pointless. Partially out of boredom, but partially out of trying to stand out, I would send passionate letters. First of all, I was passionate about what I wanted to do and I thought, if I could convey that, some people would be turned off by it, but there would be somebody out there who would respond to it. I did it once with Ray

> Stark. I wrote Ray Stark and...offered myself up
> for minimum wage. I said I would work for
> nothing, and that I was frustrated, and that I
> wanted to get into the business. I just went on
> and on. I got a call from his vice president
> ...They read my script...and...tried to help me
> get an agent. It was something, because the
> letter was a little bit different. I think it's impor-
> tant, because there are so many people out
> there looking for the same job."

In your quest to be interesting, you have to resist the temptation to be too cute. One job seeker wrote a letter to our company which began with the following sentence: "Youse guys is lookin' for some good guys to do a job for youse? Yeah? I'm your man." That was all we read. The letter went directly into the trash.

Figure 2.2 is a sample cover letter requesting an informational interview. Joe Wannabee first specifies that Tom Goldstein has referred him to Joe Smith. Without this information, Joe Wannabee's chances of getting an interview are greatly diminished. Joe Wannabee then describes who he is and what he wants to do, giving Joe Smith a solid idea of how Smith can be of help. Finally, Joe requests an interview, but he does so in a gentle way. He acknowledges that he will get an interview only at Joe Smith's pleasure. Joe Smith is under no obligation whatsoever.

Figure 2.3 is Joe Wannabee's resumé. Joe has done a lot of film-related activities in advance of seeking a full-time job in the industry. Not all of you will have had this opportunity. However, if you are in the middle of college, take a good look. Joe Wannabee has prepared himself well for work in the movie business. Try to make your resumé comparable to Joe's by the time you graduate.

Joe has prepared his resumé in a standard format, which makes it easy to read. Each piece of the resumé is concise and deals with one of Joe's various qualities. On one level, the resumé is about experience. Joe has lots of film-related experience for a student. That is important, but he needs more. The resumé then identifies Joe's high level of motivation and drive. He has won awards and sought responsible positions. Finally, the resumé mentions a few non-entertainment details because they complete its portrait of Joe. He has done serious office work and community service. Not only are these items "conversation starters" in an interview, they demonstrate

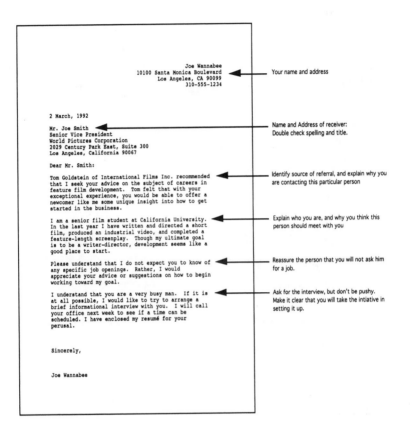

Figure 2.2   Cover letter requesting an informational interview

that there is more to Joe than just celluloid. Many candidates omit any non-industry jobs from their resumés, but this can be a mistake. If you have done something which will make you stand out as an interesting person—such as being a Big Brother or Sister—do yourself a favor and keep it on your resumé.

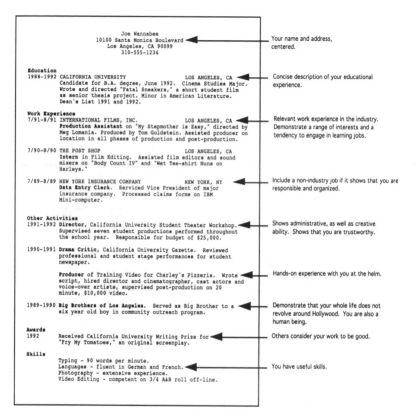

Figure 2.3   Sample resumé

2.5   JOB INTERVIEWING

Preparation

When the time comes to interview for an actual job, you will want to be well-prepared. That means learning about the company that might offer you a job, and having a general knowledge of the industry. You can learn about the company and the industry by reading the trade papers regularly. *Daily Variety* and *The Hollywood Reporter* both report on all major companies working in the industry. By keeping up with the trades you will know who is doing what, which movies are doing well at the box office, and which television shows have the highest ratings.

If the trades yield no information about the company, you can search for facts in other sources. Ask your lower-level informational interview contacts what they know about the company. Find the producer's listing in the *Producers, Studios, Agents, and Casting Directors Guide (Lone Eagle Publishing)* and cross-index his or her work in the other directories (see Appendix G). Find out what movies he or she has produced and rent them. If it is an agency, try to find out what their specialty is, who their clients are and what major projects they have packaged recently.

Learn a little history of the movie business by reading books about the industry. Present-day Hollywood is the sum of past trends and dynasties. Since everyone you meet will have been in town longer than you, it pays for you to understand the periods they have lived through. Books like *Final Cut (NAL-Dutton, 1986)* and *Reel Power (New American Library)* can give you a feel for the way business is conducted and familiarize you with the names of many major players.

If you have never been on a film set, try to visit one before you go on a job interview. You can never lose sight of the fact that the movie business always comes down to the creation of an actual film in a studio or on location. Having some insight into the challenges faced by physical production will help you in an interview. If you cannot get onto a film set, you could work on a student film. There you will see how truly difficult it is to bring a scene to life on film, and you will never again take a professionally produced film for granted.

Finally, go to the movies and watch television. This seems obvious, but you would be amazed at how many people claim to want to work in the business, yet never go to the movies! You don't have to see everything, but you should at least see every high-grossing studio release and critically acclaimed film. If a film gets good reviews, yet performs poorly at the box office, you should not only be aware of this contradiction, but have your own personal interpretation of what went wrong. For television, you should watch every series in prime time for at least one episode and sample recent television movies to have a familiarity with the format.

What They're Looking For

"Someone who is a good reflection on me," says agent Cathy Stone. "Someone who makes me look good. A kind person, considerate. I need a partner, not a secretary. Anybody can answer the phone."

Michael Barnathan is looking for "...somebody who's smart, somebody who wants to work hard. Somebody who has a sense of where they want to be, somebody who's not floundering and just dabbling in this... I like it when people come in and know who they are and what they want to be and have the attitude of, 'I want to work hard, and I want to learn. I want to earn it.' "

"The most important thing for me is sound judgment," says Chip Diggins, "by which I mean the ability to know when to make a decision and when not to make a decision. And the ability to handle the unexpected situation. That may not mean getting it all done, but knowing, for example, when to interrupt me when I'm in a meeting."

According to literary agent David Kanter, "It's not about where they went to college. It's not even about what they've done or what they know. It's about wanting to learn and work hard. It's a look in the eye."

Bill Todman, executive producer of MARRIED TO THE MOB and producer OF HARD TO KILL, prefers to hire assistants who have already had some basic experience in the industry, such as agency mailroom training. "The producer's desk is not where you cut your teeth," says Todman. "I want an assistant who wants my job. I want an assistant who wants to do what I do. That's the only way you're going to have an assistant who's truly going to get down and dirty and do the work that you do, and work as hard as you do."

Based on these ideals of what an assistant should be, figure out what is special about you and how you can emphasize it. Though each of these people is looking for something slightly different, they are all looking for the exceptional person. What is exceptional about you? Are you nicer than anyone else in the world? Smarter? More articulate? When you have figured out your best attribute, you are ready to make a winning impression in an interview.

Interview Atmosphere and Typical Questions

These people are busy. Out of a thirty-minute meeting, you may get ten minutes of actual conversation. The phone rings, and people walk into the office with urgent business. People cannot drop everything in order to speak with you. You should be sensitive to this fact and not take it personally. It is no reflection on you that the person interviewing you takes a twenty-minute phone call in the middle of your appointment. The challenge to you is to make the few five- or ten-minute patches of dialogue count.

They probably don't remember your resumé, either. It is a mistake to assume that the person who interviews you has reviewed your credentials before the meeting. You will want to be able to present a concise sixty-second description of your background, if asked. This is your spiel, an encapsulation of who you are, where you came from, and what you want to do. A good spiel is essential in the event of a "cold-fish" interview, where the person just looks at you and says, "What do you want?" and sits back. You have to be able to take the initiative and invigorate the situation or the interview will fail.

"Interviews are as uncomfortable for me as they are for the interviewee," says David Kanter. "I don't play tricks or ask stupid questions. I don't scare people. I ask people how they feel about the movies. I ask them what their favorite movies are. I don't judge them on their answer. I'm interested in the ability to answer the question, and how they approach it. This is the moment they tell me who they are."

Before your interview, think about what movies you like best and which you like least, and why. Have your favorite films been box office successes? If not, what does that tell you about your taste? It is acceptable to have liked a movie that bombed, but you should know how to defend it as a creative work. Try to answer the question "What makes a great movie?" and apply it to films you have seen recently. Try to avoid pretentious answers unless you are convinced that the person interviewing you shares your background and tastes. If you are unsure of yourself, practice discussing your favorite films with a friend.

Michael Barnathan prefers not to ask a standard set of questions. The only question he asks of every candidate is what they want to be in the industry. Michael always asks people "...where they want to be... Not that they want to come and be my assistant, but what they really want to do in this business, in this life...It really cuts through a lot of stuff because you get to see where somebody's head is at."

Bill Todman also prefers a free-form interview without set questions. "I usually tell them a little bit about what I'm doing....then listen to what their ambitions are, and decide if there is that same work ethic, number one, and number two, the same passion for doing a job like I do. Because if they don't, and they're just looking at it as a stepping stone—you know they're going to be in and out of here in a year."

Chip Diggins, who worked as a precious metals trader before working in the movie business, likes to ask ethical questions that he used in interviews in the financial industry. Diggins expects his assistants to be "...entirely honest with me. I also expect them to go above my head if they think I'm doing something unethical. This is one area where there can be no compromise."

How ambitious should you sound when asked where you want to go in the industry? Michael Barnathan finds that many people shy away from describing what they want to do for fear of sounding arrogant or grandiose, but he encourages them to share their dreams and visions with him. When Michael interviewed for his first job, he never hesitated to tell people that his ambition was to write and direct great movies. It paid off, even though his career path ultimately took him in the direction of producing. "People respond to your honesty," he says. To hold back from admitting what you really want to do is to give the negative impression of aspiring to a low position in the business.

To counterbalance ambition, there is realism. Cathy Stone asks people what they are looking for in a job. "If they want to be me in three months, I have to tell them to forget it." Stone would be delighted if you wanted to be her eventually. She's just saying that it won't happen in three months. Expressing an unrealistic short term goal indicates that you have a poor understanding of the industry, which reflects badly on you.

Other typical interview questions:

1) *What do you think of a recent deal or trend?*
An interviewer might ask you something on the order of "What do you make of the fact that Brandon Tartikoff left Paramount?" or "Did you read the Katzenberg memo?" to evaluate your awareness of the state of the industry. If you don't know what these two questions refer to, you have not prepared yourself adequately for a job interview.

2) *Do you read a lot? What is your favorite book? Do you have a favorite author?*
You are not expected to be an expert on literature, but be prepared to discuss an author you like. If you never read at all, think about what career track you are on. Think about how you would explain the fact that you never read in an interview for a development job.

3) *Do you have a favorite screenwriter or director?*
This is really another version of, "What's your favorite movie?" When people ask you this, they might be looking for an ability to analyze what makes a writer or director good. Think about movies you have liked and evaluate the role the writer or director played in making the film a success visually or dramatically. People want to see how well you have refined your aesthetic sense and language.

4) *Which TV shows do you watch?*

If you never watch TV it's probably okay to admit it, though you really ought to be watching if you want to know what's going on in the industry. Some people are testing you for anti-TV snobbism with this question. Weigh your answer carefully. If you truly detest television, think about what that says about your ability to fit into the commercial movie business, where many people got their start in television. You don't want to offend people. At the same time, if you like nothing more than to kick back and watch seven hours of TV a day, make sure that you don't come across as a couch potato with no initiative. A reasonable goal is to be able to discuss one or two programs that you enjoy and give solid appraisals of them.

5) *Is there a particular film you would like to make?*

Don't worry if you can't answer this question. People just want to see how passionate you are. If you have a favorite book that you would love to make into a film, that shows you have a high level of ambition and vision.

Turnoffs

There are an infinite number of ways to make a bad impression in an interview. Here are but a few examples:

1) *Acting like a know-it-all.*

Many potential assistants fall prey to the temptation of having a slick answer to every question. If you don't know the answer to a question, don't pretend that you do. If you make something up, people can usually see right through it. "You have to have the attitude that the people you're going to work for are smarter than you, know something you don't know, and you want to learn it or you shouldn't be going to work for them," says Michael Barnathan.

A prospective assistant was once given a script to read as part of his interview. He read the script and came in to discuss it the next day. The producer asked him what he thought of the script, and the candidate simply said, "It's a hit movie." The producer then asked, "What do you mean? Why is it a hit movie?" The candidate replied, "I'm telling you. I read it and it's a hit movie," to which the producer angrily replied, "Kid, what the hell would you know about that?"

2) *Lying.*

Cathy Stone warns, "Don't tell someone you can do something if you can't." You may get the job because of a falsehood, but not only will you not last long, you will anger the people who hired you. After all the stress of looking for a job, it may seem convenient to claim to know how to speak Japanese, but if you can't back it up, you will have wasted all your time.

3) *Giving vague or generalized answers.*

They tell nothing, and indicate that you lack seriousness or vision. Michael Barnathan remarks that when he asks people what they want to do, "you'd be amazed how many people say they don't know." He doesn't believe that they actually don't know. "I will continue to press them to tell me what it is they would do."

If someone asks you what kind of movies you like and all you can say is "comedies," without any elaboration, you have just made an exquisitely bad impression. You might be perceived as stupid, aloof, or both.

4) *Canned answers.*

Even if you have been through many interviews, you have to sound spontaneous. Remember, these people are meeting you for the first time. Speaking in automatic "sound bites" suggests either that you are not thinking, or that someone has rehearsed you and your ideas are not your own.

5) *Making an issue out of money.*

In response to a job offer, a recent college graduate said, "If we can get the numbers to work, I'm there." What was her mistake? She failed to realize that all entry-level jobs in entertainment pay little money. To act as if money were your motivation in getting the job suggests that you do not prize the learning experience of the job, which itself has great value.

"The worst thing you can do when interviewing for an assistant's job is to make money an issue," says Michael Barnathan. "When I interviewed, money was absolutely not an issue, and it wasn't because I had money, or had a family that had money. It was because I had very low expenses, and kept my expenses low because I did not in any way want to make money an issue."

Sample Coverage and Story Notes

Executives often ask serious candidates to write coverage (a synopsis and comments) on a screenplay. The assignment is designed to gauge your taste and your writing ability. Chapter 4 describes how to write good coverage in detail, so I will not go into the mechanics of coverage here. Instead, let's think about the opportunities and pitfalls of a sample coverage assignment from a job interview.

You will not know anything about the script they give you to read, so you have to be careful how you review it. They might have given you a complete bomb, so if you gush all over it you could look like an idiot. If they gave you a script they just optioned for half a million and you trash it in your coverage, you will prove that your tastes are different from theirs.

Transmitting as little attitude as you possibly can will keep you out of danger. Don't be a wimp, though. If you don't like something, say so, but don't be nasty. Explain your reasons for disliking the material, but try to avoid the fate of the following two job candidates at Edgar J. Scherick Associates:

One person covered the script to the film RAMBLING ROSE, which was written by Calder Willingham, an Oscar-nominated writer. The coverage, which was riddled with grammatical errors, ended with the brash pronouncement, "Calder Willingham is obviously an amateur. He can't write." We took a red pen to her illiterate coverage, circled the mistakes, and mailed it back to her. If you're going to come out swinging in your coverage, at least know what you're talking about, and try to write properly.

Another candidate was asked to cover a teleplay for an upcoming television movie. A comment on the coverage proclaimed that the script was "sub-standard TV filler." Since television movies are an important part of our business, we decided not to torture this guy by forcing him to work in a medium he clearly didn't like.

Some companies ask prospective assistants to write development notes on a script in addition to coverage. Notes are detailed comments on how a script should be altered to make it better. (Chapter 5 covers notes.) Briefly, notes begin with an assessment of a script's overall problems and then give specific recommended changes for each scene that contains a problem.

You face the same difficulty of second-guessing the producer with notes as you do with coverage. The big question for a note-writer is, "What's wrong with this script?" Since you have no way of knowing whether the script is a favorite of the producer's or a reject, you have to weigh your assessment of the script's problems with care. As in the sample coverage, your best bet is to make honest comments about the script's weaknesses and suggest solutions which would improve the script's commercial appeal. People are more interested in your ability to analyze than your "taste." Resist the temptation to make extreme comments or suggest changes which are intended to show off how much you know about film history. A good development executive works to make a script better, not just different.

What to Wear to an Interview

Karen Swallow, a graduate of New York's Fashion Institute of Technology who now assists Michael Barnathan at Largo, offers the following advice regarding what to wear to an entertainment job interview:

> "It's better to be overdressed than underdressed. A woman should always wear a skirt, a dress, or a business suit. Avoid overly conservative suits, however. Try a round-neck silk shirt underneath a jacket. You can dress with flair and still look nice, but don't go overboard. You can wear a pin if you want to. Keep your nails short and don't wear a lot of makeup.
>
> For men, I wouldn't wear a suit, but I would wear a jacket and tie. If a man is going to wear a suit, then, just like a woman, he should try for a suit that isn't a cookie-cutter Wall Street type. I wouldn't wear a grey pinstripe. Something a little hipper."

Follow-Up

After you've had a job interview you will have to follow up, as you did in the informational interview process. Even if you don't get the job, following up will lead to further referrals, more interviews, and ultimately, a job offer. You have to be aggressive in follow-up, but you must walk the fine line between being assertive and being pushy.

According to Chip Diggins, "You can't get up in the morning, make a couple of phone calls, and sit around bemoaning the fact that no one's calling you back. That's ludicrous. Don't put the burden on the people you're trying to reach; make it easy for them." Making it easy for the person involves frequent follow-up phone calls. Here, tone is all-important. If you are friendly, you can call every day. If you are pushy or impatient with the staff of the person who interviewed you, one call is enough to put you at the bottom of the call sheet indefinitely. An executive might interview you and tell you that he'll be in touch, but then two months will go by. By that time you have probably concluded that the job went to someone else. Then the phone rings, and it's the executive calling to offer you the job.

2.6   INTERNING, TEMPING AND READING

Working as an intern, a temporary assistant, or a freelance reader offers you a chance to gain some experience while you search for a permanent position. Temping and reading can also help you bridge the financial gap. All three activities allow you to "sample" an employer before working there full time, should the opportunity arise.

A good internship provides you with exposure to the industry within a legitimate company. Normally, an internship allows you to learn about the industry in exchange for doing some menial work, getting some college credit, and no pay. A good internship should mix office work, scriptreading, coverage and observing meetings. At the very least, you will expose yourself to the ways of the industry and make your first set of contacts for your permanent job search. Many interns get offered full-time work or production assistant positions at companies where they have worked hard and made a good impression.

Some companies lure in interns with a promise of "getting in" to the industry, but then exploit them mercilessly. These situations offer only menial work and little education. If you feel that your internship experience is teaching you nothing, leave it. However, before you quit, make sure that you have done everything possible to learn something, including asking to be included in more challenging work.

An exploitative internship is really slave labor, and if you are not getting college credit for it, the company is breaking the law. The State of California recently challenged a major studio for advertising an unpaid position, which is illegal. As a result, there are fewer internships available now except those that give college credit.

Temping, like interning, allows you to get some experience and sample a variety of work environments as you seek a permanent position. Many people got their first full-time job at an office where they temped. Chip Diggins, for example, prefers to hire temps, because he is able to give them a two- or three-day trial to check their competence before offering them the real job. And, in contrast to interning, temping pays the rent.

Freelance script reading pays you to improve an important skill, but in general it is a dead-end proposition. Reading is the occupation of choice for aspiring writers, since the hours are flexible and the job gives constant updates on the state of story development in the industry. If you want to get onto one of the career tracks, however, reading will probably not get you there. Readers have little contact with the producers and agents who employ them. A reader works at home, so he gets no exposure to the language and conduct of the business, which is so important to career development. However, like temping, reading pays and can help you bridge the financial gap as you search for a real job.

If you are in high school or college, you are probably looking for a summer job in the business. The bad news is that summer jobs are very hard to get. The good news is that you have many chances to find one, and summer jobs present a truly idiot-proof entry-level work experience in the business. If you are a sophomore in college, for example, you have two summers ahead of you in which to find a job. You have the great luxury of experimenting with job search strategies and improving them based on the results. Then, if you do get a job or internship, you have the luxury of making a complete mess out of it, and nobody will ever hold it against you.

Looking for a summer job is identical to looking for a real job. You should contact people for informational interviews and follow up conscientiously. Conduct a self-assessment and decide where you want to be. Start early in the school year and plan carefully.

The *Academy of Television Arts and Sciences*, the organization which produces the Emmy Awards, sponsors one of the only paid summer internships in the industry. Every summer, the Academy selects promising college students who have expressed an interest in a career in television and sends them to work at a major company for eight weeks. The Academy offers internships in several categories, including editing, development, directing, writing and daytime programming.

The *Directors Guild of America* and the *Alliance of Motion Picture and Television Producers* sponsor the Assistant Directors Training Program. This scholarship, which lasts for over a year, trains young people to be second assistant directors by placing them in paying positions on productions. You must be a college graduate to enroll. The trainee program is an excellent way to learn production and gain contacts on the production track. As a result, entry is very competitive.

Internships, temporary jobs and reading jobs all offer that rare opportunity to get started in the industry, but after that it's up to you. Success from that point on depends on you. The people who have climbed out of internships or temp situations to get offered real jobs have put no less effort into the job than if it were in a full-time position. If you want to move up, then be an exceptional intern, temp or reader. When an intern or temp fails to rise to the occasion, everyone feels disappointed. The company feels as if it wasted a great opportunity on the wrong person.

2.7 EDUCATION

Is college necessary? A college degree is hardly a prerequisite for success in Hollywood. Some of the truly colossal figures of the past and present barely finished high school, if that. College education has little direct impact on your potential in the movie business. However, since the majority of people in the industry have been to college, you may want to evaluate your comfort level at plunging into this educated society without a college degree. It is primarily a personal decision.

If you are in the middle of college, though, and are tempted to drop out to pursue a career in movies, then you owe it to yourself to think the issue through carefully. Quitting college is a major step which can be, depending on the length of the hiatus, irreversible. Dropping out of school can give you the stigma of being a "quitter," an image you would not want to cultivate in the movie business. Hollywood is more exciting than most colleges, so it is tempting to bail out of school. If you are really bored in school, you may be studying the wrong subject. Most people who abandon college to work in film eventually regret the decision.

Opinions split on whether graduate school is worthwhile preparation for the movie business. Some people will encourage you to get a law degree, an MBA, or a Masters in Film. Others advise jumping right in. The general consensus has it that a graduate degree never hurts, though there is a slight industry bias against overeducated people. People who have spent too much time studying, as opposed to doing, are viewed with suspicion.

Law and business schools can help you, though with such specialized professional education you run the risk of being pigeonholed. A position in the legal or finance department of a studio may pay well, but it is a long way from the creative side of the business. The tragedy is that once you have established yourself in these departments, you will probably never get out. It has been done, but real crossover success stories are quite rare.

Many job-seekers explore the possibility of going to film school, but most industry people name only one valid reason for going. "The only reason to go to graduate film school is to direct a film as a calling card," says Michael Barnathan. "If you're not intending to direct a film as a calling card, you're wasting your time...If you want to write, write. If you want to get into a craft, then get into a craft. Go to work." If you didn't study film as an undergraduate, and understand nothing about filmmaking, then film school will provide you with an expensive learning opportunity. You could probably learn most of the same skills on the job, however.

If you have the time, you might want to supplement your formal education by taking courses to learn some specialized office skills to make you a better assistant. Shorthand can come in handy if you have to take notes in a meeting or take a letter in dictation. Speedreading would put you at a clear advantage in a development or agency job. Computer knowledge will help you in almost every endeavor. The sum effect of having skills like these would be to speed you through the day-to-day details of your job and allow you extra time to learn about the more interesting aspects of the business.

2.8 MAKING THE DECISION

What do you do if you are actually offered a job? First, pat yourself on the back, because you have accomplished something that is very difficult. Then, you have to do the hard work of evaluating whether the job will give you what you need. How is the personality match between you and your potential boss? If you cannot stand him, how long do you think you will last? What is the learning potential for the job? What will this person teach you? Try to map out the advancement potential. Ask what happened to the last assistant.

Check him out. Using that burgeoning network of contacts you made during the interview process, find out what you can about the person who has offered you the job. Trusted advisors might tell you to stay away. Your potential boss might have five sexual harassment suits outstanding, for example. If your friends give you reasons to turn down the offer, ask yourself how you would handle the issues they raise. Can you live with some difficulty?

Given how hard it is to find an entry-level job, you will not want to turn down an offer unless there is an extreme potential conflict. You will encounter some kind of hardship almost anywhere you start in the business. It is a rite of passage. But if you sense that you will be unable to cope with the job, you might have to say no.

Try to determine what kind of commitment they expect from you. Most offices expect you to settle down for about a year, though many assistants leave sooner on good terms. It is a mistake to take a position knowing that you will leave after a very short time. For example, the job offer you receive might be in a different field from what you actually want to do, so you plan to stay with the job until something opens up in your area of interest. In this case, you are shortchanging both your employer and yourself. For one thing, you might find that you love the new job. Give it a chance. Remember the flexible path. If, because you really want to be doing something else, you don't give the job your best effort, the weak impression you create will stall your chances of switching to another field later.

2.9 IF NOTHING IS WORKING

What happens if you do everything right, but after nine months in Los Angeles you still have not found a job or even an internship. First of all, don't worry. You are in good company. Many successful people took a long time to find their first jobs. If you are having real trouble, though, it is a good time to re-examine your goals and approaches to finding the job.

Have you picked the wrong path? You might be seeking a position for which you are unsuitable because of education, training or personality. For example, you might have interviewed for production jobs, but you hate getting your hands dirty. Or your push has been to work at an agency, but you consider yourself a painfully shy person. Perhaps you are looking for work in all the wrong places, given who you are and what you like to do.

Evaluate the kind of impression you make. Have you had good follow-up with people, or have they uniformly not returned your calls? If everyone you have met in the business avoids you, then you can conclude that something in your presentation is lacking. Were your interviews friendly? Were you able to draw people out and let them talk about themselves comfortably? Or did you have people on the defensive all the time? Try to be objective about the kind of effect you have on people. If you can identify situations where you made a bad impression, you have begun to understand why it is taking so long to get a job.

Are you too picky with job offers, or playing hard to get? The perfect job is virtually impossible to find. If you have turned down more than one job offer, then the delay in your job search is probably your own fault. Take the plunge! Working in a less than perfect situation still beats being unemployed.

Have a friend who is experienced in the business review your resumé, cover letters and sample coverage. Does your resumé match the career path you are seeking, or does it emphasize the wrong aspects of your background? Are your letters and coverage well-written and concise? Do they display any unwanted attitude? Ask your friend to make an honest assessment of your entire job search.

Finally, there is absolutely nothing wrong with deciding that you do not want to work in the entertainment industry. Hollywood is not for everyone. Some people characterize those who leave the business as losers. Nothing could be further from the truth. The real losers are the people who stick it out for years even though they are clearly in the wrong business. Intelligent people will respect you for making the decision that's best for you. If you decide not to be in the business, move on. There is no stigma attached to concluding that Hollywood is not for you.

Chapter 3
Basics: Setting Up the Office and Getting to Work

3.0 THE INFORMATION TOOLS

Your primary goal as an assistant is to help your boss do his job more effectively. The phone log, appointment book, filing system, Rolodex and computer are all tools which enable you to accomplish this goal. Your first order of business on the job, therefore, is to become proficient in the use of these tools, among others, and get to work.

What you are really doing with these tools, though, is managing information. Every phone call, letter and verbal transaction in an entertainment office contains information which is relevant to your boss. Even if something seems unimportant, it may well hold crucial facts which will be needed later.

Most executives define an assistant's competence as the ability to manage information well. An executive must have instant access to accurate information about his deals and projects. A big part of your job is to store and interpret information in a system your boss can use. Your skill at handling information will be a significant measure of your success in the job.

3.1 TELEPHONE PROCEDURE AND THE PHONE LOG

"Show business is dog eat dog. It's worse than dog eat dog. It's dog doesn't return other dog's phone calls..."
—Woody Allen in *CRIMES AND MISDEMEANORS*

Entertainment executives live on the phone. Talent agents use headset phones to prevent sore ears. Studio heads make hundreds of calls a day. Success comes only to those who can "give good phone." Phone etiquette and protocols are well established, and assistants play a central role in the phone game. The first thing you will be expected to do, probably within minutes of arriving on the first day, is answer the phone and "do calls."

The first law of the phone is that everyone who calls your office or receives a call from your office should be treated as if they are an important person. You must maintain courtesy at all times with all people. While your boss might be entitled to lose his cool occasionally, it is inexcusable for an assistant to be rude to a caller at any time. As an assistant, you might not know who is important and who is not, so it is smart to give people the benefit of the doubt when you speak with them. Courtesy also establishes your office as a classy operation, no matter the reality of the place.

Here are three typical phone conversations for a fictitious entertainment executive named Stanley Blockbuster. For simplicity, and extra practice at reading scripts, the conversations are written in screenplay format.

1) An *Incoming Call* from Abe Troglodyte, a person *well known* to Stanley Blockbuster, your boss.

INT. ENTERTAINMENT OFFICE—DAY

FADE IN

You are sitting behind a desk, expectantly. The phone rings. You pick it up.

                    YOU
          Stanley Blockbuster's office,
          good afternoon.

                    ABE TROGLODYTE
          Is Stanley there? It's Abe.

                    YOU
          Just a moment, please.

You put Abe on hold, and buzz Stanley at his desk.

                    YOU
          Abe Troglodyte is calling
          Do you want him?

                    STANLEY
          Yeah. I'll take it.

You transfer the call to Stanley's extension, and *log it in*. (To be covered shortly.)

2) An *Outgoing Call* to a person well known to Stanley Blockbuster.

```
INT. ENTERTAINMENT OFFICE—DAY
```

                    STANLEY
          (Yelling from the other room)
          Get me Abe Troglodyte on the
          phone, now!

You look up Abe's number in the Rolodex and dial the number...
You log the outgoing call...
Abe's assistant answers the phone...

                    ABE'S ASSISTANT
          Abe Troglodyte's office.

                    YOU
          I have Stanley Blockbuster
          calling. Is he there?

                    ABE'S ASSISTANT
          Please put him on. Abe'll be
          right there.

You put Abe's assistant on hold and buzz Stanley in his office.
                    YOU
          Please pick up...he'll be right
          with you.

Stanley gets on the phone and waits for Abe to pick up the phone.

CUT! Why is Stanley waiting on hold? Why not Abe? Who waits on hold for whom? This is one of the great questions in any entertainment office. It is the single greatest determinant of power and place in the hierarchy. In our example, either Stanley is less important than Abe and he knows it, or they are such close friends that it doesn't make any difference. Major stars and moguls do not have to wait on hold for anyone unless they are calling the White House. An individual of lesser stripe has to know his or her place. It is one of the great subtle and ongoing negotiations that people engage in. Part of the game is that if one is enough of a player to have someone making calls for him or her, then he or she ought to be confident enough to tolerate a lapse in etiquette. As a new assistant, though, you have to be keenly aware of the rules. If you work for a powerful person who is not magnanimous, then you might regret making him or her wait on hold for someone of lesser station.

3) An incoming call from a person *unknown* to Stanley Blockbuster. In this case, we'll imagine that the call comes from an obscure literary agent in New York named Sue Smart.

```
INT. ENTERTAINMENT OFFICE—DAY
The phone rings and you pick it up.

                    YOU
          Stanley Blockbuster's office.
          Good afternoon.

                    SUE SMART
          Is he there?

                    YOU
          Who may I say is calling?

                    SUE SMART
          It's Sue Smart.

                    YOU
          One moment, please.

You place Sue Smart on hold and buzz Stanley in his office and
tell him Sue Smart is calling.
                    STANLEY
          Who the hell is Sue Smart?

You reconnect with Sue Smart.

                    YOU
          May I ask what this call is
          in reference to?
                    SUE SMART
          I represent a best-selling novel...
```

And so on. You cannot give the caller the impression that your boss does not care about him or her. A lot of powerful people keep low profiles. Constant courtesy and a good knowledge of who's who can prevent you from putting your foot in your mouth.

You will have to develop a way of telling your boss who is calling him beyond merely saying it out loud. If he is on the phone, he may not want the person on the other end to hear who is calling, or he may find it distracting to be spoken to while on the phone. Hand signals, lip reading and PostIts have been known to work, but there is a better way. There is a machine called an *Amtel*, which transmits written messages to your boss silently via an electronic connection. It is a cross between a typewriter and an intercom. You type in the words "Abe Troglodyte is calling" at your desk. The Amtel on your boss's desk will beep and those same words will appear in front of him instantly. He can then press various buttons, which might say, "Put him through," or, "I don't want to talk to him now."

Unfortunately, once in a while, it may be necessary to tell a small fib to someone who's calling your office. You aren't really lying. It's all part of the game. If you are deeply troubled by this idea, you might be in the wrong business. For whatever reason, though, you will at some point have to tell a caller that your boss cannot speak with them, but you can never say, "My boss doesn't want to speak with you right now." That would be rude. People would much rather be lied to. Here are a few good phrases which you can use to explain that your boss will have to call them back:

> *He's in a meeting.*
> *He's on the other line*
> *She's on an international conference call (This one is ironclad!)*
> *He's in a casting session.*
> *She's out of town today.*
> *She's working at home today.*
> *He's in his car and he's driving through the canyon, so I can't*
> *   connect you.*
> *He just picked up another line, but he does want to talk to you...*

You've probably heard all of these before, but it's good to practice them to remove any trace of guilty conscience from your voice. After all, if you must lie, you should at least be courteous about it.

The basic document of the phone game is the *Phone Log book*. The Phone log helps you keep track of every phone call your boss makes, wants to make, has received, or needs to return. The phone log book is a specially made spiral notebook sold in stationery stores. Incoming calls are listed on the left side and outgoing calls are on the right, facing each other. The typical phone log looks like Figure 3-1. You can also maintain a phone log on separate sheets of paper or even on a computer program.

When the day begins, turn to a fresh set of Incoming and Outgoing pages in the phone log book. When a call comes in, you will make an entry in the "Incoming" side of the book. Write down the time the person called in the far left column, which is marked "Time." Write the caller's name in the next column, which is marked "Name." If you don't know the caller, ask him to spell his name for you. The caller may tell you why he is calling, but if he doesn't, you should ask or at least try to figure out the purpose of the call. Your boss may not return the call until the next day, and it is possible that you will forget the reason for the call unless you write it down in the "Description" column as the call comes in.

Date 1/3/93	INCOMING CALLS		
Time	Name	Description	
10:20AM	Joe Smith		X
10:21	Abe Troglodyte	Re: Dolly Parton 555-1234	
10:22	Steven Spielberg		X

Indicates that your boss took the call

Blank space - your boss owes Abe a call.

Figure 3-1 The incoming phone log book

In the example of Figure 3-1, Joe Smith called at 10:20AM, and your boss took the call, indicated by the X (or check mark) in the far right column. Abe Troglodyte called at 10:21, but your boss was on with Joe Smith, so you told Abe that he would be called back. Abe said he wanted to talk about a movie for Dolly Parton, so under the "Description" column, you entered "Re: Dolly Parton." Under description, you also wrote down Abe's phone number for quick reference. Steven Spielberg called at 10:22, so your boss decided to get off the phone with Joe Smith. He still owes Abe a call. As the day goes on, the page will fill up with incoming calls. Some will be completed. Others will need to be returned. A quick scan of the far right column should tell you who needs to be called back.

At 10:25, your boss gets off the phone with Spielberg and asks you who else called. You tell him that Abe called, and then ask if he wants you to try to get Abe on the phone. Your boss tells you to try Abe later. Right now, he wants to call Barry Diller. He also says he wants to call Robert Redford about starring in A KILLER IN THE SNOW, Jane Fonda about Ted Turner's birthday party, and Mel Gibson about doing TWO GENTLEMEN OF VERONA with Arnold Schwarzenegger. You turn to the Outgoing side of the phone log, displayed in Figure 3-2, and write down the names of all the people he wants to call. Even if you do not place the calls immediately, the outgoing calls are logged as "Want to Call" entries.

Date 1/3/93	OUTGOING CALLS		
Time	Name	Description	
10:25	Barry Diller	555-4321	L W ← You "Left Word" with Abe
10:26	Redford 212-555-2345	Starring in "Killer/Snow"	X ← Call Completed
	Fonda	Ted Turner's Birthday Party	
	Gibson	Teaming w/Schwarzenegger for "Two Gentlemen of Verona."	

Figure 3-2 Outgoing phone log.

You dial Barry Diller's number, but his assistant says he can't come to the phone. You say "Okay, *leave word* that Stanley Blockbuster called." After you hang up, you tell your boss that you left word for Barry. Then, you put "L.W." in the far right column, indicating that you left word. Now begins a great waiting game, as people see who calls them back promptly. If Barry does not call Stanley back for two days, then Stanley can infer that Barry does not think much of him. If Barry calls back three minutes later, apologizing for the delay, then Stanley can be assured that he counts. You then try Redford, a he takes the call. You mark the right column with an X to indicate that the call went through.

As the day goes on, you will accumulate a list of calls which your boss *owes*, and has to return, and other calls where he has left word with someone and *is owed* a call back. At the end of each day, or even during the day, you prepare a summary *Call Sheet* which lists the incoming calls and outgoing calls. Figure 3.3 shows a typical, if brief, call sheet. The abbreviation "WTC" in the far right denotes a person your boss wants to call. Each listing should have a phone number, and a description of what the call is about. Important calls should be highlighted or starred.

Call Sheet for 1/3/93 as of 10:30AM
Today's calls:

Incoming

Abe Troglodyte	310-555-1234	Re Dolly Parton	Owe

Outgoing

Barry Diller	310-555-4321		LW
Jane Fonda	404-555-5566	Re: Ted T's B-day	WTC
Mel Gibson	310-555-3322	Re:"Two Gentlemen"	WTC

Calls From 1/2/93

Mike Ovitz		Returned your call
Nancy Reagan	310-555-3345	Re: Her acting career

Figure 3.3   Excerpt from phone summary sheet

Periodically during the day your boss will want to go over the calls. It is likely that there will be more calls to return than time will allow. Your job is to scan the phone log and pick out the important calls. In order to do this you must have a grasp of which projects are the most important and which people are attached to those projects. You can always hand your boss a long list of calls and say "you pick," but it saves him a lot of time and effort if you are on top of it yourself.

In addition to being an essential tool for managing the volume of calls, the phone log also serves as a diary of your boss's work life. As such it can be useful in reconstructing events after they have occurred. The phone log can even be used in legal proceedings to determine the chain of actions leading up to a decision. Steven Bach wrote *Final Cut*, a book which chronicles the disastrous making of HEAVEN'S GATE, by reconstructing phone conversations and related activities from his phone log when he was president of United Artists. For this reason, the phone log should never be thrown away. The log should be legible and meticulously maintained. It is as much a permanent record of your boss's work life as any other file, correspondence or archive.

On pages 74 and 75, there are blank phone logs. During your job search, log your incoming and outgoing calls as practice for when you are on the job.

3.2   THE APPOINTMENT BOOK AND THE FINE ART OF SCHEDULING

After phone calls, the second most popular activity for an entertainment executive is meetings. Your job is to schedule all the various meetings and appointments in an efficient and productive fashion. Your boss will probably give you a basic blueprint for his schedule when you begin working. Otherwise, you may be able to discern a pattern after a short time on the job. For example, your boss might like to have lunch out three days a week, hold story conferences from two to five only, and spend Saturday reading scripts at his house. This basic schedule will be the template for all meetings except those which are unusual, or so important that they can violate the model.

The secret to effective scheduling is flexibility. Your boss's schedule should never be filled to more than about eighty percent of its capacity, although determining what eighty percent means is more of an art than a science. There should always be room for unexpected meetings or crises. In the future, the schedule should be as empty as possible, with the only firm commitments being things like doctors' appointments, and meetings with individuals more important than your boss. Meetings which are pertinent to ongoing projects or relevant business should be put on the schedule as near in the future as possible, making sure that the schedule never fills up so much that your boss has back-to-back meetings all day long. Secondary meetings, such as informational interviews with aspiring assistants, should be kept in limbo for as long as possible. When important matters crop up, you do not want to have the schedule clogged with trivial meetings.

Some executives tell their assistants to double-book certain hours or lunches and then cancel one of the meetings. This is fine so long as it isn't overdone. One does not want to get the reputation for playing games, but it is up to your boss. It's his decision.

Geographical location can play a role in scheduling as well. Nothing wastes time like driving around Los Angeles. A good assistant will always try to trace an efficient route around town when setting meetings out of the office. If you are not sure where someone is located, you should ask. (And don't forget to annotate the Rolodex.) Location is especially important in planning meals. Breakfasts should be located between your boss's house and the office. Lunches should either be near the office, mutually convenient to the two parties, or more convenient to the more powerful party. A badly planned

Date _____		INCOMING CALLS		
Time	Name		Description	

Date _____	OUTGOING CALLS		
Time	Name	Description	

Figure 3.4 Practice Phone Log for use during your job search.

location for lunch can kill three hours of your boss's day.

The appointment book shows a full week on its two-page spread. When an appointment is written down, the entry should legibly contain the name of the person, his or her phone number, and the purpose of the meeting. Use a pencil, because the appointment book is subject to frequent revision. Anyone who is set to meet your boss should be told to call the day before to confirm the appointment. Confirming is a strong custom in the business. In fact, if a meeting is not confirmed, it is assumed to have been canceled.

When your boss leaves the office each day, he should have a copy of the following day's schedule typed on a sheet of paper. Like the appointment book, this *take-home appointment card* should list the names of people with whom your boss is meeting, their phone numbers, and the purpose of each meeting. Your boss carries this card in his pocket so he can look at it anywhere or any time.

The schedule drives your work routine. As the schedule is laid out, you scan the horizon for tasks relevant to upcoming meetings. Your boss might have to make a phone call, read a script, or have another meeting in order to be prepared for an appointment. You don't want to have to tell your boss that he has a story meeting in an hour covering a script he hasn't read.

For certain meetings, you might want to prepare a *meeting agenda card* for your boss. This pocket-sized card lists any important matters your boss wants to discuss at the meeting. For example, if your boss is going to a casting session, you will list his favorite actors under consideration for the part. With the agenda card, your boss does not have to worry about forgetting any details under the pressure of a meeting.

3.3 WRITTEN CORRESPONDENCE

Written communication is integral to all endeavors of an entertainment executive. The most common examples are the *pass letter*, which is used to reject a screenplay, and the *letter of transmittal*, which accompanies a piece of material your boss is trying to sell. (These are covered in detail in Chapters 4 and 5.) There are many others which your boss will have you writing, including summaries of meetings, complaints about consumer products, and legal letters. Part of the education you receive as an assistant is a growing familiarity with the acceptable and commonly used writing forms of the industry.

Most letters are written in similar language over and over again, so there will be some essential phrasing which will never change. Your boss might dictate letters to you, or even write them out himself, but you must be prepared to draft letters in your boss's English. His old letters can give you a sense of his writing style. It takes practice, but if you have a good ear for written English, it should not be too hard after a time to create letters which could have been written by your boss.

Figure 3.4 is a standard business letter format you can use. There is no universal format for a business letter, so you should check to see if there is a company standard, or a preferred format for your boss. Your letters should be consistent with what has come before.

When you have completed the letter, you place it on your boss's desk for signature or revisions. It is common for a letter to go through several drafts. Revisions should not be interpreted as criticism, unless specified. Generally, when the letter is signed, that means it is ready to go out in the mail. Otherwise, if your boss tells you, you can put "Dictated but not signed" under his name and mail the letter unsigned.

3-4   THE FILING SYSTEM

Filing is one of the most maligned of all office tasks. For most assistants it ranks down there with washing windows or taking the boss's dog for a coiffure. How unfair! A good filing system is a joy to work with, for you and your boss as well as other assistants, who will continually seek your help in locating pieces of information. Filing should be approached as a dynamic part of the work process — something which will enhance your image and your boss's productivity, not a chore to be deferred until the world stands still.

There are three tenets of filing which I strongly encourage you to observe. The first is continuous updating and maintenance. A file is only useful if it is current. You will never locate a document which is languishing in a "to be filed" bin. The second tenet is flexibility and adaptability. I have outlined several basic types of files below, but as an assistant you must be able to create new types of files in response to changing situations and needs. Filing is about information retrieval and management. In order for it to work properly, it must evolve with the rest of the organization. Finally, filing systems must be simple in design and easy to use. You can use a simple system very efficiently. After you are promoted, your successor will use your files, provided that you have made them easy to understand. If a filing system is too complex or inflexible, it will be abandoned by your successors.

The Rolodex

The Rolodex is the indispensable filing system. It is the *sine qua non* of office existence. Every desk has one, but few are used effectively. The

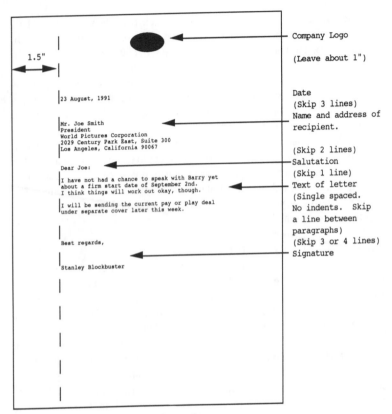

Figure 3-4   Standard Business Letter format

Rolodex is much more than an address book. If maintained properly, a Rolodex can be a comprehensive list of everything your boss would ever want to know about anyone he has ever contacted.

The key to having a good Rolodex is continuous and thorough updating. Every time you place a phone call for your boss, make sure the proper number is listed in the file. If someone's name, title or address changes, you should record the new information as you discover it. If a card is missing an address, ask for the address when you call. That way, if you have to write a letter to the same person later on, you will have saved yourself the effort of making another phone call.

Periodic updating is an alternative to continuous updating. Periodic updating means that once a year you sit down and call everyone in the whole file and verify their information. This can take weeks! The problem is that this task is often deferred and rarely ever completed. Listings become stagnant and obsolete. Some assistants compromise by updating one letter of the alphabet each week.

Your boss may not call everyone in the file every year, and some of the listings will indeed become obsolete through no fault of your own. The solution to this problem is to place the date of the last updating on the card. Figure 3.5 shows a sample card from the ideal Rolodex. If possible, you should try to use "3x5" cards, as the smaller ones cannot hold enough information. The date in the upper right corner is the date of the card's creation or most recent updating. The date should remind you to update old listings. Then, once in a while you can go through the file and weed out cards from people your boss doesn't call and whose creation date is so old that they're no longer of interest.

The card should contain the name, title, company name, and address of the person in complete detail. The spelling of the person's name should be checked carefully. Their title and the proper spelling of the company they work for must be verified with the company itself. Remember, it is a major embarrassment to get the name, title or company name wrong in written correspondence. The address should be as complete as possible, including suite number and the nine-digit zip code, if available.

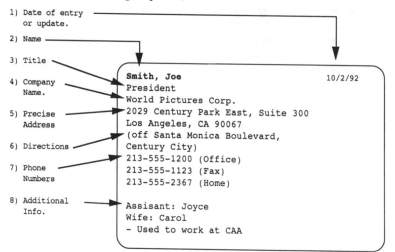

1) Date of entry or update.
2) Name
3) Title
4) Company Name.
5) Precise Address
6) Directions
7) Phone Numbers
8) Additional Info.

Smith, Joe   10/2/92
President
World Pictures Corp.
2029 Century Park East, Suite 300
Los Angeles, CA 90067
(off Santa Monica Boulevard,
Century City)
213-555-1200 (Office)
213-555-1123 (Fax)
213-555-2367 (Home)
Assisant: Joyce
Wife: Carol
- Used to work at CAA

Figure 3-5   Sample Rolodex Card

It is helpful to list directions to an address on the card. For example, your boss may not remember how to get to a place where he has a meeting. If the directions are written on the card, then once again you save time by avoiding a phone call to get directions.

Finally, you should annotate the card with additional information about the person listed. The name of the person's assistant is a useful thing to know, and an easy thing to forget. Making the annotations also helps you become familiar with who's who, who does what and who reports to whom. One particular assistant clips photos of executives from *The Hollywood Reporter* and pastes them to the backs of cards. That way, she and her boss know what everyone looks like. Picture clipping is a little extreme, but it is a good example of how an assistant used an information maintenance task to her advantage. While keeping her boss's Rolodex up to date, she also made herself pay attention to what was going on in the industry by being an avid reader of the trades. Before long, she was an expert on various executives and agents around town — a first step to becoming a real insider.

With a computer, the Rolodex becomes a much more powerful tool. A computerized address database is really a sophisticated memory bank for you and your boss. In the course of a year you will place and receive thousands of calls. It is unlikely that you will remember the name of every person your boss speaks to and the purpose of the call. With a computer, the annotation section of the card becomes a key by which you can trace calls and names. Let's say your boss calls an agent who represents an obscure writer to discuss an obscure script. Six months later you and your boss may not be able to recall the name of the agent. However, if you annotated the computerized address database and listed the name of the script and the writer, you will be able to find the name of the agent by doing a *search* on the computer, asking it to find the name of the writer or the title of the script. Either clue will lead you back to the name of the agent.

Smith, Joe President World Pictures Corp. 2029 Century Park East Suite 300 Los Angeles, CA 90067	213-555-1200 (Office) 213-555-1123 (Fax) 213-555-2367 (Home)	Assisant: Joyce Wife: Carol Used to work at CAA	(off Santa Monica 10/1/92 Boulevard, Century City)

Figure 3.6   Sample computerized Rolodex printout in notebook form

Computerized Rolodexes have several other advantages. You can print the whole file and make multiple notebook copies. You then place a copy in your boss's home and/or car, or yours, for that matter. Figure 3.6 shows a typical format for a file printout. The computerized list can also be used to generate mailing lists. Christmas cards, changes of address, and press releases all become infinitely simpler. See Appendix G for software which can be used for an address database.

The *personal phone book* your boss carries with him is an offshoot of the Rolodex. Normally, the personal phone book is less exhaustive than the Rolodex, and may contain sensitive private numbers that your boss does not want available to anyone in the office. As you update the Rolodex, you have to be sure to update your boss's personal phone book at the same time. If you can convince your boss to carry around a fresh computer printout, then you have eliminated your updating chore.

Project Files

Each new project your boss undertakes requires a file. All relevant correspondence and written material should flow into the project file. If the project is a development deal, then every set of story notes should be in the file. If the project is a pitch, then the file should contain every draft of the treatment or notes which were prepared, in addition to any correspondence.

As a project file grows, you will want to subdivide it into separate folders. The objective is to be able to retrieve a specific item, be it a letter or a report, at a moment's notice. If there are more than a handful of papers in the folder, this becomes difficult. The project file is the only complete record of activity on a project, so it must be meticulously maintained. Long after you are gone, some new assistant may have to crack open the file and trace the history of the project.

Project files are generally split into *current* and *inactive* projects. Current files are those which are in use on a daily basis. These include ongoing development, current clients, and active pitch/presentation projects. Inactive files are for dead projects which will never be produced, and backlist projects, which are old ideas that could theoretically be sold, even though they are not being pursued vigorously at present. Minimizing the number of current files on hand in your work area will help eliminate wasted space and effort. Inactive files can be put elsewhere, even in long-term storage, but they should never be thrown away. Sometimes yesterday's garbage is tomorrow's hit.

One thing you will notice right away about the entertainment business is how many times a project can change names. To avoid confusion, an assistant should maintain an *A.K.A. list*, which keeps track of the old names of current projects. When a new assistant starts work, he or she may have to find a folder on a project which has changed names several times. Without an A.K.A. list, old information can get lost.

Chronological File

After your boss has written a letter, the norm is to make one copy for the project file and one for the *Chronological File*, or *Chron File*. The chron file is a continuous chronological file of all written correspondence sent by your boss. The chron file is usually a ring binder with dividers for the months of the year. If your boss is a prolific letter writer, you can use a manila folder for each month of the year. The duplication of filing makes it is easier to find old letters. It helps to have two places to look.

Personal Files

Most executives require their assistants to perform a certain amount of personal work for them. As a result, you will have to maintain personal files for your boss. You don't have to segregate personal files from business files, but you might choose to, because personal files have much more subjective labels than work files, which generally bear the working title of the project. For example, is "Children's Elementary School Report Cards" filed under "C" for children, "S" for school, or "R" for report cards? It will be easier to find if it's contained in a small subsection of the business files marked "Personal." If you do not segregate the personal files, you may still want to color code their labels differently from the others so you can spot them easily.

As in any other endeavor, the personal files are an opportunity for you to improve the effectiveness of your boss. Many executives waste time on poorly-organized personal events, such as charity fund-raisers or parties. If you can help him or her cope with these extracurricular activities, then there will be more time for getting real work done, and you might get home early.

Legal Files

You may or may not prefer to segregate the legal files which pertain to current projects in the office. However, if any group of files deserves special attention, it is the legal files. There is much disagreement and litigation in the business. The only real rationales for resolution are the contracts and deal memos. If your boss finds himself involved in a legal wrangle, he will want to have the most up-to-date legal files available. Unfortunately, in many small offices, legal records are not vigilantly kept. The result is incomplete files and missing documents. The documents are always available—often from opponent —but by the time a paralegal from your law firm has found the items in question, your boss may have spent hundreds of dollars in legal fees.

The essential problem is that negotiation and deal-making in entertainment is often done on a handshake. Very often, the closest thing to a signed contract you will ever see on a deal is a letter of intent. Equally often, the deal will not be signed until after the film is made, if it is signed at all. There is an expression that goes, "The basis for negotiation in the film business is the signed contract." The trick is to recognize the importance of a letter of intent when it floats across your boss's desk and put it in a specially labeled folder inside a project's legal file. It may be the only evidence your boss will ever see that a deal was made. Some executives maintain a desktop file of deal memos in a three-ring binder so they can have instant access at all times.

The custom in legal filing is to create a new folder for each separate deal or agreement. The drafts of the deal and related correspondence all go into the specific file folder. When a contract is finally signed, a copy of it is pinned to the left side of the folder. Drafts are then pinned to the right side. The folder opens neatly, and the signed agreement is accessible instantly.

Clippings File

Most executives clip articles out of the newspaper with some regularity. He or she might clip reviews of films, true stories which could become movies, or profiles of rising young wallpaper designers. Clippings are also frequently used in support of projects which are being pitched to the networks and studios. When your boss clips out an article, or circles it and tells you to clip it out, you will want to put it somewhere it can be located later.

To file a clipping, first prepare the clipping for copying. Cut away any extraneous text or images. Then, glue or tape the clipping onto white paper. Newsprint is very flimsy and becomes brittle as it ages, so mounting preserves a clipping's life. Prepare a folder with the title of the article, the name of the newspaper, and date of publication. Run off as many copies of the clipping as are required and file the folder away. You can integrate the clippings into the project files, but since many clippings don't belong to a particular project when they are cut out of the paper, your best bet would be to keep clippings in their own file drawer. Or if you have enough time, keep copies of the clippings in both a clipping file and in the appropriate project file.

Master Script File

When a writer turns in a script, you will invariably have to make copies of it for reading by your boss, his associates, the studio, and other interested parties. Everyone must always have the most up-to-date draft. The *master script file* is a place where you store the *master copies* of scripts that must be duplicated with any frequency.

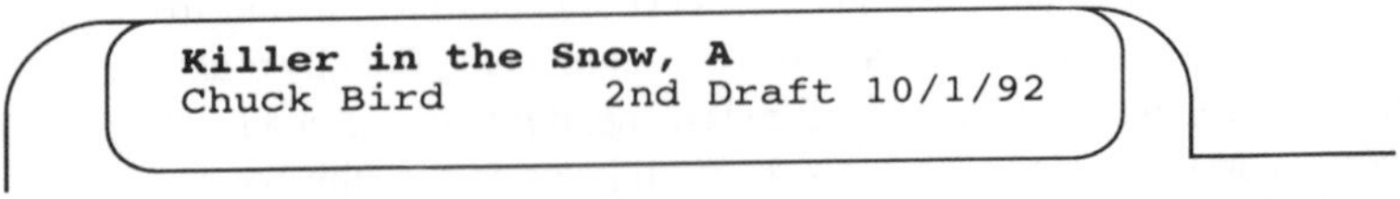

Killer in the Snow, A
Chuck Bird   2nd Draft 10/1/92

Figure 3-7   Sample label for Master Script file showing title in bold, author's name, draft, and date of submission.

Each script is placed loosely in a folder, so it can be removed and run through the copying machine with a minimum of trouble. Paper fastening brads tear up the paper, leading to jams in the copier, and successive generations of photocopying make a script dirtier and more difficult to read. For the sake of appearance, as well as for ease of copying, it is better to make all distribution copies of a script from the original provided by the writer.

People tend to borrow scripts they see lying around. If you keep your master copies bound and sitting on your desk instead of in a file, someone in the office might assume that they are for general consumption and walk off with your only copy of an important script. Searching for missing master copies of scripts and books is a big time-waster in a lot of offices. You can avoid this by filing your masters.

Film Reviews, Ratings and Box-Office Files

Some executives like to clip all film and television reviews from the trade press. Others do not. It's a matter of personal preference, so a systematic file for reviews should be considered optional for an assistant in setting up an office. It is a labor-intensive activity, so it may not be feasible if you are working alone. However, these files can be quite useful if maintained properly.

More films and television programs are produced every year than can be watched by one person. Your boss will only be able to view a small selection of the avalanche of new releases and shows. Reading trade reviews is one way to keep abreast of new films. The file will keep him completely up to date on what's happening in town. You will learn, too.

Filing the reviews creates a resource for story and credits. The trade papers always publish detailed film credits with their reviews. As your boss comes into contact with producers, directors, and various other technical people, he will have to evaluate their credits, both in advance of meeting the people and afterwards. Often, the films that people have worked on are quite obscure, and neither you nor your boss may have seen them. At this point, you can go back to your review file and find out what *Variety* and *The Hollywood Reporter* thought of their efforts.

Box office results and television ratings are a natural complement to the reviews file. Box office is published in the trades on Tuesdays. TV ratings are published on Wednesday. Box office and ratings files are useful for determining the "bottom line" aspect of a person's credits, since many executives equate financial success with talent.

The review and box office files are another good candidate for a computer database. Reviews are normally taped onto sheets of looseleaf paper and stored in notebooks, but if they remain in that form, cross-indexing and searching for non-title elements becomes virtually impossible. You will want to be able to enter a search command for one person's name and call up all the films he or she was involved with. If you only have the reviews organized chronologically or alphabetically, then you will never find the person's complete credits. With a computer you will be able to do this with ease.

Your boss will probably be interested either in film or in television, but usually not both, so you will only have to concentrate on one subject, such as features, TV pilots or TV movies. (If you do TV movies, you ought to track original made-for-cable product as well.)

The method to use is as follows: 1) Grab the trade papers every day and photocopy any reviews relevant to your database. 2) Paste them onto looseleaf paper. 3) Key the vital statistics of the film into a database. The choice of data to include is up to you, but at the very least the entry should list title, director, producer, writer, star, log line, studio or network, and ratings/cumulative gross. 4) File the looseleaf into a notebook, sorted either alphabetically or chronologically. 5) As box-office and ratings information is published, enter the figures pertaining to each film into the database.

At the end of each month, you can prepare reports which summarize the state of the release schedule or the primetime season. These reports help your boss get a handle on the current season at a glance. They also point up which kind of movies are doing well and which are not.

Creating a ratings, box office and review file and database is quite time-consuming. If your company can afford it, most of the this information is available for a fee from Entertainment Data, Inc. at the end of each month. (See Appendix G for details on Entertainment Data.)

Credit Files for Talent

Assistants spend a fair amount of time tracking down credits on directors, actors, writers, and many other pieces of talent involved in putting a film project together. To save time later on, it pays to create a thorough file of credits. Otherwise, you and your successors will repeat the same credit searches over and over again.

Most people in the industry have their credits listed chronologically on a sheet or two of paper. When they are under consideration for an assignment, their agent will fax these credit sheets to your office. A ring binder file organized alphabetically can serve as a place to store all credit information. Or, you can segregate writers from directors or production personnel. The main thing is to file every credit sheet you get. You will find that the same people frequently appear on different lists for work with your company.

Credits are a natural application of a computer database. Notebooks can become voluminous, while a computer can store thousand of people's credits easily. You can cross-index and search, as well as compile condensed listings which are easily read and carried around. With a good database program, you should be able to create an abbreviated but usable, filofax-size talent directory for your boss.

There are also several published directories of talent credits. If you do not have time to maintain a database, you can purchase these directories and update them by hand until the new edition comes out the following year. (See Appendix G for specific titles.) You can also use the published directories to supplement your computer database of credits.

Coverage Files

As readers and assistants read scripts, their coverage, or reader's reports, begins to accumulate. Though coverage is usually copied and circulated to many different executives, it is a good idea to keep a central file of master coverage copies in one place. Executives habitually throw away coverage because they assume that someone else is keeping it on file. Coverage, which is normally a three- or four-page report stapled together, is best filed in a ring binder. As time goes on, you will amass several binders full of coverage, all filed alphabetically.

3.5   LENDING MATERIALS

Occasionally, your boss will lend a videocassette or a book to someone in the industry. In contrast to times when your boss gives someone a script to read, your boss will expect the book or tape to be returned. Your job is to keep track of who borrowed what, and get it back within a reasonable time.

Most producers lend tape copies of their films to other people in the business as a sort of reciprocal courtesy. For example, a producer might want to see a certain director's work, so he will call your office and ask to borrow a tape. When you field such a call, you have to get down the exact name of the person who wants to borrow the tape, and their specific reason for borrowing it. Then, ask your boss permission to lend the tape. It is possible that the person who called has borrowed half a dozen tapes over the years and never returned them. Always give your boss the opportunity to decide whether or not to honor the request for the loan.

You can create a *Materials on Loan* log book which will track the material lent, the date it went out, the name, address and phone number of the person who borrowed it, and the reason they borrowed it. Periodically, you can go over the list and see who has not returned their material. Many people are irresponsible, and never return tapes that were lent to them. You have to begin to request the return of the material early, because if you wait too long, the borrower might lose it. Since good quality videos are costly to duplicate, and replacing tapes from masters is a hassle, it is important that you make every polite effort to get the material returned.

One way to assure the return of valuable materials is to enclose a postage-paid, addressed envelope with the material. Though this adds expense to the loan process, it improves returns dramatically. The borrower merely has to insert the material into the envelope and drop it in the nearest mailbox.

3.6   HIS OR HER DESK

Most of us don't like to have people messing around with our desks. In entertainment, though, if you *don't* mess around with your boss's desk you might get fired. Everyone is different, but most entertainment executives want their desks cleaned up and organized before they arrive in the morning. The desk is merely another tool which you use to enhance the boss's effectiveness in his job and reduce stress and wasted time in your own.

The basic commandment of desk management is to observe any traditions which precede you. If your boss likes to have his newspapers in the same place every day, then don't move them unless specifically asked. At the same time, you should look for ways to improve the organization of the desk, as long as they don't interrupt a stable pattern which your boss finds comfortable.

Before your boss gets in, go over the contents of the desk and open all *incoming mail* unless it is marked "personal." Then position anything which is important within your boss's primary visual field. Your boss will invariably have more paperwork hitting his desk than he can handle in a day. Place secondary items like junk mail on the periphery. Remove any obsolete items from the desk, and empty the "out" box. If there is no "out" box on your boss's desk, then you would do well to campaign for one. It creates a focus for your boss: get paper off the desk!

If the desk becomes a jungle, then radical action is needed. Once in a while I used to scoop every last piece of paper off my boss's desk (with his say-so, of course) and place the contents into a large envelope. Over coffee on Sunday morning at his house we would go over the mail at a leisurely pace. By doing this, we cleaned his desk and freed him of clutter anxiety. Some executives see a messy desk and assume they are forgetting something important.

3.7   THE BOSS'S CAR

Los Angeles is the capital of the automobile culture. If you work for anyone of note, you will spend part of your time caring for the number one possession and status symbol your boss owns, his car. The assistant's role in car maintenance is an unfortunate one. If the assistant does his or her job properly, the good work is invisible. If something goes wrong, the assistant is blamed. Do a good job, so you can get promoted and have an assistant take care of your car.

Develop a maintenance and cleaning schedule for your boss's car. Consult with the mechanic to arrive at a good plan. Then, enter future tune-ups and oil changes into the appointment book even if they are months ahead. They will serve as reminders to you. Cleanings will occur at regular intervals. Your boss will have a preference for how often he wants his car cleaned, and how he wants it done. Sometimes a simple car wash will be enough, but more often than not, executives want *detailing*. Detailing, for the uninitiated, is the ultimate car wash. Done by hand, it involves cleaning and polishing every surface of the car with an exquisite tenderness usually reserved for show dogs. The results are fantastic, though the price can easily be over one hundred dollars! Several detailing services even come to your office and detail the car right in its parking space. (See Appendix G for these.)

Be sure that your boss's gas tank is always full. You may develop a routine for filling the tank. Otherwise, you have to check it once in a while and fill it if necessary. You will want to have your own set of keys to the car, as well as a gas credit card in your boss's name.

Automotive affairs requires a whole new file devoted to the car. You are the official keeper of records for insurance, repairs, maintenance, lease payments, and whatever else is required to keep the car running. Remember, the L.A. car fantasy has two parts: 1) You have this great car and get to drive around in it all the time, and 2) You never have to worry about a thing...someone else takes care of all the paperwork. A good assistant will try his or her hardest to make the boss's L.A. car fantasy come true.

Repair and emergency information should be accessible everywhere your boss might need it. Phone numbers for repair service and AAA must be plastered all over the car, the car phone, your boss's personal address book and your Rolodex. Usually, if your boss has a mechanical problem or an accident he will call you, but you must be prepared to have the situation handled swiftly in your absence if you are unavailable.

Come up with a procedure to follow in case of car emergencies. Don't wait for them to happen. You should have in your Rolodex the names of more than one mechanic who can fix your boss's car, in case the first one is too busy to repair it quickly. A luxury rental car should be available in short order. There are several luxury rental agencies in Los Angeles. (Again, see Appendix G.) A charge account with a cab company is also a convenient thing to have in the event of a car crisis.

Car Crisis Drill:

Your boss calls you at home at 7:00 A.M. In a panicky voice he tells you that his car won't start. He has important meetings starting in an hour. What will he do? Without even getting out of bed, you should be able to tell him:
1) To take it easy.
2) To expect a cab to come in twenty minutes, and to be ready.
3) That he will be behind the wheel of a red Porsche 911 rental with a working phone in no time flat.
4) Goodbye.

Then,
1) Get the number out of your home copy of the office Rolodex and call a cab for your boss.
2) Reserve the luxury car for your boss.
3) Reserve a portable cellular phone for your boss.
4) Call AAA or a tow truck.
5) Call the mechanic.
6) Go back to sleep.

You probably will not have to drive your boss around, but driving is a staple of many entry-level jobs. It was for me. Some executives do not like to drive while speaking on their car phones, so they prefer to have their assistant drive for them. At the very least, you will probably have to take your boss to the airport occasionally. When that time comes, you will have to know how to drive in a manner which is pleasing to your boss, and you must know where you are going.

There should be a *Thomas Guide,* the most comprehensive map of Los Angeles, in the office and the car. Before you drive your boss anywhere, look up the best possible route, keeping in mind likely traffic buildups. Listen to traffic reports on the radio before you get started.

If your boss does not know where he is going, you have to make a map for him. One way to do this is to photocopy the page from the *Thomas Guide* which contains the destination. Using colored markers, highlight your boss's point of departure and his destination. Trace the best route he should take with a highlighter. Call the destination and verify that you have chosen the best route. Then type the directions, including the phone number of the destination, and attach it to the map.

3.8 PETTY CASH AND EXPENSE ACCOUNTS

Your boss will need you to buy things for him from time to time. Lunches for meetings in the office, newspapers, books, videotapes and flowers are just a few of the items you will be asked to run out and pick up for your boss. You have two objectives. You want to make sure that your boss gets whatever he wants instantly, and you want to get reimbursed.

Every company has a slightly different policy regarding cash expenditures made by employees, but generally there are two types of accounting. Under the petty cash voucher system you sign out a certain amount of cash, perhaps $50 or $100, and keep it in a special envelope. As you purchase items, you mark them down on the outside of the envelope and place the receipt for the item inside the envelope. When the cash runs out, you take the envelope to the accounting department. They take the receipts and give you more cash. The expense account system is slightly different. With an expense account, you make the purchases out of your own pocket. At the end of the week or month, you fill out an expense form and receive reimbursement by check.

You have little control over the choice of systems used by your company. Obviously, the petty cash envelope is better, since you don't have to lay out your own money. Asking an assistant who has take-home pay of $290 a week to run out and spend $40 on lunch for a couple of writers does seem a little excessive. You can probably set up a private system of your own if you are not happy with the expense account system. Ask your boss to give you the necessary cash. You maintain your own envelope with him. At the end of the week, the receipts go on *his* expense account, not yours. This can work if you trust each other.

3.9   A GENERAL NOTE ON COMPUTERS

As discussed above, computers can greatly improve your effectiveness in the office by automating such tasks as alphabetizing, filing, and searching for information. With a computer, you can also save time by editing documents in a word processing program. If applied properly, a computer can make you a much better assistant. If your office does not already have a computer, I would make every recommendation to get one. The following very brief summary should help familiarize you with the rudiments of computer systems.

Computers are far from obligatory, however. Many paper-based systems are equally effective, and the best office computer systems are based on an efficient and well-understood manual system which preceded it. Without the underlying structure, the computerized office becomes a nightmare of "garbage in, garbage out."

Hardware

The dominant type of computer in offices is the personal computer. Personal computers, which first appeared in the mid-1970s, are designed to be used by one individual. Before then, computers were large, centralized machines which served many users through terminals. Now, everyone can have their own self-contained computer.

There are two established personal computer systems available today, the Apple Macintosh and the IBM Compatible. The *Apple Macintosh* is a very user-friendly, easy-to-learn, and intuitive computer. The Mac allows you to select files and programs by using a *mouse* —a device which controls the position of the cursor on the screen—to point at *icons*, which are symbols of programs and files. The mouse also enables you to perform a variety of tasks such as selecting pieces of text and moving them around the page, or converting text into italics just by pointing at commands. You can become adept on the Mac in a matter of hours, which makes it an excellent computer for an office where staff turnover is high. You can train new employees quickly to do computer tasks on a Mac.

The Mac has its own special *operating system*. A computer's operating system is the program which tells the computer how to function. Without the operating system, the computer is just a hunk of metal. Apple's proprietary operating system for the Mac is what enables the Mac to have icons and a mouse. No other company can sell a "clone" of a Mac, because they do not have access to the Mac's operating system.

The IBM-compatible computer, or PC, has historically been cheaper and more popular than the Mac, though it is more difficult to use and harder to learn. All IBM-compatible computers contain the same microprocessor chip (the Intel 286, 386 or the 486) and run off the Microsoft Disk Operating System (MS-DOS). Because all IBM-compatible computers have the same chip and operating system, their disks and software are usually interchangeable. For this reason, PCs are said to be an "open system." IBM-compatible computers are manufactured by IBM and a whole range of companies, including Compaq and Dell. Since many manufacturers make PCs, competition has driven the price down.

Microsoft Corporation has created a new operating system for PCs called *Windows*, which emulates the Macintosh style of working, using a mouse and icons. The PC with Windows is a strong competitor for the Mac, but there are many experts who believe that if you want to have a Mac, get a Mac, not a PC with Windows. However, if you already have a PC and you want the ease of a Mac, then it does make sense to convert to Windows.

A computer's *core memory* (also known as *Random Access Memory*, or *RAM*) is the space where it stores programs and data for immediate use. Memory is measured in *bytes*. A byte is the same as one character. A *kilobyte*, or K-byte (or just K), is a thousand bytes. A *megabyte* is a thousand kilobytes. A 3,000-name address database fills about one and a half megabytes, for example. A page of text is about three kilobytes. Most computers available today have at least one megabyte of core memory.

In addition to core memory, computers also have *disk drives,* which store information when the computer is switched off. A *floppy disk* is a small, removable magnetic disk which stores about 800 kilobytes of information. A floppy disk is made of the same material as a cassette tape, only a little more rigid. Floppy disks fit into a slot on the side of the computer known as the floppy disk drive. The floppy disk drive reads and writes information onto the floppy disk using a magnetic stylus similar to what you would see on a record player. A *hard disk* is also a magnetic storage medium, but it has much more capacity than a floppy disk. Hard disks available for personal computers range from 20 to 160 megabytes and beyond. Virtually every personal computer sold today has a hard disk installed inside it.

Personal computers are available in three sizes. *Desktop* computers are the familiar large boxes with detachable keyboards, and *monitors* (screens) that look like television sets. *Portable* computers are substantially smaller and contain a fixed keyboard and a flat screen. Portables can be battery-powered. *Notebook* computers are the smallest, usually weighing about seven pounds and fitting into a case about the size of a large notebook. Of the three, desktop computers are usually the most powerful, though a new notebook is much more powerful than a five-year-old desktop, given the pace of innovation in computers.

Whatever system you choose, however, the most crucial thing is *compatibility*. It is difficult and expensive to make PCs compatible with Macintoshes. Recent innovations such as Mac's *Superdrive*, which can read data off an IBM-compatible disk, have made compatibility between systems easier. However, the results are much better in an office where everyone is on the same standard. With compatible computers, people can share disks, printers and files with little fuss. If someone knows how to run one computer in the office, then he will know how to run them all.

Software

Computer *software* is the term used to describe the programs which enable computers to perform useful tasks. Software comes in two basic categories: 1) *Custom software* is created by professional programmers who write a program to fit your exact needs, and 2) *Off-the-shelf software* is available at software stores. Off-the-shelf software is designed for a certain range of functions which you can adapt and customize for yourself.

There are three main types of off-the-shelf computer programs. *Word Processing* programs allow you to write and edit documents. A word processor is like a typewriter with an endless piece of paper. You can type in text, which is stored in the computer's core memory, and make changes and insertions anywhere in the document. When you are finished, you can store the document on a disk or print it on paper. Word processors offer an advantage over typewriters because you can make many changes on a document quickly without the necessity of retyping.

Database Programs store information systematically, so you can sort it, process it and search through it. A database is the electronic equivalent of a filing cabinet. It consists of *records*, which are bundles of separate pieces of information, each known as a *field*. In the phone company's directory assistance database, for example, your record contains fields for your name, address and phone number. When you design a new database, the software allows you to designate the fields you want in a given record. Databases are useful for any type of categorical information storage, such as a Rolodex or a project list.

Spreadsheet programs arrange numbers on a grid so you can perform calculations on them. A spreadsheet is like an enormous sheet of ledger paper, with hundreds of rows and columns. You can command the spread sheet to add, subtract or multiply any series of numbers in any combination of locations. In addition, spreadsheets allow you to perform advanced mathematical operations and statistical functions on the numbers. Spreadsheets are ideal for budgets, expense accounts, accounting, financial forecasting, and scheduling.

While computers come with operating systems, the choice of software is up to you. As shown in the table below, an entertainment office has uses for all three types of software. Programs are expensive, often costing more than $500, so you may not want to buy all three types of software unless you have a proven need for it.

Database	Word Processor	Spreadsheet
Rolodex	Letters	Expenses
Script Logs	Coverage	Budgets
Talent Credits	Development Project List	Forecasts

Figure 3-8 Table of office tasks by software type

In addition to the three main types of generic software, there is a wide range of specialty software for the entertainment industry. For example, scripting programs enable you to format a screenplay with all the appropriate page breaks and "cut to's" in position — a task which, if done manually, can take hours. Other specialized programs enable you to schedule and budget a film. Appendix G contains listings of several major computer programs with applications for the entertainment industry.

Beyond these listings, there are literally thousands of programs available. Graphics and illustration programs allow you to draw pictures and lay out printed pages on the computer. Computer-Aided-Design (CAD) Programs and engineering programs allow you to design three-dimensional objects and architectural drawings. In the near future, the personal computer will be powerful enough to control videotape editing and digital image production.

Printers

Printers provide the paper output, or hard copy, from a computer. There are several basic types of printers which vary widely in price and performance. Your boss's printer will depend on your office's budget and needs.

Dot Matrix Printers utilize a nylon inked ribbon and mechanical print head which contains anywhere from nine to twenty-four pins. The pins punch the ribbon onto the paper to make the printed images. They are inexpensive, but dot matrix printers tend to be noisy and slow. Their output smudges and the printing is not letter-quality.

Daisy-Wheel printers are like electric typewriters which are driven by a computer. A daisy wheel is a plastic disk which has the letters of the alphabet molded onto its surface. Using a ribbon, the daisy wheel spins and imprints the letters onto the paper mechanically. Daisy wheel printers are letter-quality, but they are also noisy and slow. They can only print text, not images of any kind. Since they are falling out of favor, they should not be anybody's first choice in purchasing a new system. The only reason to buy a dot matrix or daisy-wheel printer these days is to print multi-part forms.

Laser printers put an image on paper using a laser beam in combination with a machine similar to a photocopier. The result is a letter-quality printout which feels like a photocopy. Laser printers are remarkably fast, and they can create the widest range of images. Though they are the most expensive printers, laser printers offer the greatest speed and versatility. They are also considerably quieter.

Inkjet Printers, which spray ink from a cartridge onto the page, offer print quality similar to that of laser printers for a lower price. However, most inkjet printers are slower than laser printers. If you do high volumes of printing, an inkjet printer is probably not adequate.

Modems and Networks

In order for a computer to receive or transmit information to another computer, it must be attached to a *modem*. A modem is a special kind of telephone which allows a computer to talk to anther computer over phone lines. With a modem, you can connect your computer to information services which can give you stock market prices, banking information, or entertainment statistics. You can also send and receive files to and from another computer with a modem. Some new computers have a modem built into the machine itself, but most of the time you will have to buy a separate modem.

A *fax modem* is a modem which allows you to transmit data from your computer to a fax machine, and vice versa. This is extremely useful if you want to send, for example, the same letter to many people at the same time. Simply program in the phone numbers and the best time of day to transmit the fax, and the computer does the rest.

Computers can be connected to each other through a *network*. A network enables multiple users to share the same files by connecting the machines through cables or over phone lines. Most large companies have a computer network. Each person can tap into the central files of the company using his own personal computer. In a corporate legal department with a network, for example, several secretaries can access the same contract on one centralized hard disk drive.

As networking computers becomes more important, computer manufacturers and software companies are making it easier to set up a simple *Local Area Network* or *LAN*. A Local Area Network is a small group of computers in an office which are connected to each other with cables or phone wire. (In contrast, a Wide Area Network might link hundreds of computers over a large geographical area using a dedicated telephone system.) A number of LAN software packages are currently available. In the case of Apple's Macintosh System 7, the networking capability is built into the operating system. With some phone wire and connectors, you can create a LAN in a matter of minutes.

Chapter 4
Handling Written Material

4-0 THE VITAL AND SENSITIVE NATURE OF WRITTEN MATERIAL

WRITER FILES SUIT OVER 'LEAP' ORIGIN
    A. Kevin Schine has sued producer Donald P. Bellisario [Quantum Leap, Magnum PI] for allegedly taking the idea for the Universal-NBC series Quantum Leap from a treatment Schine submitted in 1983. The Los Angeles Superior Court suit seeks at least $250,000 in compensatory damages and unspecified punitive damages. Schine's treatment, which he says he finished in 1982, was called "The Time Well."—**Daily Variety, September 24, 1990**

    This tiny notice from the trades speaks volumes about the importance of handling written material properly in an entertainment office. One can see articles detailing such lawsuits every week in Hollywood. They range from unknown writers filing frivolous claims to Art Buchwald taking on Eddie Murphy and Paramount Pictures in a multi-million-dollar lawsuit over COMING TO AMERICA. In the above-mentioned case, a major producer is being sued over the alleged theft of an idea. In order to respond to the suit's claim, Bellisario must first ascertain when and if his office ever received *The Time Well*. Then, if it was received in 1983, he must figure out who read it, and what response, if any, the treatment was given.
    In the best-case scenario, if Bellisario's office is well run and his assistants over the years have done an adequate job of handling submissions, he will simply have to look up *The Time Well* in the record books. Bellisario

will then be able to say with confidence that the treatment was read and returned to the writer on a given date, and he will be able to prove that the idea for *Quantum Leap* came from a different, coincidental source.

However, if Bellisario's office is run like the vast majority of entertainment companies, with revolving door assistants and record-keeping on a firefighting basis only, he could be in a lot of trouble. Going back seven years, he probably would not know for sure if *The Time Well* ever came into his office, if it was read by anyone, or if it was returned. It would be possible for Schine's attorney to claim that Bellisario's office had received *The Time Well* in 1983 and, rather than respond to it or return it to the author, had appropriated the idea. Bellisario would have little evidence to present in his defense.

A busy entertainment office handles hundreds or even thousands of pieces of written material every year in an unceasing cycle of receipt, analysis and response. It is the job of the assistant to keep track of the whereabouts and status of every single item. The producer, executive or agent must respond personally to each of these *submissions* in a timely manner in order to maintain a close working relationship with the writers and agents who send them in. As a result, he or she will rely on you to keep scrupulous records, and to be familiar with the content of as many individual stories as you are capable of absorbing. It is one of the main reasons you are around.

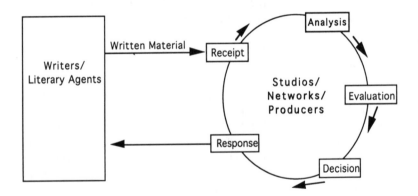

Figure 4-1   The Industry cycle of receipt, analysis and response

The most common form of written submission is the feature-length *screenplay*, though your office may also receive books, manuscripts, treatments, videotapes and newspaper articles. (More on this in Chapter 5.) A screenplay is a highly technical written version of the film, exactly as it would be shot. It is a blueprint for the physical production of the film. In addition to dialogue and stage direction, a screenplay contains character descriptions, and a myriad of production details used by the director and production departments in making the film. If you have never read a screenplay, you must do so before embarking on a job search in the entertainment industry. There are several published scripts from popular movies available at bookstores.

The screenplay also serves as the vehicle of communication for the disparate individuals who join together to make a movie. The screenplay is a surrogate for the movie. Without a screenplay, there is no film. People send screenplays to each other as a way of saying "I want to make a film with you—*this film*." So, when the star actor commits to a film role, he or she is doing it after reading the screenplay. When the studio or network gives the greenlight to produce a film, it does so because it likes the screenplay, and because certain key people, usually a director, star and producer, are "attached." These individuals became attached after reading the screenplay and making known their interest in the project. Every piece of written material flowing through your office is theoretically an employment opportunity for your boss, though, to be sure, some are more legitimate than others.

Your job is to make sure that this process of receipt, analysis and response flows as smoothly as possible. It is not easy to do well, but regular attention to detail in the present will pay for itself many times over in the future, in the form of career opportunities for your boss, and avoidance of wasted work and legal hazards.

4-1   THE INCOMING SCRIPT LOG AND DATABASE

You will want to keep some sort of organized record of the written submissions flowing in and out of your office. If you don't, you are virtually assured of becoming overwhelmed by the volume of detail and material. The result will be lost scripts, incomplete information on submissions, prolonged response times, tarnished relationships between your boss and the submitters, and even litigation. None of the above are desirable outcomes. In fact, a bad case of any one of these could cost you your job.

The best way to keep track of material is with a regularly main-

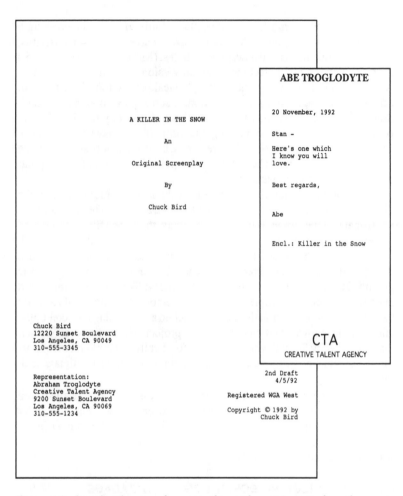

ABE TROGLODYTE

20 November, 1992

Stan -

Here's one which
I know you will
love.

Best regards,

Abe

Encl.: Killer in the Snow

A KILLER IN THE SNOW

An

Original Screenplay

By

Chuck Bird

Chuck Bird
12220 Sunset Boulevard
Los Angeles, CA 90049
310-555-3345

CTA
CREATIVE TALENT AGENCY

Representation:
Abraham Troglodyte
Creative Talent Agency
9200 Sunset Boulevard
Los Angeles, CA 90069
310-555-1234

2nd Draft
4/5/92

Registered WGA West

Copyright © 1992 by
Chuck Bird

Figure 4-2   Sample title page of a screenplay, with covering note from the agent

tained *incoming script log* or *submissions log*. The log could be a spiral notebook or a network of computer terminals. The choice would depend on the availability of a computer and the volume of material the office has to handle. However, regardless of the log's format, the processes are comparable. The idea is to create a baseline of information about every item the office receives. The log should contain the following information for each written submission:

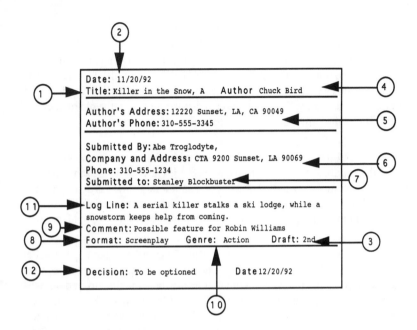

Figure 4-3   Sample submission log card or database screen

1) *The title of the material.*

Be precise. There is a difference between *The Killer in the Snow* and *A Killer in the Snow.* Titles sound alike, and are often identical from script to script, so attention to detail can help you manage the process better. (The story editor's wisdom is that one in four scripts is called *Fire and Ice.*) If your boss is being sued seven years and ten thousand scripts later, the distinction between "A" and "The" could make all the difference.

2) *The date of receipt.*

The date of receipt will dictate proper response time. In this case, the script was received in the office on November 20th, so a response date can be scheduled by working forward from this date. If the submission is an active development project, the writer's paycheck will be due within a certain time span after receipt of the material (usually three weeks). In legal actions, many suits are based on date of authorship. If you, the defendant, can prove that you received a piece of material before the date of authorship claimed by the other side, you may have solved your legal problems.

3) *The draft or version of the material.*

This applies more to active development projects, where writers are completing successive drafts of a script and sending them in to the office, but it is also relevant to regular submissions. For example, a writer may get rejected in 1986, but then rewrite her script and resubmit it in 1987. It is important to realize that the new script is different from the old one, even if the title is the same. It could be a lot better. You never know.

4) *The full name of the author.*

You might have also received a script from someone named Chuck Byrd, in addition to the one from Chuck Bird. They sound the same, but they could be completely different works and authors. If there is an inquiry into the submission after years have elapsed, you want to be confident that the variation in spelling is due to different identities, not typographical error.

5) *The address and phone number of the author.*

This information is often omitted from the title page by the writer. Or, just as likely, the address and phone number on the title page is obsolete. If the address and phone number are missing, take the time to find out what they are upon receipt of the material. You will need this information if you have to return the material with a pass letter, or if your boss decides he is interested. If you are responsible for not being able to get in touch with the writer, you could be in serious trouble.

6) *The name, address and phone number of the author's agent, or the person submitting the material.*

The above explanation, times two.

7) *The name of the person receiving the material in your office.*

You may have to maintain a submissions log for more than one person. To help them organize their reading and responses, it is good idea to note who received what. If *A Killer in the Snow* gets lost, then you will know that the most likely culprit is the recipient, Stanley Blockbuster. Or, if your company passes on *Killer* and someone else turns it into a smash hit film, you will know that Stanley Blockbuster's judgment is not completely sound.

8) *The format of the submission.*

A Killer in the Snow is a screenplay. If it gets lost, then you will know that you are looking for a script, not a book or a tape. If your boss decides that he likes the concept of *Killer*, then he should know at a glance whether it is a full-length screenplay, ready to shoot, or a two page treatment.

Logging the format and length is also a good way to gauge the reading workload of the office staff and your boss. If your office receives ten large book manuscripts on the same day, all with response deadlines, you may have to hire some freelance readers. It is important to know how much material there is to cover.

9) *The purpose of the submission.*

This information has been put in the all-purpose "Comment" slot to save space. Sometimes a writer will send in a script of a movie which has already been produced, just as a writing sample. You should be able to distinguish between these writing samples and actual story submissions. You don't want to go running into your boss's office with a script of CHINATOWN in your hand, screaming about how he has to make this movie.

Also relevant in this category is the response expected of your boss. Every script has a context which determines its urgency and manner of handling. If a spec script by a hot writer comes in on Friday afternoon with a note from the agent beginning, "Only three studios get to bid on this one...", that is quite different from receiving a script by an unknown writer with a note from the agent which says, "This is a young kid with a lot of promise. Give it a read when you have a free weekend."

10) *The genre of the piece.*

You may not be able to know this when you receive it, but it is a good idea to keep track and enter it into the log after the script has been read. Sometimes, stars and studios get inspired and say things like, "Let's do a ski-bunny serial killer picture." It is always good to be able to comb through the database and come up with a few gems to answer the studio's needs.

11) *The log line.*

After the material has been read, you should enter a one-sentence description of the story into the log. The log line is a useful shorthand for identifying a script at a glance.

12) *The decision made on the material, the action taken, and the date it occurred.*

If a script is returned, you have to keep track of when and how it was sent back. The sender may have poor records himself, so he may accuse you of not returning his script. However, if you can look at your log book and say with confidence that you returned *A Killer in the Snow* on December 20th, you're free and clear.

Often, though, material is not returned. Instead, your boss will call the author or agent and thank him for the submission, but let him know that he can't do anything with it. The material is sometimes returned after such a *telephone pass*, but often it is simply thrown away. Sometimes, a piece of material will be put *on hold*, pending some kind of delayed decision or rewrite. This status should be noted in the log and on any subsequent follow-up reports.

You can treat library books as if they were regular submissions. If your office does original story research, then your work space will probably be awash with library books. With everything else going on, you may lose track of these books and incur replacement costs or ill will from the library. By logging in the library books, you can figure out which ones are due back when. Under the comment section, you can put "Library Book — due on 1/23/93." You also create a research record at the same time. Half the time in research is spent finding the right book. Logging in library books tracks work done by the researcher for future consultation.

If your boss receives story submissions in the form of verbal pitches delivered in meetings, you have to create a way to keep track of these stories as if they were scripts. One approach is to log in the pitch, noting the date of the meeting, the people who delivered it, and the essence of the idea. For a fuller record of the pitch, you can keep a *pitch book*, a spiral notebook containing your summary notes of the pitch, which you took while observing the meeting. By maintaining a pitch book and logging in the verbal pitches, you make it easier for your boss to respond to the pitches and keep track of exactly who brought in what idea when.

The incoming script log is the basis of a story department database which will contain a record of every idea ever submitted to the company. Daily logging in of titles creates a skeletal record of each submission. You then complete the record by entering the log line, name of reader, genre, date of return, and action taken. Anyone in the company can access the database and find out the name, log line or author of any script submitted to the company in its history. If you can achieve this level of database integrity, you will have done a great service for your boss.

The database should be easy to use, or your co-workers and successors will ignore it, rendering it useless. If you use off-the-shelf database software, you should create an instruction sheet which outlines the steps clearly and simply for others to use. If you buy customized submissions software, make sure the documentation is readable and clear. Then, create cross-indexes and printouts which anyone can read. It is a mistake to assume that everyone will learn to use a computer. Make it easy for them.

Rigorous maintenance is the only way to make a database work. If the database is incomplete, it will rapidly become unworkable. You have to allocate enough time during the day to enter all the new information which is relevant to the story department. It may seem like a lot of time, but it is time well-spent. If you have to search for a lost script six months later, you will appreciate the value of regular database maintenance.

Even if you don't have a computer, it is possible to keep an excellent submissions database by writing the log information on index cards in addition to the log notebook, and filing them by title. Some offices do both computer and manual index card systems. This is a lot of work, but it can save time and heartache if there a computer failure or a computer-phobic person in the office. Also, the index card system can tie in with your physical materials flow. Acting like a librarian, you can "check out" scripts to readers, but keep the card in a special place so you know who has what. If they lose the script, you can exact punishment.

All of this may seem like common sense, but you would be amazed at how few entertainment offices, even major ones, utilize a solid, long-term record-keeping process like the one described above. A lot of executives have a laissez-faire policy whereby material comes in, gets neglected, and is ultimately disposed of when the mess gets out of hand. Inquiring phone calls are not returned, and in the end the office has missed opportunities, damaged relationships, and exposed itself to legal liabilities. If you inherit a bad system, you can be a turnaround hero by implementing an effective incoming script log.

4-2   UNSOLICITED SUBMISSIONS

George Lucas just spent five years in litigation fighting a lawsuit brought by a Canadian writer who claimed that the Ewok characters in RETURN OF THE JEDI were based on *Space Pets,* an *unsolicited* script he sent to 20th Century Fox in 1978. Lucas had to take the witness stand in a Canadian courtroom several times to claim that he had never seen *Space Pets* (*Daily Variety, 11/14/90*). Lucas won the case, but imagine the time and expense which could have been avoided if someone at the studio had been paying better attention to a fundamental rule in any entertainment office: **Don't accept scripts which just arrive in the mail from unknown writers**. To do so is to invite an expensive lawsuit like the one which plagued Lucas for five years.

If your office receives a script unannounced, from an unknown writer who is not represented by an agent, you should ask your boss for his or her policy on unsolicited or unrepresented writers. Your office probably does not accept them. There are thousands of people all over the country working on screenplays. Some of them may be good, but most of them are not. Aside from legal liability, your office probably does not have the resources to read and respond to all of them. Certain producers have made a business out of discovering new talent through unsolicited material, but their secret is usually a large staff of unpaid interns to do the reading for them.

It is quite likely that someone in America has written a screenplay which is similar, if not identical, to a project your company is developing. Think about how many scripts there are about two tough cops on the trail of a crazed killer — probably thousands. The risk of a misunderstanding arising with an unrepresented writer outweighs the probability that a viable, commercial idea will come from a totally unknown source. However, this is a judgment call to be made by your boss and the legal department, not you.

Most production companies and agencies have a *release form* which they require unrepresented writers to sign before accepting their material. The release limits the production company's liability if the unsolicited story is similar or identical to one currently being developed. It also absolves the production company of any obligation to read or return the unsolicited material. If the writer is unwilling to sign the release, you must return the material immediately. Your company's legal department can draft a release form for your office if one does not already exist.

If a writer sends in material without calling beforehand, return it with a release and explanatory form letter on the day you receive it. This practice minimizes the chance that the writer will think that you secretly read his script, photocopied it, and sold it to a major studio.

4-3   THE PHYSICAL FLOW OF MATERIAL THROUGH AN OFFICE

Your desk should be near the area where submitted material is kept. A good office will allocate sufficient space for this purpose. If yours doesn't, you may want to recommend a change. Physical location of scripts and books should correspond to their status in the evaluation process. Material to be read should be in one place. Material which has been read and now awaits a decision, should be in another distinct place. This makes it easy to find things, and eliminates the chance that a script will get read twice (a sad but common occurrence). Ideally, the storage area should be large enough that the title of a script can be read at a glance.

Over time, scripts, books, coverage and tapes will pile up in an entertainment office. When you start your job, you will probably inherit someone else's pile. You must organize this mess into a neat, accessible *library*. Because of physical incompatibility, scripts, books and tapes may have to be segregated. For easy access, it is smart to shelve everything according to title. Standard bookshelves can accommodate almost anything, but remember to leave enough room on each shelf to expand.

Most of the scripts in the library should be either under option, in development, or already produced. Your office should have enough space to hold such a library. If there is no room on the shelves, you may be retaining too much material, or you may need a larger office. If you work for an old company, it may be necessary to weed out really old, dormant material and put it in long-term storage. Never throw anything away unless you are absolutely certain that a copy exists in safekeeping somewhere.

The purpose of a library is to keep written material accessible for anyone who needs it, and to provide dependable long-term storage for the company's development projects. For more current scripts, it is probably a good idea to maintain a second, temporary library which consists of multiple copies of frequently requested titles. For instance, a script which is in active development may have to be circulated to a large number of people inside and outside the company. To save time, it's worth making multiple copies and keeping them handy. If a starring role is being cast, or a director is being sought, a script may have to be sent out to dozens of agents.

4-4   PRIORITIZING YOUR READING—THE TRIAGE CONCEPT

Triage—*"The sorting of and allocation of treatment to patients and esp. battle or disaster victims according to a system of priorities designed to maximize the number of survivors."*—Webster's Dictionary

Triage? That's something they do in wartime, right? Yes, but triage is a also useful concept to apply in the story analysis department of an entertainment office, a place which at times may resemble a battlefield. As a script reader, you must triage the submitted material. That means setting priorities by reading important submissions, and deferring dubious selections. If you were to read everything which came into the office in the order in which it was received, and paid equal attention to covering every script no matter how bad it was, you would fall far behind in your job. Not only that, your company would miss valuable opportunities, and executive reading piles would bulge with excruciatingly precise analysis of completely irrelevant material.

The first step toward prioritizing reading is understanding the perspective of your company. What kind of movies does your boss make? What kind of clients does your boss represent? What is his or her specialty? Has any new direction or style been announced recently? What is already being developed? These are the questions you must ask yourself when reviewing incoming material. Set your priorities accordingly. If you do not address these issues, you may waste a lot of time reading scripts which the company would never take seriously.

Some companies have prohibitions against certain genres—period pieces, blood-and-guts movies, Vietnam subjects, comedies, you name it. If a script falls into one of the proscribed categories, you'll probably still want to read it, but you may not want give it priority and write an extensive analysis. In these cases, many companies encourage an abbreviated, half-page coverage format for recording purposes only. (See Appendix B for an example.) The trick is to give everything a solid chance without wasting your time. A really good script, no matter what the genre, is always in demand.

How urgent is the submission? Is it a "hot" script, or a casually submitted writing sample? For some material, response time is critical. Major literary agents will send out a script or book manuscript on Friday afternoons, and expect to receive large offers from producers and studios by breakfast on Saturday. That is an extreme example, but there are plenty of times when a script will have to be read within a few days of receipt, if your company is to be in the running for acquisition of the material. These scripts should go to the top of your reading pile. The coverage you write could be part of a major deal.

4-5   READING SCRIPTS AND WRITING COVERAGE

Coverage is industry jargon for a condensed summary of a submission prepared by a reader, for use by anyone who does not have time to read every screenplay and manuscript in full. The reader's summary "covers" subjects such as story and characters, hence the name. Other names for Coverage include *Reader's Report, Analysis, Synopsis, Breakdown* and *Story Report.* Coverage varies from company to company, but the standard begins with a one-sentence log line, proceeds with a two- or three-page

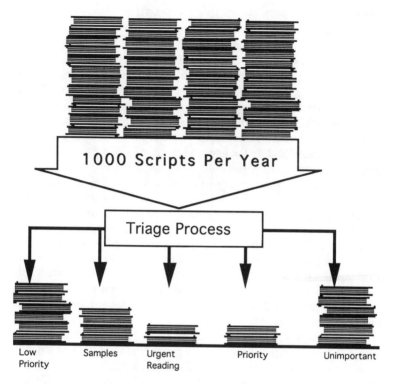

Figure 4-4   Schematic diagram of prioritizing reading through triage

summary of the plot and characters, and concludes with about a page of comments on the quality of the writing and commercial viability of the idea. Often, there is a chart on the front page of the coverage form where the reader rates aspects of the script, such as dialogue, on a scale from one to five.

Coverage serves different needs depending on who is asking for it. Studios need to know if a screenplay can make a commercially successful film. Networks want to derive future star vehicles and high ratings from story ideas. Agencies are interested in how a piece of material could be exploited by their individual clients. As a result, agency coverage tends to call for a more detailed description of individual characters. Whatever the specific purpose, though, the essentials of coverage are clear, concise writing and balanced, sensible comments.

FIVE STEPS TO WRITING GOOD COVERAGE

Step 1—Determine the Intended Medium of the Material

This is a simple question, but it is the cause of much heartache in the world of script coverage. Before you analyze anything, you must know, or at least have a good idea of, what type of film the writer had in mind. Is it a feature script, a miniseries proposal, a true story for a TV movie, a sitcom concept, or a Saturday morning kid's show? You would look for very different qualities when reading scripts from each of these categories.

Misunderstanding the intended destination of a piece of material can lead to misjudgments of suitability. For example, a reader at a company which specialized in television read the manuscript to *A Bright Shining Lie*, which is about an American officer's experience in Vietnam. The reader recommended a pass on the grounds that it was unsuitable for a commercial television movie. A week later Peter Guber and Jon Peters bought the book for a feature at Warner Bros. The reader was correct in his assessment, but he judged the book by excessively narrow criteria. It was a good book, bound for critical acclaim and bestseller status. The reader should have been aware of the potential it held as a feature. More importantly, whoever was supervising that reader should have had a more flexible and attentive system of evaluation in place.

Sometimes, a writer will create a feature script which actually belongs on television. For example, you might read a script about a family and all of its humorous dynamics and relationships. The script rambles plotlessly for a hundred pages and ends pretty much where it began. Sounds like a loser, right? Maybe, but it is worth considering converting the story to a situation comedy. It could work. Many major studios circulate all coverage between the television and feature divisions, hoping for just this type of conversion.

Sometimes the format is written right on the title page. It will say "screenplay" or "teleplay," though TV writers often label their work "screenplay." If the title page is a dead end, check the covering letter from the agent. A phrase in the cover letter such as "Spielberg wants to direct" should tip you off that the script is for a feature film.

Length is another indicator of the screenplay's intended medium. Feature film scripts are usually about a hundred and twenty pages or more. Television movie scripts, which must always conform to the network time standard, are somewhat shorter, but rarely are they under a hundred pages for a two-hour MOW. Hour-long episodic television scripts run about sixty pages. Sitcoms are typically about forty or fifty pages, double-spaced.

The main thing is to be able to recognize quality, regardless of format. If it is not evident what type of movie the material is intended to be, then read it and *you* decide. The only way to become adept at this is through practice and feedback from others, which will show you the range of possibilities which exist for any idea.

Step 2—Reading

Scripts should be read attentively, but not obsessively. In the beginning, you will want to read every word and take copious notes. This will get you into the habit of writing good, clear summaries for the first few scripts. However, it is a good idea to wean yourself off note-taking at an early stage. It can be very time-consuming, and can lead to dense, overly detailed coverage, if done to excess.

After a while, you will be able to see the flows of stories and characters, and reading will become a lot easier. Some experienced readers read the first thirty pages of a script, then skip to the last ten. I wouldn't recommend this to anyone with less than a year's experience, but most professional readers can guess with a high degree of accuracy what is contained in the middle seventy pages. In general, skipping pages is a bad way to run a story department, but it can be an effective way of screening dozens of submissions in your triage process.

One way to read a script is to lock on to the main character, and then concentrate on what happens to him or her as the script progresses. Readers of coverage are not interested in trivial aspects of the plot, so as a story analyst, your best bet is to follow the continuity director's motto of "Keep your eyes on the money." Follow the star. If the script is an ensemble piece, concentrate on the major players.

Break the story down into its three acts as you read. Most movies have a *three-act dramatic structure*. The *first act* introduces the characters and situation, then ends with some critical incident. Think, for instance, of the fire starting in THE TOWERING INFERNO, or Bruce Willis deciding to fight the terrorists in DIE HARD. Those scenes are the *first act breaks*.

The *second act*, usually the longest, takes the characters through the process of discovering what needs to be discovered, or fighting the forces which need to be fought. In DIE HARD, the second act consists of the extended cat-and-mouse game which Willis plays with all the terrorists, and the continuous unraveling of what they were doing in that building in the first place.

The *third act* is the finale and resolution. Third act breaks are usually noticeable. There is a quickening of pace. In action films, the third act often begins with a cataclysmic car chase on about page 90. In dramatic films, characters usually make important decisions about themselves or their relationships in the third act. In JAWS, the third act begins when the men get on the boat to hunt the shark. They have realized there is a shark (Act I), seen the shark kill a few people and panic the town (Act II), and now they have decided to kill the shark and end the movie (Act III). Next time you go to the movies, try to locate the act breaks for practice. Even if a script does not have readily discernible act breaks, you can sort the story into its relevant parts and dramatic "beats" as you read it.

Visualize the movie as you read the script. If the script is well-written, you should be able to imagine specific stars playing the parts. Run the movie in your head. Does it look like the kind of movie you would pay to see? Visualizing helps you identify problems with a script. For example, the writer may describe a scene that would be physically impossible or completely absurd. If you are just reading as quickly as you can without visualizing, you may miss these problems.

Step 3—Writing the Log Line

The *log line*, a one- or two-sentence description of the material, is shorthand for the complete film idea. Ideally, a log line should be a simple sentence which describes the underlying concept, story flow and characters contained in the script. At the very least, the log line should serve as a convenient way to identify a piece of material.

Some movie executives say that if you can't explain a film in two sentences or less, it won't work. Though this is a glib oversimplification, it is not a bad idea to consider when writing log lines. If you have great difficulty condensing a script into a simple sentence, then it's likely that decision-makers will have a similar problem grasping the essential film idea contained in the script. Log line writing can be an acid test for a script. If it is impossible to come up with a good log line, then the idea is probably uncommercial. For practice, try to think of log lines for films you have seen recently.

The log line should concentrate on the star of the film. A good way to think through a log line sentence is to distill *what* happened to *whom* in the simplest terms, leaving out all detail. Did someone get killed, or kidnapped? Did the star do something to someone? The log line for JAWS would be, "Shark attacks town, forcing sheriff, shark hunter and oceanographer to risk their lives hunting it down." Let's try a more difficult example.

Pretend, for the sake of argument, that you have been given John Steinbeck's *The Grapes of Wrath* to read and analyze. Your first stab at a log line might look like this:

> The Joad family of Oklahoma loses their farm to a bank foreclosure in the 1930s, buys a used truck, which they load up with all of their belongings and set off to California, where they have heard that jobs picking fruit are available. However, their journey is long and stressful, and in the process, their grandmother dies and when they get to California they find that there are thousands of other 'Okies' already there, the fruit growers exploit them and the pregnant daughter's child is stillborn.

A bloated and incomprehensible log line such as the one above is a common occurrence with the inexperienced script reader. The problem comes from trying to tell the whole story in the log line. This is impossible. Let's try it again, only this time concentrating on the main ideas.

> The saga of a displaced Depression-era family that travels to California to find, not the advertised paradise, but a jungle of union-busting and misery.

With my sincerest apologies to John Steinbeck, this is an adequate log line for *The Grapes of Wrath*. It serves the basic purpose of identification and gross summary. One would not confuse this book with a Sidney Sheldon novel. However, this log line can be improved by adding some character description and detail:

> Tom Joad, oldest son of a displaced Oklahoma farmer in the Depression, leads his family through a grueling odyssey to California, where, as migrant workers, their dreams of paradise are shattered by the vicious practices of big business and the prejudice of local people.

It may be apparent to you by now that log lines and good English grammar are not always compatible. People will forgive you for butchering the language if you can get the idea across successfully. Your high school English teacher will never know.

Step 4—Writing the Synopsis

The synopsis should tell what the film is all about in two or three pages. If you have read the script attentively, noting the central characters and story structure, writing the synopsis will be easy. A synopsis is nothing more than a book report, a literary form you should have mastered by junior high school. Expectations vary from place to place, so you should read a large sample of coverage written by your boss's favorite script reader to get a sense of what style to adopt. However, the following general structure and approach would do well for you in almost any reading job.

Begin with a paragraph which introduces the most important characters and the basic premise of the film. Include period, setting, and contextual information if it's relevant to understanding the story. This opening paragraph, which is something of an augmented log line, further orients the reader of the coverage and sets the stage for the narrative description that forms the body of the text. Keep in mind the journalist's questions: Who, what, when, where, why and how?

The narrative description is the simplest part of the coverage, but it presents the biggest challenge to some script analysts. If you keep your eyes on the main character and major story points, you will not go far wrong. If you find yourself getting bogged down in lengthy and intricate descriptions of plot, it may be because your opening paragraph is missing some important stage-setting information. For example, if you read a spy script and describe the story in your opening paragraph as a "Byzantine espionage thriller set in four countries," you will be absolved from having to chronicle every twist and turn in the plot. The complex plot is a given. You need only concentrate on the major beats of the story. Paying too much attention to small story developments will only confuse the reader of the coverage.

A rule of thumb is to allocate one paragraph for each major turn of the story, which will bring you to about eight or ten paragraphs of normal length over three pages. This is not a hard and fast rule, but it can guide you if you feel like your report is getting too long. If you haven't wrapped up describing act one after two pages, you need to condense. However, if you are writing coverage of a novel, different standards apply. With long books, you may want to take up to ten pages to get into the kind of detail necessary to do justice to the author's work. Such books are often the basis for long television miniseries. Conversely, the encapsulation of a treatment can be as short as half a page.

If you can write clearly and concisely, you will be loved and admired by your boss. Many readers get into trouble by trying to be too sophisticated in writing their coverage. Remember, your synopsis is not a review in *The New Yorker*. Use simple, straightforward English. You can take a few liberties in your comments, but the synopsis should be readable. Producers and executives have to read piles of coverage. Don't make their job harder by using coverage to show off what you learned at the Iowa Writer's Workshop.

Above all, don't editorialize in the synopsis. If you think a script is good, highlight what you think are the best parts of it in your narrative. If you think a script is bad, then try your hardest to write the narrative honestly and fairly. Nothing is worse in a synopsis than sarcasm or a hostile attitude. Not only does this bias the coverage, it also clouds the description of what is going on in the story. A good producer can sometimes pick out one thing from a bad script and turn it into gold. You should not get in the way of this process.

Sample sentence from a poorly-written synopsis:
Robert, a cliché tough cop character who is middle-aged and divorced, breaks into the warehouse where Alphonso, the drug lord who had an affair with Robert's ex-wife Celia, causing their breakup, hides his dope.

Problems:
Aside from awkward, run-on construction, this sentence is overly detailed and confusing. In addition, the editorial opinion about Robert's character does not belong in the synopsis section of the coverage. It is an attempt by the analyst to show off that he has read so many scripts that he considers the tough cop a cliché.

Revised:
Robert, a tough cop, breaks into a dope-filled warehouse owned by Alphonso, a drug lord.

The other facts in the story, if relevant, should be described in separate sentences.

Step 5—Comments

Someone is actually paying you to tell them what *you* think of a movie idea! Can you even believe it? It is a great thing to be able to render an opinion on a script, but it's also a power and a responsibility which must be approached with respect. The *comments* section of a coverage is where you can air your views on the state of American film in general, and one specific writer in particular. Be advised, however, that the comments section is included in the coverage to serve the needs of your company, not your creative visions.

It is an irony frequently pointed out in Hollywood that the individual with the most direct responsibility for judging a piece of material, the reader, has the fewest credentials for doing so. "If readers were smart enough to know what was going to be a hit" observed one producer, "then they wouldn't be reading scripts for $40 a pop. They'd be running the studio." There is a lot of truth to that remark. It underscores some important guidelines for writers of coverage: Be analytical. Be fair. Be honest, but exercise humility.

You begin your career brimming over with enthusiasm for the movie business. You have not seen too many scripts, so everything may read like a masterpiece. Novice readers frequently suffer from expressing excess optimism over nondescript ideas, or trying to say something nice about every script. A typical comment from a novice reader might be, "It's about time Hollywood did a major movie on the life of Sister Maria Cherubusco, a thirteenth-century nun who lived a life of silence... I bet Madonna would leap at the chance to be in a $30 million period piece, filmed in Latin but with English subtitles."

The negative feedback you receive for being a Pollyanna leads you to cynicism, the inevitable next stage of the reader's life cycle. After about six months, you will hate everything. And, if you don't hate a script, you invent a petty excuse to hate it, or at least be smug about it. It is usually at this point that the producer sneaks a script written by his wife into your reading pile and gets back a comment such as, "I wouldn't disgrace my backside by wiping it with this most trivial piece of Philistine sub-moronic fluff..."

It is seldom a good idea to trash a script completely. Does anyone benefit from it? If anything, trashing a script with harsh comments evokes the negative image of a lowly reader trying to "talk big."

The other major pitfall in writing comments is pretentious intellectualism. Citing Roland Barthes and Aristotle may have gotten you a lot of A's in college, but it can give you the stigma of being an aloof nerd in the movie business. Your PhD colleagues will not read your coverage, so you shouldn't try to apply the standards of academic journals to your work. Once in a great while, an intellectual idea may be warranted in the comments section. If you cannot resist making highbrow allusions, then pretend they are desserts while you are on a diet. Allot one for yourself when you've been very good about not doing it for weeks.

Finally, if you survive gushing, cynicism, and pretention , you can find salvation by adopting a balanced and professional attitude toward the material. After all, this is why you were hired. Your boss will be pleased with you, because you can now expertly differentiate good from bad and commercial from art-house. Your comments now sound more like this: "The Sister Maria Cherubusco story is compellingly written, but it is too obscure and soft to be a commercial film." This gets right to the point: the writing is good, but the idea is untenable. No attitude was necessary was to communicate this opinion.

All you have to do to write useful comments is state whether the piece is good or bad, and give your reasons. In doing this, you should evaluate the quality of the dialogue and the depth and appeal of the characters and story. Then match the quality of the script with the perspective of your employer. Figure 4.5 illustrates the trade-offs between quality and suitability which drive most story selection. In essence, a script will fall into one of the four categories shown in the matrix. Some scripts will be perfect. That is, they're just the type of story your company wants, and they are well-written. Most of the time, however, scripts will fall short in some area. They will either lack quality of writing, or suitability of concept. As

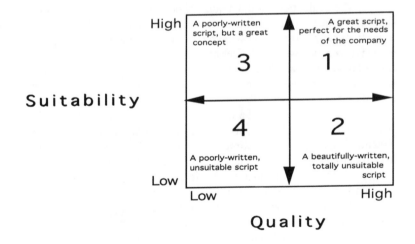

Figure 4.5   The quality-suitability matrix

117

you read scripts, try to position them on the matrix shown in Figure 4.5. The ones closest to category 1 are the ones you will want to recommend.

You have to gauge a script's suitability based on your company's perspective, even if it is at odds with your own. If you work for a schlock horror producer, you may have to shelve your disdain for the genre in writing comments. Evaluate the horror script according to the standard of, "Will this make a good horror film?", not "Will it compare to Fellini's 8 1/2 ?" The trick, though, is to avoid being overly rigid in the application of your company's standards. If a script catches your attention, but seems at odds with what you have been told to look for, you will probably want to ask other people what they think of it. You may have found something out of the ordinary, and great.

If you are confused by this process of subjective evaluation, ask yourself if the script reminds you of a movie you liked, or didn't like. Maybe it is MOONSTRUCK in a Puerto Rican family, E.T. underwater, or a cross between THE TERMINATOR and THE WIZARD OF OZ. Comparing is an effective way to express an opinion, but it is very widely used, and some people find it tired. Every series producer in town is peddling a format which combines *M*A*S*H*, *Hill Street Blues* and *The Odd Couple* all at once! You can also get into real trouble if you compare a script you like to a film which your boss hated, or one which lost a lot of money. You need to know what you are talking about when you make a comparison.

The evaluation should assume shooting starts tomorrow. Forget what the script could be. Is the script good enough now? Do not make suggestions for rewriting unless asked. Notes for a rewrite are a separate, more involved process, which does not belong in coverage. They are also a waste of time if they aren't necessary. One could easily generate a couple of pages of notes when all that's needed in the comments section is at most one page of opinion.

The comments section will culminate in a brief recommendation. Usually, the reader will recommend a pass, an enthusiastic "Buy it," or a "Potentially good idea." Sometimes the recommendation will be "Consider this writer for project X," or, "See if this writer has any other work. I like her style, etc." The recommendation should be visible at the bottom of the comments section, so your boss can know the basic decision at a glance.

A worthwhile goal in writing coverage is to improve your writing quality and speed. The better you are and the faster you work, the more highly valued you will be in the development area. Ask people for feedback and take their opinions seriously. If an experienced person thinks your coverage is too long, or too confusing, you would do well to listen and try to change your style. While it may take you several hours to write decent coverage in the beginning, you ought to be able to do it better in an hour or less after a few months. If you can't, you are probably still paying too much attention to unimportant details in the story. Samples of coverage for a film script and novel are contained in Appendix B for reference, but the best way to learn how to write good coverage is to practice writing it yourself.

4-6 MAKING A READING LIST FOR YOUR BOSS

To get an overview of all the material coming into the office, your boss will want to see all the coverage. From this, he or she will decide to read certain pieces in their entirety. Even before the coverage is written, your boss will want to know what material has arrived, in case something must be read that night or over the weekend. For this reason, in some offices, the cover letter from the agent or author is copied and placed in front of the boss within minutes of receipt.

Before you can prepare a reading list for your boss, you must be totally familiar with every piece of material yourself. Most companies have more than one reader and executive, so there will be a constant stream of coverage generated by other employees which you must integrate into your boss's information flow. You should position yourself so you read every piece of coverage before it gets to your boss, though you shouldn't cause a delay. If you work in a two-person office, you won't have this problem, but the principle of total knowledge still applies. You should be able to identify every piece of material in the office by title and plotline.

Given the high volume of material most busy offices receive, it is easy for the boss to get overloaded with material for the *hot*—or *weekend reading*—*list*. Bosses who are avid readers will want to read everything personally, but this is neither feasible nor desirable. If you do not pay close attention to your boss's home reading pile, it can grow to gargantuan proportions. There are two things you can do to prevent this situation, which can have disastrous consequences in missed opportunities and embarrassment.

First, you should keep your boss posted at least once a day on what has come in to the office, what has been covered, and what has been designated as "hot." Second, you should make an orderly list, on a daily or weekly basis, of material which he or she has requested for personal reading. Some executives only read on weekends, so in this case a Friday afternoon weekly report will suffice. The reason you're around is so scripts can be read on weeknights, while your boss is hobnobbing with famous people at cool restaurants.

The home reading list should contain title, author, format and agent. Your job is to coordinate the physical flow of material into and out of your boss's briefcase, car and home, and to make sure it matches the reading list. You can avoid an irate Saturday morning phone call if you follow this policy with enthusiasm and dedication. On Monday morning your job is to know what left the office and what returned, what he read and didn't read, and whether anything got lost. Sometimes the surf at Malibu gobbles up a masterpiece or two if your boss does his reading in a flimsy deck chair. Losing material is a forgivable sin as long as you call the agent to apologize and ask for another copy. To lose something and ignore it is inexcusable.

4-7   EVALUATING AND RESPONDING TO MATERIAL

Your boss must evaluate and respond to written material as he receives it. If your material handling process is working properly, most submissions can be handled within a week or two. The most effective way to facilitate the response process is to review the *submissions report* or *consideration list* when the subject is fresh in your boss's mind, and get decisions then on various scripts. Figure 4.6 shows a sample submissions report. Like the home reading list, it lists the title, author, agent, log line and date of submission for every piece of material which requires a response from your boss.

If there is not a regular story meeting in your office, then Monday morning is a good time for getting responses on material. Run down the names of the scripts, and find out exactly what action needs to be taken. In the overwhelming number of cases, the decision will be to pass on the material. Your boss will say "I'll call him," "Hold on that one," or "Write a letter" for each item on the list. The phone calls can be entered into the outgoing section of the phone log book. The "on hold" projects should go back to the appropriate storage area.

The *pass letter* is a delicate art form. The content of the letter will depend on the status of the author or agent, and the relationship between that person and your boss. The pass letter should take into account the fact that enormous personal feelings are tied up in a piece of written material. No matter how bad a script is, someone spent a lot of time on it. One should be cordial but not condescending in a pass letter. Bear in mind that the agent

---

Material under consideration as of 12/1/92   Page 1

<u>Prince of Waves, The</u> SP by E. Scrivener   Submitted by Max Marx, Literary Assoc. 10/30/92
   A man in mid-life crisis runs away from his wife and kids in the South to confront ihis
   violent childhood while learning to surf at Waikiki Beach.

<u>Caine's World</u> SP by X. Hack   Submitted by Moe Gull   11/1/92
   Former ship's captain starts public access music television show in a small town after
   facing a disgraceful navy court martial.

<u>Basic Manners</u> SP by B.G. Bux Submitted by Abe Troglodyte, CTA   11/5/92
   Famous writer of etiquette books succumbs to the temptation of a torrid affair and
   becomes a serial killer.

<u>Bon Bons of the Inanities</u> BOOK by Walt Fox Submitted by Sue Smart   11/15/92
   Maker of candies has an auto accident in a bad area of town, but he is able to survive by
   handing out gift packs of his Christmas selection and singing show tunes until the cops
   arrive.

Figure 4.6   Excerpt from a sample submissions report or consideration list

who sends you a bad script this week could stumble on DRIVING MISS
DAISY next week. You want to be at the top of his list.

   After the decision to pass has been communicated to the agent or
author (usually the agent), it is standard practice to return the material in the
mail. Sometimes agents will tell you to throw out the submission, but
generally they want it back. For one thing, they paid to photocopy it, and you
can save them a few dollars by returning it, but mostly it's a simple courtesy.
In these days of recycling, returning a script makes ecological sense.
Returning it also adds finality to the pass decision, and quiets fears that you
are showing it all over town, which would be a disaster for the agent and a
major breach of trust.

   On the next pages are a few sample pass letters.

1)   The simple, to-the-point version.

> Mr. Abe Troglodyte
> Creative Talent Agency
> 9200 Sunset Boulevard
> Los Angeles, California 90069
>
> Dear Abe:
>
> Enclosed is <u>The Memoirs of Henry VIII</u>, by Peter MacMillan,
> which we are returning. Thank you for letting us have a
> look at this script, but we are going to pass.
>
> Best regards,
>
>
> Stanley Blockbuster

This letter is effective, if a little short and cold. It identifies the material, author and decision being taken. There is no ambiguity about what is happening.

2)   The explanation.

> Dear Abe:
>
> Enclosed is <u>The Memoirs of Henry VIII</u>, by Peter MacMillan,
> which we are returning. Though we found Peter's script
> enjoyable and well-written, we decided after extensive
> discussion that it was not in a subject area which we want
> to pursue at this time.
>
> Thank you for letting us have a look at this script. We
> all love Peter and his work, and we hope to see his next
> one as soon as it is ready.
>
> Best regards,

The risk of this letter is that the recipient may perceive it as patronizing. It is often better to say less.

3) The personal note.

```
Abe -

I'm sending back the
Henry VIII piece. It's
not for us, but thanks.
Talk to you soon.

Love and kisses

Stan
```

Obviously, this is only appropriate when you know the person well.

4) The form letter

```
Mr. Peter MacMillan
135 South Marwell
Los Angeles, California 90090

Dear Peter:

Enclosed is your screenplay,The Memoirs of Henry VIII,
which we are returning to you. We review thousands of
screenplays every year, and can only proceed with a very
few. Thank you for thinking of us, but we are going to
pass.

Sincerely,

Stanley Blockbuster
```

The main point here is to demonstrate to the writer that his work was read and taken seriously, but physically returned to him.

4.8 THE PACE OF EVALUATION

The flow of material into your office is likely to be steady and unceasing. As a result, the material has to flow out your office and back to the submitters at an equal rate, or the office will become completely swamped. Imagine a bathtub filling up with water. Your office is the tub, and the water flowing out the faucet is the weekly load of scripts and books arriving from agents. The drain is the evaluation and response process. If the drain blocks up, the tub fills up and overflows. As the person in charge of processing scripts, you operate the drain.

Like the bathtub drain, which can only release a certain number of gallons of water per minute, your office has a maximum capacity for reading and analyzing scripts. Assume that it takes ten minutes to log in a script, two hours to read it, half an hour to cover it, ten minutes to discuss it, and ten minutes to return it. In total, it takes three hours to process a script from beginning to end. If you work on scripts and submissions for thirty hours a week, your *response capacity* for processing scripts is ten per week. That is, working at your average rate, you can read, analyze, discuss and return ten scripts a week.

The difference between the number of scripts your office receives in a week and your response capacity will determine two things: 1) *response time,* the average length of time your office requires to respond to a script, and 2) the *inventory* of unread scripts, the number of scripts waiting to be read in the office at any given time. If your office receives exactly ten scripts every week, you will be able to read and return all of them with a response time of just one week. There will be no inventory of scripts left at the end of the week. In reality, your office will probably receive more scripts in a week than you can read and return. You will only be able to respond to ten scripts every week. After those first ten scripts have been processed, the others will have to wait in the inventory until next week.

If there is a big delay in responding to material, the cause might be an imbalance, or *bottleneck,* within the response process itself. Each phase of the response process, from logging in to reading to evaluating, is a discrete operation, with its own response capacity and average response time. For example, we assumed in the above example that it took ten minutes to log in a script. What would happen if the computer broke and it took two hours to log in a script? The result would be a pileup of scripts at the log-in phase of the response process. Logging in would be a bottleneck, and the downstream process of reading and evaluating would be "starved" of scripts. Everything would slow down, and the delay at logging in would cause a delay in the entire response operation. The whole office would not be able to respond to scripts as quickly as it normally could. The entire response process is only as fast as its slowest operation.

Chapter 5
The Script and
Story Development Process

"Right now it's only a notion, but I think I can get money to make it into a concept...and later turn it into an idea."

—from ANNIE HALL by Woody Allen

5.0   DEVELOPMENT HELL

Development refers to every facet of creating a finished screenplay, beginning with the initial genesis of an idea and ending with a polished production draft. Between these two points occurs a phenomenal range of activities involving dozens of people in numerous and varied contexts. Development is everyone's business.

Producers, executives and agents all spend a large proportion of their time on development. Some say that too much time and attention is devoted to development. Since the studios and networks only produce a fraction of the scripts they commission, most producers and executives are developing projects which will never get produced.

Ever-growing staffs of development executives at production companies and studios assure that a script will be rewritten several times. Successive rewrites by different writers and notes upon notes by meddling executives can sometimes obliterate the original idea and unique voice of the creator. The process, which is quite costly, can easily last for years. "Development Hell" is the term used to describe this endless, destructive development cycle.

How does "Development Hell" affect you? For one thing, it is the current status quo in the industry, so you will inevitably find yourself working in the middle of the exhaustive development practices described in this chapter. Just as important to you, though, is the burgeoning sentiment in the industry that "Development Hell" must stop. The future may well bring a drastic reduction in the amount of development work and the number of development executives. Though it is now a way of life, the overemphasis on development could end, having a great impact on your career.

5.1 THE DISCOVERY OF THE IDEA

Development occurs in two broad phases: creating of the basic idea, followed by writing the actual screenplay. The first phase encompasses story selection and preparation, and presentation of the idea to financing entities. The second phase involves a series of drafts, story meetings and rewrites.

Each phase of development functions like a funnel for ideas. Many are considered, but few are adopted. Figure 5-1 shows the two phases as two funnels through which ideas pass on their way to becoming finished films. Given the studio ratio of development to production, a producer must develop at least ten or more projects to get one film produced. Getting ten projects to the development stage means considering hundreds of ideas and selecting a handful for a more intensive examination. As a project progresses along this path, it will require greater commitments of time and money. A well-run development department will look like a funnel with a wide mouth and a narrow spout. Few ideas are pursued, to maintain maximum focus and minimum waste of resources.

The thousand ideas shown at the top of the funnel can come from just about anywhere. There are dozens of sources of ideas, including, but not limited to, books, plays, scripts, newspaper articles, history, and your own imagination. Writers, stars, agents, lawyers, and other producers will all submit ideas to your company. Your boss can take the initiative and call them to solicit ideas. Even an assistant like you can pursue ideas if you think they have potential.

Books

Many great films have been made from books, so producers are always on the lookout for good books to adapt. Since the publishing industry is based in New York, the studios and some powerful producers maintain development offices in New York, which serve as "listening posts" in the publishing world. When a well-known author is finishing a new book, the

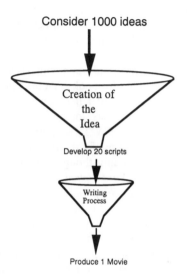

Consider 1000 ideas

Creation of
the
Idea

Develop 20 scripts

Writing
Process

Produce 1 Movie

Figure 5-1   Development as a two-step funnel

studios and producers quietly attempt to get a peek at the manuscript. Their New York representatives take advantage of long-standing relationships with editors, agents and authors to gain the all-important first look at a major work.

A typical book rights situation might look like this: An important author is rumored to be completing a manuscript for a novel which will be published a year hence. The publishing house refers all inquiries to the author's agent, who tells everyone that the manuscript will be ready for viewing at a certain date. However, a select few good friends of the agent get to have a look at the manuscript a week early. (The manuscript might at this point be copied in breach of the informal *sneak peak* agreement, and everyone in town will have one on their desks within twenty-four hours.) The select few get to express their interest early. If one of them can hustle enough, the film rights to the book will be bought before anyone else even knows it exists.

In addition to new releases, book agencies also have extensive *backlists*. Several of the most powerful book agents in New York represent authors who are dead. Many great authors have books which have never been made into movies. Talented development executives will know where to look for these backlist titles, which are often lower in price than new bestsellers.

Producers can't sit back and wait for agents to submit good books. A producer constantly searches for books that hold promise as film ideas. Often these are not on the bestseller list. Development executives (and assistants who are interested in development) read *Kirkus Reviews* and *Publisher's Weekly* (known as "PW"), two publications which offer condensed reviews and plot summaries of virtually every book being published. *Kirkus* and *PW* are just the beginning, though. People also read the *New York Times Book Review, The New York Review of Books, Library Journal,* and *The (London) Times Literary Supplement,* as well as Fall and Spring catalogues from many different publishing companies.

As an assistant you can, with your boss's permission, solicit copies of books from book agents. But watch out. You can make a lot of work for yourself by soliciting too many books. Friends at studios or big talent agencies might be able to share with you the coverage done by their readers as an occasional favor. However, if you solicit a book, you usually have to read and cover it yourself.

Spec Scripts

Writers sometimes sit down and write a finished screenplay *on spec*, which is short for "on speculation." In doing this, the writer is taking a risk. He works for free for the amount of time it takes to write the script. However, the payoffs for spec scripts can be substantial if they are auctioned off to a studio. The price of spec scripts has escalated in recent years. Until recently, around $250,000 was considered the most a studio would pay for a spec script. Then, in the wake of the writers strike of 1988, the prices started to climb, culminating in the spectacular $3 million deal for Joe Eszterhas's BASIC INSTINCT in 1990. Prices have declined since these highs, but they are still well above what was once considered the unsurpassable upper boundary.

Theoretically, spec scripts represent an advantage to all parties concerned. The writer receives the kind of money and recognition usually paid to directors and actors. The studio gets a script which is ready to shoot instantly, circumventing the long development cycle. This saves the studio time and, even with the high prices, money. The prices for spec scripts don't look so high when compared to what it actually costs the studio to develop material from scratch. The agent gets to conduct an auction and bid up the price of the material. The high-profile sales, which are reported in the trades, are useful publicity for the agent and his client.

Spec scripts are rare in network television. It doesn't make sense for a writer to take the time to write a script which will only have four possible outlets. The odds of rejection are too high. The networks also have a distinctive development process which produces the highly structured, low-budget, concept-driven, fact-based movies which do well on television. These scripts are quite different from spec feature scripts.

Networks do look at spec scripts, though, because any script can potentially help fill the need for entertainment programming. And, like the studios, networks want to circumvent the lengthy development process once in a while by buying a script outright. For writers, the networks can be a secondary market for old scripts that did not work out as features.

Cable programming services like HBO, Showtime, TNT, The USA Network and Lifetime do look at spec scripts, since their creative franchises and budgetary needs are different from those of the networks.

Treatments

A *treatment*, sometimes called an *outline*, is a short prose description of a movie idea. It reflects how the writer would "treat" the story in a screenplay. The treatment gives basic character descriptions and dramatic structure. It may also include some suggested dialogue. Many executives prefer treatments because they are easier to read than a full-length screenplay. Some writers also prefer treatments because they normally take less time to prepare. In the time it takes a writer to draft a spec script, he can create several treatments and circulate them to producers. There is no set limit on length for a treatment, but most range from two to thirty pages in length. If they are longer than that, they begin to defeat their purpose.

The treatment is shorthand for the finished screenplay. In the early phases of development, the advantage of a treatment is that it can be modified much more easily than a screenplay . A treatment allows all the parties involved in the development process to make a rapid series of changes in the overall story without the pain of a script rewrite each time. Once the treatment has been shaped to everyone's satisfaction, then the writer can go to work on the screenplay knowing that there will be fewer drastic changes later.

Plays

The live theater offers many potential film ideas, as well as talented writers and actors. New York has some terrific theater, both on and off Broadway. Los Angeles also has a vibrant theater scene. If you see a play you think would work as a movie, you can easily get complimentary, or *comp* tickets for your boss to see the play. The management of a theater company is always interested in having a prospective producer or agent come to see the show. If your boss can't come, you can prepare a packet of reviews and a video tape to supplement your verbal pitch of the material to your boss.

History and Biography

History and biography can provide the material for great films (REDS, A MAN FOR ALL SEASONS, etc.). If you have an idea for a movie based on history or biography, you can write your own treatment from library research. The only challenge is to make something old feel fresh and relevant. You might find the story of George Washington's nanny fascinating, but you should be prepared to answer some tough questions from your boss about the appeal of such a story to a broad audience.

Producers tend to like history and biography because they have an air of quality about them. Best of all, the costs of development are usually minimal. You can portray a dead person in a film without having to buy the rights to their life story. History, especially that which involves people who are no longer alive, comes to producers free of charge. A bargain! The only offsetting disadvantage is that you'll be creating a period movie, which will tend to be quite expensive.

Classics

The realm of classic literature is yet another place to find ideas for movies. Here at last is your chance to prove to your employers how well educated you are. You can dig back into your college English courses and find the one Chaucer tale which would make a perfect vehicle for Cher. However, before you let your good taste make a fool out of you in a development meeting, you have to look at yourself in the mirror and ask yourself if anyone really cares. Have they even heard of the book you're proposing to make into a "quality" picture? The idea must have the same appeal and commercial elements as any other pitch coming in to the shop. Literature as a story source does not give you quality automatically. That is a mistaken assumption frequently made by development executives.

If you do find a literary classic that meets the commercial needs of your company, prepare yourself for the reality that no one else but you is ever going to read that book until a development deal is in place. Big old books with small print scare executives and producers. As a result, the need for good coverage is more critical in the case of a literary classic than almost anywhere else. There are no press clippings to bundle, no tape to show. The coverage has to be compelling, *selling coverage.* If you are in a hurry, you can look at the synopses listed in *Cliff Notes* or *Master Plots,* the latter a collection of descriptions of classic books.

True Stories

Once in a while, a person will do something which brings the attention of movie producers. Examples include being the first man to cross the Atlantic in an airplane, being the most highly decorated soldier in a War, or murdering everyone in one's family and telling the police that crazed hippies did it. Whatever the reason, many individuals in America and around the world find themselves selling their life story rights to film producers, precipitating a deal which is technically simple, but emotionally demanding.

Because the networks and studios gravitate toward sensational and recent true stories, the news can be a fertile source. Most true story movies originate from newspaper articles, radio reports, or TV news. Some production companies subscribe to a range of newspapers and magazines from around the United States. Others tape the major news magazine shows and scan them for interesting true stories. Your job might entail responsibility for scanning the news in search of potential movie ideas.

The volume of news media can quickly become overwhelming, however. There is no way you that you will be able to read five newspapers and watch three news shows every morning in addition to your other assistant duties. You have to skim the media and restrict your search to company parameters of content and story.

If a good story breaks nationally, it will be hard to acquire the rights without a messy, competitive negotiation. For this reason, it is almost not even worth it to look at headline stories in *The Los Angeles Times* or *The New York Times.* Unless your company has a lot of pull, it could be an expensive waste of time to try for the rights, though it's always worth trying if the story is good enough. Just move quickly.

Assuming you have your boss's permission, can you contact the people who are the subject of an interesting true story. These people are called the *rights holders* because they control the critical *underlying rights*. It is *their* story, and you cannot make a movie about it without their permission and life story rights.

If the people have unlisted numbers, a phone call to the newspaper should get you in touch with the reporter who wrote the article. In a situation like this, reporters can have differing degrees of ego involvement. Some are friendly and offer to contact the family for you. Others demand an exclusive, give you their lawyer's phone number, and insist on making an expensive consultancy deal before you even get through to the rights holders. You can make a deal with a reporter, but the deal is of little value except as entrée to the story's protagonist. The reporter controls no underlying rights unless he or she is the subject of the story.

Other true stories are snapped up by *rights hustlers*, who are usually lawyers and fringe players that arrive on the scene quickly after a story breaks and pressure rights holders to make a deal immediately. Rights hustlers bill themselves as producers but they make their living by reselling true story rights to established producers and piggybacking on the project as consultants under some sort of *buyout* arrangement.

When you begin to track down a true story, it is best to affect a friendly but serious tone with everyone you contact. Though your boss or the legal department will do the actual negotiation, you might be the first person who has contact with the rights holders. The rights holders often sell their story to the person they like the most, not the one with the biggest name. Homespun folks who do things that wind up on the Monday Night Movie have an ingrained distrust of sleazy Hollywood types (mostly from watching too many Monday Night Movies to begin with), so you have to come across as respectable, honest, and willing to pay top dollar if you want to stand a chance of getting the rights.

5.2   THE INTERNAL SELL

Unless a story is truly sensational it will not stand out from the flood of ideas streaming into your office. If no one pays attention to a story, it will wither. If you find a story which you think could make a good movie, you will have to sell it to the people in your office as if you were an outside producer coming in with a pitch. Otherwise, the idea will be ignored and rejected.

Let's say that you see an article in a regional newspaper about a young boy, Gaines McSweeney, who ran away from home, hitchhiked to Las Vegas, made $10,000 playing blackjack disguised as a dwarf, and flew home first class. It looks like a workable idea. The story does not appear to have made the major papers, so you have an opportunity to be the first producer to contact the people in the story. You have to act immediately or you will lose that vital edge.

By phone you reach Ida McSweeney, the mother of the little boy who went to Vegas. You want to make sure that she understands what your company does and that you have a strong interest in her story. With luck she will say that she, too, is interested in working with your company. You ask her to keep you in mind, and not sign with any other producers until she has spoken with you again. She says yes and requests some information on your company, which you promise to send off later in the day.

So far, so good. You've found a commercial true story and made certain that the rights are available. Now you have to get someone in your company interested in the story. The approach you take to selling the idea will depend on your relationship with your boss. You might be able to walk into her office anytime, deliver a three-sentence summary of the idea, and get a quick yes or no. Or you may have to do a whole spiel to get your boss to take up the project. She may then say, "I don't know...*Sell* it to me."

If you really have to sell the idea, you will need a working title, a pitch, a *one-sheet* describing the story, and possibly a *clippings packet*, casting ideas and videotape. Even if these accessories are not required, it can be good practice to create them for a story you love.

The working title must be commercial and convey the high-concept, high-boxoffice idea you're dealing with. Play around with variations on different words and expressions. Try to imagine a poster for the film hanging in a theater. Think about what a trailer for this film would look like. After some head-scratching, you arrive at the working title *The Vegas Kid.*

A one-sheet is a cross between coverage and a very short story treatment. A good one-sheet will tease the reader and show the possibilities for the movie, including casting and promotion. On the following pages is a sample one-sheet for the internal sell of *The Vegas Kid.*

The idea of the one-sheet is to give your boss a brief summary of the film idea - just enough to get her interested. You don't have to work out the entire story in detail. Less is more when it comes to one-sheets. Usually, the snappier and more commercial you can make it, the better, though excessive hype can work against you. A good one-sheet should help an executive visualize how he or she will pitch the story at the studio. A one-sheet is a step away from a pitch. In all probability, nobody outside your company will ever see it.

The Vegas Kid
A Feature Film Idea, based on a true story

Concept: A poor ten-year-old boy runs away from home and hitches a ride to Vegas, where he wins $10,000 at blackjack and flies home first class.

Life was never too great for GAINES MCSWEENEY, a bright and charming ten-year- old boy. His parents are divorced, so he lives with his mother, IDA MCSWEENEY, 41, in a trailer park in Birmingham, Alabama. Ida works as a short order cook to make ends meet and hangs around with the wrong kind of men. Gaines is left alone a great deal of the time, playing in vacant lots and getting into trouble. Ida loves him, but can't always pay enough attention to him. One day, after a confrontation with one of Ida's many boyfriends, young Gaines decides to split.

He packs up his favorite worldly possessions into his knapsack and hits the road, thumbing a ride on the Interstate. Gaines is picked up by FRANK JONES, 35, a Mickey Rourke-ish down-on-his-luck gambler headed for Vegas. The two hit it off just fine. Gaines doesn't see Frank the way the rest of the world does—as a loser—and in a strange way Frank becomes a sort of father figure to the kid. The two play cards all the way to Vegas, with Frank showing Gaines many card hustling tricks of the trade .

Once in Vegas, Frank quickly loses everything and gets into hot water with some old mob friends whom he's into for some big dollars. They bar him from the casinos. Frank needs help and Gaines knows it. So, to rescue his friend, Gaines befriends a showgirl who makes him up to look like a man so he can pass himself off as a dwarf.

Gaines wins $10,000 at the blackjack table and pays off Frank's mob friends. But, Frank has skipped town, scared. Gaines flies home first class and gives Ida the remaining money to use as a down payment on a house.

Now that you have the one-sheet, you will need to find additional news media evidence of the story to back it up. A packet of clippings gives additional definition to the story. The rights holders may have a bunch of clippings which they can send to you. Otherwise, you will have to go to the library and dig through newspaper and microfilm.

Identify the major roles and think of major stars who could fill them. This is the time to think like a packager. For example, does your boss have relationships with the agents of any child stars? Who represents the stars you have in mind? Do any talent packages come to mind? Your cast list prepares you to discuss casting if asked about it in a meeting. You may or may not want to show it to your boss during the internal sell.

A videotape is the the final element of your internal selling package. Tape sells a true story more effectively than any other medium. Even an excerpt from a newscast can be powerful. A fully edited tape with voice-over and music is a terrific sales tool, if a little ambitious for this early stage of discussion. Tape is optional. Putting a video together can be time-consuming, and nobody expects it from you in an internal pitch. If you have tape, use it. If not, don't worry about it.

After you have assembled some or all of the above pieces for your pitch, you are ready to take the idea to your boss and get her to commit time and money to it. When you pitch to your boss, you cease to be an assistant. For a brief moment, you're a young writer who's come in to talk about an idea. You have to think of yourself that way to get up the confidence to make the "sale." Unfortunately for you, your boss is not obligated to treat you like a talented young writer with an idea. You're still her assistant. She can still take phone calls, interrupt you, and tell you to pick up her cat at the vet just as you are warming up to the best part of the story. However, if you have done a good one-sheet and thought through the idea, you stand a chance of getting a hearing.

You can't do this whole workup for every idea which floats past you. There simply isn't the time. The mathematics of internal idea generation dictates that you work with extreme selectivity or else you are bound to waste your time. Assume that the basic work required to explore an original idea takes ten hours, including reading, research and writing. If you're lucky, you will be able to find ten unconflicted hours a week at work.

Based on these figures, your capacity for creating internal pitches is about one a week. If you take on five original idea projects, then they will take an average of five weeks to be completed, given your rate of work. If you take on twenty projects, you are looking at a six-month turnaround time for an idea. By the time it's ready, the opportunity to develop the movie may be gone. A decrease in quality and organization is equally likely to occur if your load gets this big.

The competitive approach, then, is to keep your slate of original ideas limited to maximize your flexibility and response time. Ideas should be worked on until you can judge whether they have any chance. That might mean a cursory glance that takes half an hour, or a more in-depth study that takes a couple of hours. At any point along the way, if you decide that a story is not salable, you should get rid of it. Otherwise, you will accumulate a backlog of lukewarm projects, and that will slow you down and add to your organizational work load. If something doesn't work, kill it.

It is hard enough to reduce your own slate of ideas, but it becomes even harder when one or two bosses are assigning you original story work. It's easy to accumulate over a hundred assignments. Given the rate of work, none of those hundred will ever be completed to anyone's satisfaction. At the very least, you will have to maintain a worksheet on the projects you are pursuing, just to keep track of your progress. Give your bosses realistic estimates of the time until completion. Ask them to prioritize your work.

5.3   DISCUSSION AND REFINEMENT OF THE IDEA

In most companies, the development executives convene once or twice a week in a *story meeting* to discuss new story ideas and hear internal pitches. After you have presented your work on *The Vegas Kid* at a story meeting, the executives will either accept or reject the idea just as if it were coming from an external source. In some companies, the project will be taken out of your hands once your have presented the story. Or, depending on your boss, you may be able to participate in the project as it continues in development.

Development executives rarely hear a story and say, "That's perfect. Let's not do a single thing to it." They want to twist the idea around, reshape it and examine it from all angles until everyone feels it's ready to sell. This is the stage where the idea is refined and matched to the needs of the company. The talent of a development executive is partly measured by her ability to interpret and restructure a raw idea, and turn it around into something which can be sold.

In this case, you will assist in the process of revision. Your boss will look at the work you did and ask you for additional ideas, making changes as she shapes the idea into something she can use. The formulation stage of an idea is a good place for you to practice ego control. Even if it seems that your boss is ripping your work to shreds, she is only trying to get the idea into its most appealing form. You should not take it personally when executives cut and paste your presentation and distill it into something unrecognizable to you.

You wrote your one-sheet based on the concept of a children's movie, a star vehicle for a major child actor. However, your intuition turned out to be wrong. Let's say there is not a single studio in town interested in making a movie about a kid. Your boss still likes *The Vegas Kid*, though, for her own reasons. She takes you through a number of variations on the storyline. The following new log lines suggest the process involved in refining a story and formulating a pitch:

Star vehicle for a major actress
A single mother cashes in her life savings and goes to Vegas with her ten-year-old son, wins big, loses it all and learns something about herself in the process.

Romantic comedy
A single mother of a ten-year-old boy is courted by a down-and-out gambler who, as a way of winning her heart, "adopts" her son and teaches him how to play cards.

A Vegas showgirl and her down-and-out gambler boyfriend take her ten-year-old son and move to Los Angeles, only to have the boy hitch a ride back to Vegas to save her boyfriend from the mob by winning $10,000 disguised as a dwarf.

Drama
By threatening the son of the woman he loves, Vegas mobsters force a down-and-out gambler who owes them money to cheat the casinos.

A bitter custody battle over a ten-year-old boy between his mother, a Vegas showgirl and the boy's father, a shadowy underworld figure.

Screwball comedy
A ten-year-old boy, posing as a dwarf and playing cards the way he was taught by his stepfather, a down-and-out gambler, goes on the biggest winning streak in Vegas history and is pursued by an assortment of showgirls, widows and mobsters.

Television movie

A woman and her estranged husband start to engage in a bitter custody battle over their ten-year-old son, but the boy runs away to Las Vegas, bringing the husband and wife back together.

This is an example of the kind of reinterpretation which can occur at the formulation stage. You and your boss will probably go through several iterations in refining the idea. It's as if you are refracting the basic idea through a series of lenses. Each lens represents a different genre, star vehicle or overall concept. Eventually, you will arrive at one which feels right and meets the criteria of the buyers.

Your boss is trying to be a matchmaker of ideas. She knows who is looking for what kind of project, and she looks within her own development pipeline for a fit. Or she might just be looking for a kind of idea she feels will sell, regardless of what people tell her they are looking for. Experienced executives and producers will tell you that they rarely ask the studio or network "What do you want?", but rather try to figure out what it ought to want. Either way, the process involves a lot of imagination and an open mind.

5.4   RIGHTS DEALS

After your company has decided to develop a movie, it has to make a deal to acquire the film rights to the story, whether it comes from a book, screenplay or true story. There are dozens of ways to make a film rights deal, but most deals follow a distinct pattern. We will outline some of the basic deal structures as examples, but these deals have many permutations.

Film rights are expensive because the rights holder has the opportunity to sell these rights just once. Your company buys the films rights to a story in perpetuity, worldwide. Your company can sell them to someone else later on, but the original rights holder is out of the picture. As a result, the original rights holders and their representatives want to receive the maximum possible value.

Almost all deals involve an *option*, a fee paid to the rights holder in exchange for the exclusive right to buy the rights to a piece of material for a set period of time. The option serves the needs of both the rights holder and the rights buyer. During the option period, the producer has the exclusive right to buy the theatrical rights to a piece of material. Options normally equal a fraction of the final *rights purchase price*, so they save the buyer money. If a producer takes an option on a property but cannot get a studio to produce the movie, he has only lost the option money, not the full rights price. At the same time, the rights holder gets his material back once the option has *lapsed*. He can take it to another producer. If there were no option, the original producer would own the script, and despite his inability to get it produced, would hold on to it for life. The rights holder usually wants the flexibility to give more than one producer a chance to produce his script.

The option runs for a specific period of time. When that time is up, the producer may or may not have the right to *renew* the option for another set period of time. In many rights deals, the first sum of option money is applied to the final purchase price of the rights, but the renewal fee is not applicable. The renewal aspect of the option agreement allows additional flexibility to the producer and the rights holder. It gives the producer more time to work with the material, but it provides for additional payment to the rights holder.

The producer works for free at this stage of the development process, so he might ask for a *free option* on the material. He will argue that if he can spend time on it for free, then the writer should be willing to do the same. The producer can plead poverty, or overextended development funds, and in many cases the agent relents and grants the producer a free option. A free option deal works just like a regular option, only the up-front fee is zero dollars. Some free option agreements have high renewal fees after a very short free option period (one month, for example), as an incentive to the producer to work quickly in getting the project set up at a studio.

One notch below the free option deal is the *handshake deal*, which is more common than you might think. If a writer likes the producer, or at least knows her, he might say, "If you like the script, run with it." The two parties trust each other to negotiate in good faith if the project is set up anywhere. The advantage of a handshake deal is that it saves everyone a lot of wrangling over getting a project started. Lawyers' and producers' time is valuable, so if the deal can be executed just by two people agreeing to deal with each other later, the whole affair gets going a lot more smoothly. What's more, a good handshake deal lends an aura of confidence to the working relationship between writer and producer.

Handshake deals are not merely for low-level, unrepresented talent. Some of the biggest names in the business work without contracts and signed deals. Of course, a handshake involves a delicate balance, which can go haywire if one party takes advantage of the situation. However, if the participants are paying attention — which can involve a diligent assistant's eye — then a handshake deal can work pretty well.

Rights deals provide *stepups*, which guarantee extra payments depending on the ultimate use of the material in a film. If the material is used in television, that triggers one purchase price. If the material is used for a feature film, the price steps up to a higher figure.

Bonuses and *consulting fees* are thrown into a rights deal to give extra money to the rights holder in the event that a film is made. The rights buyer tries to spend very little money up front and defer as much of the rights holder's fee as possible. The option comes out of the rights buyer's pocket. Later, the rights purchase price, bonuses and consulting fees are paid out of the film's production budget. At that point, the company is already spending millions, so it makes less of a difference that the rights holder gets a few thousand extra dollars. In getting a rights holder to make a deal, however, those extra fees at the *back end* might have been the deciding factor.

Finally, rights deals almost always allow for some form of profit participation, series rights, and ancillary rights to a film. While these are usually meaningless, the rights agreement provides for the possibility that the film will be spun off into a television series with huge profits and merchandising. The rights holder wants to be sure that he will receive some royalties from that enterprise, if it should come into existence.

Terms of a typical book acquisition deal:
1) The producer gets a year's option for $5,000. The first year's option is applicable to the purchase price of the book.
2) The producer can renew the option for an additional year for another $5,000, which is not applicable to the purchase price of the book.
3) The purchase price of rights to the book for a two-hour television movie will be $50,000.
4) If the book is produced as a miniseries, the purchase price will step up $25,000 for each additional two hours of programming.
5) If the book is produced as a feature film, the purchase price will step up to $150,000 if the film has a budget of less than $10 million, and $250,000 if the film's budget exceeds $10 million.
6) The producer will pay the author a bestseller bonus of $2,500 added to the purchase price for each week that the book remains on the bestseller list.
7) The producer will pay the author a $2,500 technical advisorship fee upon commencement of development of the screenplay.
8) The author will receive 7.5% of the net profits of the film.

9) The author will receive royalties on any series, merchandising, or other ancillary products created from the film, to be negotiated in good faith.

The deal for rights to The Vegas Kid, a true story:
1) Producer will pay $2,500 to the family of Gaines McSweeney as an option for one year, applicable to the purchase price of $45,000. The producer can renew the option for a second year for an additional $2,500, not applicable to the purchase price.
2) The Producer will have the right to portray Gaines and Ida McSweeney as characters in the film.
3) Upon commencement of principal photography, the family will receive a $5,000 production bonus.
4) The family has the right of consultation on the selection of a writer and the development of the screenplay.
5) The rights purchase price for a feature film based on the story is $100,000.
6) The newspaper reporter who wrote the original article will receive a $5,000 consulting fee for helping the screenwriter during the development period.

Spec Script Deal:
1) Studio will acquire the rights to the screenplay for $500,000.
2) The writer will receive $250,000 now, and $250,000 upon commencement of principal photography.
3) The deal will be subject to a creative meeting between the studio and the writer.
4) The writer will receive executive producer credit on the film and an executive producer fee of $100,000.
5) The writer will perform two additional drafts and a polish on the script.

Option Rewrite Deal:
1) Producer will pay $10,000 for a one-year option on the screenplay, commencing on the delivery of the rewrite. The first payment is
applicable to the purchase price of $100,000.
2) The option fee will include the writer's fee for completing the rewrite.
3) The option is renewable for a second year at an additional $10,000, not applicable to the purchase price.

5.5   SELLING THE IDEA

After all the revising, discussing and negotiating, it is time for your boss to sell *The Vegas Kid*. We'll assume for our purposes that your boss has decided to sell *The Vegas Kid* as a television movie, since television movies provide a relatively straightforward model of screenplay development.

If *The Vegas Kid* were already a finished screenplay of acceptable quality, it would be a fairly simple matter to sell it. Your boss would just call up network executives and tell them about the script. If they were interested, your boss would send it to them. They would read it, and if they liked it, your company might have a deal. With less developed ideas, though, there are several different approaches to selling.

A pitch over the phone is the simplest form of presenting an idea to a buyer, though people try to avoid doing one. Though it is the least time-consuming way to sell, the phone pitch can be seen as denigrating the quality of the idea. It is "only" a phone pitch. A phone conversation has the least impact of any form of selling. However, if an idea is highly commercial and easy to grasp, your boss might want to give it a try over the phone just to see if there is any interest, before investing more time.

Your boss could go to the network and pitch the idea in person. The aim of a pitch is to generate enthusiasm on the part of an executive by telling a great story and enticing the executive with great potential in the idea for casting, drama and, where relevant, quality. Producers usually don't leave any written material behind when they pitch an idea. The fear is that the emotional moment of the pitch will be lost if the executive can later pick apart some document and find fault with the idea.

The selling process usually begins with a short phone call from your boss to the network executive to say something like, "I have a great piece of material which I'm going to send over to you today." Your boss then writes a *cover letter* and sends the material to the executive by messenger. The cover letter might be a detailed letter, or a handwritten card which just says "Read this. You'll love it." A cover letter is also called a *letter of transmittal*. A copy of the cover letter should go into the chron and relevant project files.

Your boss might dictate these letters for you to type. If you take dictation, allow your boss the opportunity to read, sign, and reread notes and letters before they go out. Control over wording and nuances is important for most executives. Hint: Double-check the spelling of people's names. The fallout from one mistake will probably be enough to make you a believer in this habit for life.

You can write cover notes yourself. Many submissions arrive with typed notes which say something like, "Per Mr. Blockbuster's instructions, enclosed are the clippings concerning *The Vegas Kid.*" This is a necessity if your boss is out of town and something has to go out. However, make sure you understand your boss's policy on assistants writing notes before you take the initiative. Under no circumstances should you send a handwritten, personal note as an assistant.

Sample cover letter

```
20 December, 1992


Mr. Ray Ting
Director, Motion Pictures for Television
NBC Entertainment
3000 West Alameda Avenue
Burbank, California 91523

Dear Ray:

Enclosed are the clippings and videotape on The Vegas Kid, the
story I told you about yesterday. I look forward to hearing your
thoughts.

Best regards,


Stanley Blockbuster
```

Selling is the submissions process in reverse. As with submissions, you have to create a system for keeping track of what went to whom on what date. An *outgoing material log* is the most effective way to organize the selling process. The log should contain all relevant name, title, address and phone information. It should also give an explanation of why the material was sent out. Was a script sent out for star attachment, director attachment, or just to give an old friend a chance to read it? This is especially important at an agency, where one agent may send out hundreds of scripts a month. It is easy to forget the exact purpose of each outgoing submission, given the large volume of material.

The database concept also applies to outgoing material. A title-indexed database is the easiest way to see where a script has been. It is embarrassing to send a studio the same script twice, but it could easily happen if you don't keep proper records. You should check the records for prior activity when your boss asks you to send something out. It is not good enough just to check the name of the studio, either, because executives move around. A script may have gone to Fox in 1989, but the same executive who passed on it then may now be at Warners.

As in the submissions process, it should become standard policy to issue weekly, quarterly and annual reports of outgoing material. The weekly report can be a limited account of what left the office that week, but the longer-term reports should be cumulative. This is the only way that anyone can chronicle the history of a development project. You will find that the outgoing summary is one of the most useful documents in the office. It points out projects which are being neglected, and it helps generate follow-up lists.

(1)	(2)	(3)	(4)	(5)	(6)
Title	Author	Form	Sent to	Date	Comment
Killer In the Snow, A	Chuck Bird	SP 1st	Joe Smith, World Pix	9/15/90	
Killer In the Snow, A	Chuck Bird	SP 2nd	Oscar Ampas, Fox	10/30/90	
Vegas Kid, The		Clips	Ray Ting—NBC	12/20/90	
Vegas Kid, The		Clips	Abe Troglodyte, CTA	12/21/90	Writers

Figure 5.2   Excerpt from outgoing material log summary

Figure 5.2 is an example of an outgoing log summary. By scanning the outgoing material log summary shown in Figure 5.2, your boss can figure out whom he wants to call to follow up. The summary contains the following information about each outgoing submission:

1) The title of the material being sent out
2) The author's name
3) The format of the material, and the draft number.
4) The recipient of the material, and their company
5) The date the material was posted or delivered
6) The reason for sending the material out

Some producers who are close to spending money on options might call the network and pitch the idea before they commit to spending the money. This practice, known as *shopping an idea around*, is fairly common, but it is regarded as unethical. The problem is that a producer who picks up the option later has acquired a used car, something which he will have trouble selling because everyone will already have seen it. When agents get involved, and realize that their projects are being shopped around without their permission, things can get ugly.

5.6   SELECTING A WRITER

Three days after receiving the packet on *The Vegas Kid*, the network calls up to tell your boss that it will commit to develop a script. Your boss says "Great. Let's put a writer on this thing and get busy." Your boss's job now is to find a writer who will turn the raw idea into a finished script which is good enough to produce. Your boss will have to find a writer who is right for the project, acceptable to the network, available to do the job, willing to do the job, and works for the right price. Finding such a person is not always the easiest task.

Your shop now has an *open writing assignment*. Word gets around that you have an open assignment, and agents will begin to call up to suggest their clients for the job. These agents may end up talking to you first, if your boss is busy. An assistant can confirm that an assignment is open, though you should not feel obligated to discuss any other aspect of the project. (A big no-no is to talk about development with reporters, since networks and studios like to clear publicity in advance.) Depending on what instructions your boss gives you, you can refer all inquiries about the assignment to her, or you can handle them yourself. Either way, you should be familiar with the process which occurs when there is an open writing assignment.

If you are allowed to handle the inquiries yourself, then you will want to get three pieces of information from each agent who calls. First, if you are not familiar with the writer you should request a *writing sample*. A sample might be the shooting script from a previously produced film, or a relevant spec script. Then you have to get a list of credits from the agent. These will go onto your *writer list* in abbreviated form, as well as being filed in your writer credits database (see Chapter 3). Finally, you have to ascertain the writer's *availability*.

The first stage in selecting a writer for a project is creating a list of all available writers who might be appropriate for the assignment. The list contains a mix of writers who have been suggested by agents, and writers who have worked successfully with your company in the past. At first cut, such a list might contain more than thirty names.

The first factor in selecting a writer is appropriateness. Unless everyone involved in the project knows the writer, he has to fit the project in some way. While typecasting and pigeonholing writers is never a good idea, one has to be realistic about how the network will react to an unusual choice. A writer of suspense dramas would be an inappropriate choice for a romantic comedy. The decision of appropriateness will probably not be up to you, though you may be involved in evaluating the writing samples which are submitted.

If a writer is appropriate, he must also be *network acceptable* (also known as *network approvable*). The networks have certain writers they like, and others they consider strangers to television. It is not simply a matter of quality. Indeed, some fine feature writers and playwrights have had to struggle to be accepted by the networks because they have never written for television before. A network acceptable writer has usually written for television before and has the respect of the network.

Figure 5.3   Sample writer list format

As names get dropped for reasons of appropriateness and network acceptability, the writer list now begins to take shape. You are involved, evaluating sample scripts and writing coverage to judge the suitability of writers for the project. At this point the list might have ten names on it. Now you have to ascertain availability and desire to do the job.

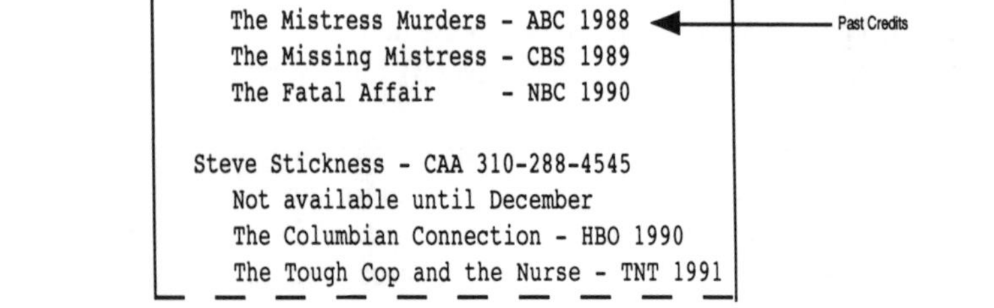

Availability is a ticklish subject with writers, as it is with most talent. A writer may well be available to write your script, meaning that he is currently unemployed or will be in the near future. However, he may be hoping to get some more interesting or higher-paying assignment instead.

Assuming a writer is available to write your script, at least in terms of his calendar, the next crucial step is to find out if he actually wants the assignment. Your boss asks the agent if the writer is interested in the project, and the agent asks the client. Unfortunately, a lot can get lost in translation.

The writer may want to discuss the idea with your boss before accepting or rejecting the assignment. This is known as a *creative meeting*. At this point, the agent might insist on your boss making an *offer* to the writer *conditional on the creative meeting*. The agent will claim, justifiably in some cases, that his client does not have the time to sit around with producers discussing ideas without a guarantee that the project will go to him.

Before the creative meeting, you will have to send any project-related material to the writer. If the project is a book adaptation, for example, the writer must have the book to read before the meeting. At the creative meeting, the writer and your boss discuss their views and interpretations of the project. The creative meeting is a chance for your boss to evaluate further the writer's appropriateness and level of enthusiasm. The writer, too, can ascertain whether he wants to work for your boss.

Often, it is necessary for your boss to sell the idea to the writer. Sought-after writers have many competing assignments at their fingertips. The project will be well-served by such a writer. It is up to your boss to convince the writer to write this script instead of the others. It is a process similar to selling the network, only writers are more fickle and may take a long time to decide whether they are interested.

You have to track the frequent additions, deletions and changes being made in the writer list. You might even be involved in receiving and transmitting the changes in status which affect the list. Then writing samples arrive. You log them in and designate them for the project in question. You make sure your boss sees which samples have arrived for the project. Then you read and evaluate the samples. For samples which your boss reads, you track her reaction to the writer. As the writers of most interest are selected and creative meetings are set, sample scripts and project-related material will flow back and forth among your office, the writer's agent and the network. Using the outgoing log, you will track the flow of material.

Your company finally finds a writer who is available, acceptable to the network, and interested in doing the job. Before he can go to work, a deal must be made for his services. Deals are typically negotiated between your company's business affairs department and the writer's agent. At times, though, your boss might negotiate the writer's deal herself. In either case, you should know as much as possible about the deal-making process to track the proceedings.

The first stage in a making a deal with a writer is usually listening to the writer's agent state his terms for the deal. For *The Vegas Kid*, a true story adaptation, the agent asks the following for his client: $60,000 fee for writing two drafts and a polish, $10,000 production bonus *reducible* to $5,000 in the event of a *shared credit* (meaning that if there's a rewrite by another writer, the first writer only gets half the production bonus), a $10,000 fee to serve as a producer (with a credit) on the film, a research budget of $5,000 to hire a researcher, 10 percent of the film's net profits, and $250 *per diem* for any travel days. The agent claims that since this project is a true story, the writer will have to travel to God-knows-where and research such obscure topics as gambling. To help write a better script, the agent insists that his client needs a researcher to help him. In addition, all standard *Writers Guild of America* (WGA) terms apply. The Writers Guild, the screenwriter's union, has a standard contract which is the same in every deal, covering pension and health payments, participation in any series pickups or spinoffs, first-class airfare, residuals, and the like.

Your boss now asks for the writer's *quote*. A writer's quote is the amount he got paid on his last project. The agent says the writer's quote was $55,000 for writing his last project, and he feels his client deserves a $5,000 raise. A Business Affairs person or an assistant must now *verify the quote* by calling the network or the producer of the writer's last movie. Producers and studios frequently ask each other to verify quotes on talent. It is a common practice. When the quote is verified, it is discovered that the writer only got $50,000 for his last movie. The agent was exaggerating.

Now comes the negotiation. Your boss is motivated by two conflicting factors. On one side there is the network. They will only reimburse your company for writer's fees up to a given amount, which is usually based on the writer's previous quotes. At the same time, however, your boss does not want to lose the writer if a deal cannot be made. The agent is aware of these two pressures, and he is likely to exploit the fact that your boss wants his client, and that finding a replacement can take a substantial amount of time. If the writer is perfect for the job and everyone really wants him, the agent can get away with asking for more money than the network will pay, and your company will have to make up the difference. In television, this practice is known as *deficiting*.

Your boss agrees to give the writer a $5,000 raise, but based on the real quote, which was $50,000. So the writer will receive $55,000, but for two drafts, a set of revisions, and a polish. The money will be paid in the following sequence: $10,000 upon commencement of writing, $20,000 upon delivery of the first draft, $10,000 for the second draft, $10,000 for the revisions, and $5,000 for the polish. Your boss okays the production bonus but rejects the demand for a producing credit, asserting that the writer has limited experience in actual producing. A compromise is reached—the writer will get a $2,500 consulting fee upon commencement of *principal photography*. The profit participation demand is reduced to 5 percent of net profit, with net profit precisely defined. The demand for a $5,000 research budget is reduced to "a researcher will be provided as needed." The per diem demand is reduced to $100 per day plus "reasonable expenses," such as car rentals.

Your boss and the agent will go back and forth on these points for a while, though writers' deals are fairly standard. When they agree that they have settled everything, the deal is said to be *closed*. Otherwise, any terms on which the agent and your boss have not agreed are said to be *open points*. Most writers will go to work if a deal is essentially closed, give or take an open point.

When the deal is closed, your company sends the agent a *deal memo*, which is a concise description of the terms of the deal. Any points in the deal misunderstood by either party will be revealed in the deal memo. In certain cases, the deal memo is the only written documentation of a writer's agreement. While most business affairs executives will generate a *long-form agreement*, which is a fully written contract, the deal memo is usually enough to express commitment to the deal. If both parties can honor a deal memo, they can save the expense of drafting and revising a long-form agreement.

Sometimes the network will have made a previous *open commitment* to a writer. This means that the network has made a promise that a writer will be used to write some upcoming script, with the specific project to be assigned at a later date. When this happens, the writer selection process works in reverse. Your company's project comes along, and the network decides it can fulfill its commitment to the writer with your film. Open commitments exist in every phase of the business. Networks and studios frequently make promises to producers, directors and stars. Open commitments are also known as *blind commitments*.

The television movie offers a good model for the process of selecting and hiring a writer, and the process is comparable in film, though with some important differences. In feature writing, the four-way dance of availability, appropriateness, desire to write the script and ability to make a deal still holds, but the terms are a great deal more flexible. Writers have more latitude to defer assignments and sign on for projects that they will commence six months later. Studios have preferred writers, but the field is more open than in television. Since feature films are rewritten more than television films, there is more of a sense of giving someone a chance to work on an idea to see how it works out, versus the one-shot approach of television.

5.7 THE WRITING PROCESS—NOTES, REVISIONS AND THE THREE-WAY INTERFACE

At the center of the writing process is the screenplay, a piece of writing which evolves continually through a series of notes and revisions. Three forces shape the screenplay: The Writer, the Producer and the Network Executive(s). The balance among these three forces will shift and change over time as the script is written. In many cases the balance will go out of alignment, and the script will favor one of the three forces. Developing scripts involves more or less the same process, whether for television movies, miniseries or feature films. Once again, the television movie provides us with a good basic model for the process.

After the writer has been hired and given enough time to digest the material, he and your boss will have a meeting to discuss various interpretations of the story. This initial story discussion will follow the themes of the earlier creative meeting, but it will be more focused on pinning down the actual story of the script. The writer then goes home and develops a story outline, which he will present in either written or verbal form, first to your boss and then to the network.

A few days or weeks later, the writer finishes the story outline and reports to you that he's ready to come in and discuss the story. You book a *story meeting* at the office as soon as it can be scheduled. In the story meeting, the writer will tell your boss the entire story of the script he intends to write. At the same time, he will provide a written story outline for your boss to read. Your boss will invariably suggest certain changes. Thus begins the process of negotiation and compromise which is central to the writing process. The writer will fight for points which he believes in and compromise on others. Your boss will do the same. At the end of the first story meeting, the writer is sent back home to modify the story outline. A story meeting is then scheduled at the network.

The story meeting at the network is similar to the story meeting at your office. The writer and your boss go in to see the network executive, tell the entire story of the movie, and get feedback. If the network executive likes what he hears, he *approves* the story and the writer can start to work on the script. Otherwise, the meeting will be a discussion of different ideas and interpretations of what could happen in the story. Everyone likes to resolve these differences of opinion at the story stage. Once the script has been written it is much more difficult to make changes.

Now the writer goes to work. Some writers will vanish for two months and then deliver a finished script. Others need daily hand-holding. Others still need supervision, even if they don't admit it. Your boss's style figures into this issue. Some executives like to leave writers alone, figuring that the writer will ask for help if he needs it. Others like to have their hands in the process the whole time. It usually takes about eight to twelve weeks for a writer to complete a finished script. The writer's agreement might stipulate a delivery period, though it will probably not be enforced unless the writer is extremely late.

When the writer hands in his first draft of the script, your boss evaluates it before sending it to the network. Your boss might bring the writer in for a meeting or speak with him on the phone regarding changes which have to be made before the network can see the script. Whether your boss's comments are delivered in written or verbal form, this is the first set of script notes.

Notes are offered to the writer as possible changes to the script. Sometimes a note is an order to change the script. The writer will argue against a note which he feels will hurt the story. The argument over a note might reveal an underlying weakness which needs to be addressed, so the conversation could produce a compromise.

You might get to write your own script notes, to which your boss can add her own assessment of the writer's work. There is no set way to write notes. Notes are simply your suggestions to the writer for how to improve the script. Like the comment section of coverage, notes should be based on the company's particular strategy or goal for the project. They should not be oriented toward realizing your fantasy of cinematic genius.

Example of a well-written story note on a first draft:

Scene 10, pp 12-14—Gaines' motivation seems ambiguous in this scene. It is hard to tell whether he is angry at his mother or merely playing a joke on her.

Example of a poorly-written story note on a first draft:

Scene 10, pp 12–14—Gaines' line, "Mom, I don't want to take a bath" goes over like a lead balloon. Change it to, "Mom. I'm not getting in the bathtub."

The second note is so imperative and critical that it might alienate the writer. It is also too detailed for a first draft. Notes progress toward finer detail as the script evolves. In the early drafts, notes tend to focus on broad changes, or scenes which don't work. In later drafts you can give *line notes*, which highlight problematic dialogue or language in the script. The above example is really a line note. It is a mistake to give overly detailed line notes too early. The scene in discussion will probably be rewritten out of existence by the time the script is finished, so the premature line notes are a waste of time, and irritating to the writer.

After the first draft has been touched up and is finally ready, it can be sent to the network. It is common practice to send multiple copies, since more than one person at the network will read it. You will also send an accompanying transmittal letter, which can be as simple as:

Enclosed is the first draft of *The Vegas Kid*. We look forward to meeting with you shortly.

Keep careful track of the dates when drafts are received and sent to the network, since these dates trigger payment to the writer. The standard writer's agreement provides for payment within three weeks of delivery. For the contract described above, what is the actual date of delivery? The first draft was handed in on one day, but your boss requested changes, so as far as she was concerned, the first draft came in on a later date. The writer can claim that he delivered his first draft on the earlier date and insist on payment three weeks later. It is a grey area with no clear answers. Most companies try to pay writers promptly. An orderly system of record-keeping will help your boss keep the situation from turning into a needlessly painful dispute.

The network reads the script and schedules the first network notes meeting. It is at this meeting that the three forces acting on the script begin to struggle against each another. The network presents one vision of the script, the writer another, and the producer a third. The network is the strongest force, since they are footing the bill, but they can be dissuaded from certain points of view. The art of producing lies in coaxing the best script out of the development process without alienating anyone.

Whether or not the network gives written notes after the meeting, the writer has his instructions. Once again he goes home and works on the next draft of the script, which according to the contractual language might be called either the *second draft* or the *first revision*. Each time the script is rewritten, the story will change a certain amount. Sometimes the initial story is kept intact and the revisions merely refine the idea. In other cases, the transformation which occurs in the revision and notes process can be staggering.

The process of writing, discussing and revising at the producer and network level repeats itself for each successive draft in the writer's contract. After the writer's contractual obligation has been fulfilled, he does not have to deliver any additional revisions. In practice, though, the writer may perform subsequent polishes to the script if he feels that it is close to being produced.

When the final draft of a script is delivered to the network, there are four possible outcomes. The network can give the producer a *production order*, which gives the greenlight for making the film. The network might make the order *cast-contingent*, which means that the producer has to attach a specific star to the project to get it made. The network can place the script in *turnaround*, a situation where the producer can take it to other networks. Or, if the network likes the idea but is not happy with the work of the writer, they may request a rewrite by another writer. Though rewrites are standard practice in feature films, they are less common in television. Nonetheless, the process of hiring a writer and developing the script in a rewrite would be similar to the one undertaken the first time around.

In the event of a production order, the writer may be called in to perform a *production rewrite*, or *polish*. Production rewrites are typically minor alterations which address specific directorial, casting or location changes which were not anticipated when the script was developed. For example, a script might contain a scene in a restaurant. Because of location problems, though, the director decides to shoot the scene in a park. The dialogue might have to be altered to adjust to this change. By this time, however, the revisions will be tracked by the production office coordinator of the film, so you will have a less direct role in handling the changes. Production rewrites are covered in more technical detail in Chapter Six.

5.8   DEVELOPMENT BUYING PATTERNS

The studios and networks fund development in many different ways, so there are numerous buying patterns. Here are a few typical development scenarios. Though every development situation is slightly different, these basic types cover the general structure of most development you will see as an assistant.

Feature Films

1) A studio options/purchases a piece of material directly, then assigns it to a producer.
2) A studio options/purchases material for a specific person, i.e. a star, director or producer.
3) A producer options material and convinces a studio to fund development of a script.
4) A producer options material, finances development of a script out of his own pocket and then takes the script to a studio for production financing.
5) A producer pays a writer to develop a story based on the producer's idea. The producer and writer then pitch the idea to the studio, hoping to get further development funding.

Television

1) *Series pilot development*—The network commissions pilot scripts after hearing pitches from producers. The network then proceeds with production of the most promising scripts.
2) *Backdoor pilot movie*—A movie script commissioned by the network movie department will be evaluated by the drama development department as a possible series pilot. If the movie is successful, the network may order episodes.
3) *Feature film as pilot* —The studio which produces a successful feature can sell the concept to a network as a series. Famous examples include *The Odd Couple* and *M*A*S*H*.
4) *Current series development* —For shows on the air for the season, the network commissions and evaluates scripts through the current programming department.
5) *Miniseries and movie development* —The network movie department commissions scripts based on pitches and material brought in by producers. The network reimburses the producer for options and writer fees.

5.9   THE ASSISTANT'S ROLE IN DEVELOPMENT

It seems silly to distinguish a specific development role for assistants, because most of the assistant's work is in development. However, you should cultivate an awareness of how your actions and decisions affect the entire process of development. Realize that you personally can have a great impact on the success or failure of a development effort.

Day to Day

Pure organization on the part of the assistant is a necessity when dealing with the huge volume of detail generated by development. Think for a moment about how many pieces of information a typical development assistant has to carry around in his head during an average day. Assume the office has five development deals, fifty pitches and a hundred scripts under consideration. Each development deal has six individual people associated with it, and three drafts and sets of notes in the works. Each pitch has two people associated with it, and five pieces of related media in its packet, and is under consideration at ten financing entitities. Each script under consideration has an agent, a writer, coverage and a response. Throw in a few open writer assignments, and our assistant is handling about two hundred people, five hundred scripts and presentations, and at least a thousand related bits and pieces of data at any point in time!

Your other tool in managing this unwieldly process is familiarity with the permutations of a development project. This chapter was written to aid you in understanding the procedures and language — the rhythm — of development. If you can achieve an overview of the different paths a project can take, you will be able to anticipate events before they occur. An untrained assistant functions like a clerk, only doing what he is told. An assistant who is familiar with the development cycle can suggest alternatives to his boss, and eventually take on a limited decision-making role in preparation for a promotion.

Narrowing the funnel of development projects in the works will streamline your boss's development operations, and reduce the amount of time she spends on low-potential ideas. You will only have limited authority (or none at all) to eliminate projects from consideration. But, you do have some discretion in positioning projects in front of your boss. It is up to you to gauge how interested she is in each project. Then you steer her toward the ones she likes. The result is focus, and the achievement of important milestones. The focus is achieved by keeping phone calls, correspondence and meeting activities concentrated on the primary projects. The other projects will wither, but that is the whole point.

The centerpiece of the assistant's role in development is the development status report. This report lists all ongoing projects and their relevant information. It is a driver of action, a medium of consensus, and a record of activity. With a correctly prepared report, your boss should be able to find out the status on any project at a glance, without having to ask you for clarification.

A report contains three sections, which rank projects by their status. First, it lists all development deals with financing entities paying for the writer. Second come projects which the company is actively trying to sell to financing entities. This category is called *active development*, or *A-List development*. The third grouping is *backlist projects*, which are projects too old to be active, but still with the potential to be sold.

```
Development Status Report     11/15/92                Page 1 of 3
Title                   Writer           Format  Network/Studio    Status
Vegas Kid, The          Open             MOW     NBC               Deal
Origination Date 8/24/92         Option Expiration Date  8/23/93
Logline:  A Ten Year old kid hitchhikes to Las Vegas and wins $10,000 while his
divorced parents search frantically for him.
Comments/Progress Update
11/1/91 In negotiation with Fred Samson to write.
10/24/91 Family of kid must sign release forms.

Killer in the Snow      Chuck Bird       Feature  Paramount         Deal
Origination Date 9/1/90          Option Expiration Date  12/20/92
Logline:  A serial killer stalks a ski lodge.
Comments/Progress Update
11/15/91 Option Expires in one month.  One year extension (non-applicable) allowed.
11/1/91  Paramount wants to do a dialogue polish on script.
         Writer list being prepared.
```

Figure 5.4   Sample Development Status Report Format

Figure 5.4 shows one way to format a report. The idea is to convey all pertinent information on the company's development in a minimum of space. Each listing contains:

1) Project title.
2) Name of writer—if unassigned, note that it is an open assignment.
3) Format of the finished product. In the above example, MOW stands for (Television) Movie of the Week.
4) The status of the project: Deal, Active, Inactive, or Backlist.
5) The financing entity, if appropriate.

6) Origination date—the day the project was launched.
7) Option expiration date.
8) Log line.
9) Comments/Progress update. This is where you list the most recent status changes. The comments section should stimulate decisions and action from your boss.

The development status report should be issued regularly, depending on the your office's schedule. If your company convenes a weekly meeting to discuss development, then you should prepare a report on a weekly basis. Otherwise, less often may be suitable.

Your boss can use the report to determine any actions which need to be taken in the near future. The report can prompt you to ask your boss if she wants to make certain phone calls or arrange certain meetings. If used wisely, the report can become a powerful tool for organizing your boss's time.

An adjunct to the development status report is the tracking system for writer payments. As each draft of a script comes in, the writer is usually entitled to an incremental payment per his contract. You have to monitor the whole process, making sure that the writer gets paid on time for the work performed. There is no set way to do this, because the payment process differs widely from company to company. You will have to adapt to whatever mechanism for paying writers exists at your company. If you are lucky, the business affairs department will handle everything and present you with an accurate report every week. Usually, though, you have to go to business affairs and find out who has been paid and who is about to be paid. When a writer on one of your boss's projects does not get paid on time, his agent will call your office asking for the money.

Within a short period of time after a writer has turned in a draft, the writer's agent will send an invoice to your company requesting payment. Your boss has to approve the invoice before a check can be cut. This means your boss has to be satisfied that the writer has done the work as promised. (Remember, many drafts handed in to the company are simply intermediate attempts to get a script to the "first draft" or "first revision" stage.)

When your boss signs the invoice, it can now be paid. In some companies, the invoice can be sent directly to the Accounting Department for payment. In others, the invoice must also be signed by the Business Affairs Department before Accounting can cut a check. In either case, the invoice will leave your safe hands and flow into some dark corner of the bureaucracy. This is where problems arise for you.

When you field phone calls asking about missing checks, you want to have as much information as possible so you can avoid saying, "It's in the mail" too often. A simple chart such as the one shown in figure 5.5 is a good way to track writer payments. The chart can be printed on a 5x8" index card and stapled to the project folder. The draft sequence listed in the left hand column of the card should match the sequence dictated by the writer's contract. Every time you receive an invoice from an agent or a photocopy of a check from Accounting, you fill in the corresponding box on the card. In the example of Figure 5.5, the writer has turned in the first draft of the script and his agent has invoiced your company, but the invoice has not yet been paid. Appendix F shows a much more exhaustive approach to tracking writer payments, using a spreadsheet program.

Project Uegas Kid Writer F. Samson		Deal Total 55K		
Draft		Date Delivered Invoiced		Paid
Comm	10,000		8/25/92	10/1/92
First	20,000	9/10/92	9/15/92	

Figure 5.5   Writer payment chart

One convention which assistants follow in tracking writer payments is to maintain rigorous specificity in transmitting payments. For example, when mailing a check to a writer, you should type a cover letter phrased along the following lines:

Dear Agent:

Enclosed is check number 445667, in the amount of $10,000, for the services of Fred Samson, which covers payment for commencement of services on the NBC project *The Vegas Kid*.

The Accounting or Business Affairs Department should follow this practice. If they do not, convince them to. Copies of these cover letters, and of the checks themselves, have to be filed either in the project folder or in the Business Affairs file.

The Long Term

The process of selling an idea, hiring a writer and delivering a completed script can take years. The average gestation period for a television movie is two to three years. Features can take even longer, with a year being the absolute minimum. This was not always the case, but lately "development hell" has become, at the very least, a rather long purgatory.

How does this affect you? In contrast to the multi-year lifespan of a development project, most assistants last about a year or so in their jobs before leaving the company or getting promoted. This mismatch between project and assistant lifespans can wreak havoc on smooth development operations. Try to effect a seamless transition from you to your successors. Otherwise, costly and time-consuming disruptions will plague your company's development process every time your boss changes assistants.

Your best hedge against the march of time is to create a development archive. The project files described in Chapter 3 can comprise one part of your archive. If the project files are well-organized, your successors can find what they need in these files. To make a proper archive, though, you need to create a database on all development activity.

The database will contain the development status of any project which was ever developed at your company, regardless of the eventual outcome. The archive database will contain all information, while the weekly status report will merely be a selection of relevant projects which deserve attention. Figure 5.6 on the next page shows the structure of such a database. The status report just skims the current projects off the top of a huge pool of information on past projects. Incoming submissions constantly feed new projects into the pyramid.

Why is it important to have a database? For one thing, some development projects resurface after a time and become quite salable. This is likely to occur a long time after you are gone. You want to create a system where someone who steps into your job years after you are gone can access the hard work you performed. If the work is just left in the files, it will be impossible to search for projects using key words, such as an author's name. It will never be found, and your work will have been wasted.

Ambitious database designers can integrate the incoming submissions database described in Chapter 4 with the development database. That way piece of written material can flow from receipt through development,

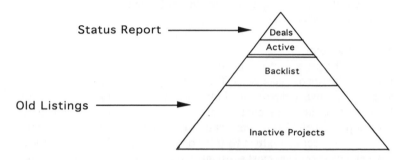

Figure 5.6   Schematic of database design as a pyramid

all in the same database. When a new script comes in, it can be given a ranking of 1. The submissions report would be generated by telling the computer to compile a list of all projects having a ranking of 1. If a project is put on the A list, its ranking is changed to 2. If the script is rejected, it's ranking is reduced to 0. Backlist projects are ranked 3, and development deals 4. The development status report is created by asking the computer to show all projects with rankings of 2, 3 or 4. The advantage of organizing the projects in this hierarchy is that it saves you time and confusion in data entry. People will always know where to look for development information, since it can only be in one place.

Chapter 6
Production

6.0 WHY ASSISTANTS NEED TO KNOW ABOUT PRODUCTION

In the old days, when an aspiring Cecil B. DeMille wanted to make a movie, he wrote a scenario, hired some actors and a cameraman, built an outdoor set with three walls and said, "Action!" Look how far we've come. Production is Chapter 6. It should be Chapter 1! Production is what the movie business is all about, but in the intervening eighty years a mighty system of writers, agents, lawyers, power-brokers and stars has emerged. This system has grown to the point where *production executives* and producers (so named because they are supposed to make something) often have a poor grasp of how a film is actually made.

Do not fall into this trap. A working knowledge of production is a personal asset worth cultivating. Even if you envision yourself working solely on the development or deal-making side of the business, you will be helped by having an understanding of physical production.

This chapter is written from the perspective of an assistant to a production executive or producer who must oversee a production. This is in contrast to a producer who works on location (local or out of town), the so-called *line producer*. This chapter will not cover setting up a production office or being a production assistant. Nor will this chapter give you a full technical indoctrination into production. Instead it should give you a broad overview of the production process, so you can be familiar with the happenings and situations of production as they pertain to your office.

6.1   PRE-PRODUCTION
Hiring a Director

After your company has received the *greenlight* from a studio or network, the first task is to hire a director for the film. On a feature, there may aleady be a director involved, but in television, the director is almost always attached after the network gives the go-ahead.

Selecting a director is comparable to hiring a writer. The director must be appropriate, available, acceptable to the financing entity, interested in doing the job, and affordable. Finding a match can be quite difficult. One critical difference between writers and directors is that while a writer can always be rewritten, a director only gets one shot at making a film. The director also has to have the strength to overcome the difficulties and politics rampant on a movie set, especially where temperamental personalities are involved.

When a directing assignment is open, various talent agents will submit their clients for the job. Normally, the agents will send over cassettes of one or two recent films by the director in question, as well as a printout of credits. You will have to prepare a *Director list* in the same manner as the writer's list described in Chapter 5. Some directors will send over a *director's reel*, which is a cassette or film compilation of work done by the director. Your boss will decide which films she wants to watch. You have to coordinate the sending home of material with your boss. For instance, you don't want to overload her with viewing on any one night, and you don't want any tapes to get lost. It's good practice to log in the tapes as you would incoming scripts, just to assure that you will know where to return them. Each tape should have a Post-it attached, giving the name of the project for which the director is being considered.

Feature film directors sometimes want producers to see their work projected in a theater. If this is the case then you will have to arrange a *screening,* so all the relevant people can watch the work of a directorial candidate. Arranging a screening can be a nightmare. You have to make sure that everyone is available, and that you can get a screening room, a projectionist and a copy of the film to show. If there are more than two parties coming to the screening, you will probably have to lock in the date with the screening facility and force the people attending the screening to change their schedules to fit yours. You can always change things, but if you try to allow everyone maximum flexibility, it will take a month to get the screening off the ground.

The major studios lend *prints* (copies) of films to each other on a reciprocal courtesy basis. If your company is working on a feature for a studio, or has offices at a studio, then you can usually borrow a print from another studio to watch a sample of a director's work. You still have to find a screening room, but the availability of prints is not a problem. Each studio has a person who takes care of lending prints. Your responsibility is to make sure that the print is returned safely to the studio that lent it out. At $5,000 each, you don't want to have to replace a missing print.

When a suitable director has been found, the director and the producer will have a creative meeting to make sure they are on the same wavelength. Any changes to be made can be discussed at this meeting.

Casting

Casting is the process of hiring actors to fill the dramatic roles in a movie. The *Casting Director* is in charge of finding actors for each role, both for starring and for minor parts. The casting director coordinates the hiring of each actor. The skill of the casting director revolves around his or her ability to maximize the value of the casting budget by making imaginative casting suggestions, and by playing an intermediary role between the production and the agents who represent the actors. A good casting director has an encyclopedic knowledge of actors and a shrewd but friendly negotiating style.

For leading roles, the casting director creates *casting lists*, which name the top ten or twenty available stars for each part. Like the writer or director lists, the casting lists contain the actor's name, availability, agent, and agent's phone number. You might get asked to make your own suggestions for the casting list. This is a good opportunity to act important. No matter how lowly you are, you are allowed to say things like, "Kim Basinger is all wrong for this part."

Assuming that no star is already attached to a production, casting the lead role is a complex affair. It is structurally similar to hiring a writer or director, in that your company and the actor must make the same match between availability, acceptability, desire to perform the part and ability to make a deal. There are significant differences, though. Since the star is the most visible and arguably the most important marketing element in a film, the studios and networks are ruthless about who gets to play the lead role.

The actors themselves are often quite sensitive to the meaning or perceived quality of the role they are about to play. For example, actors are concerned about being typecast in certain roles. Or an actor might worry that a television role will hurt his image. For these reasons and others, an actor might actually turn down a lucrative starring role even if he has no other work lined up.

Casting can be a tense time for a production. As William Goldman writes in *Adventures in the Screen Trade*, "...everything is soft till principal photography...."* There is always the possibility that the studio or network will pull the plug on a project if it cannot assemble a cast within a reasonable amount of time. The director joins a production assuming a specific start date. If casting drags on too long, the director might look around for another, more solidly packaged production that he knows will get going right away. The director may have a prior commitment to direct another film that has a firm start date. If the director abandons your production, you are probably dead in the water. So casting can become an urgent process as time passes.

The studio, the director and your boss reach a consensus on which star to approach. Your boss makes a phone call to the actor's agent and discusses the role and the project to determine if there is any interest from the star. The agent might say that the actor won't do such a part, for whatever reasons. Or he might ask to see the script. Your boss then sends the script to the agent. The covering letter to the agent should probably state which part in the script is intended for the actor, unless it's totally obvious. When you enter the script in the outgoing script log, you have to enter in the comment section the actor for whom the script is being sent.

Some actors require a reading offer before they will look at the script. A reading offer is a guarantee that the actor would be offered the part for a certain amount of money before even reading the script. The reading offer serves two purposes for the actor. It decreases wasted time, in the sense that if an actor is going to read a script, he should not have to do so unless guaranteed the part if he wants it. What is more important, the reading offer is a negotiating tool used by the agent. Typically, the agent will use the reading offer figure as an opener in negotiating a deal for his client. The reading offer establishes an effective minimum the production is willing to pay for the actor's services. After that, it is "merely the reading offer."

If the actor likes the script and wants to play the starring role, then the deal can be made right away. Frequently, though, the part is accepted subject to a creative meeting between producer, star, director, casting director and studio. The dynamics of this phase in the deal depend on the relative power of the participants. If the star is a colossal name and the production is relatively small potatoes, then the onus is on the producer to sell the worthiness of the project to the star. If the star is up and coming or semi-washed up, and the director is a powerhouse, the creative meeting is more a time for the director and producer to make doubly sure they want to be in business with this actor.

Star deals vary enormously, so I will not try to delve into their numerous permutations. A basic star deal is an enhanced version of the standard *Screen Actors Guild (SAG)* clauses for compensation, work rules, per diem, pension, health and welfare and residuals. In addition, the basic star deal usually contains provisions for a personal assistant, hairstylist and/ or makeup person, and a trailer. A star deal almost always provides for the star's *billing* in the movie, whether it is *top billing*, meaning it's listed above all other actors' names, or *above the title*, which means the star's name goes above the name of the movie in all advertising and appears before it in the title sequence of the actual film.

At the extreme, a mega-star deal can allow the star liberal authority over script, choice of director, and advertising and publicity for the film. A mega-deal generally carries *profit participation,* ranging from a portion of the net profits to a percentage of the box-office gross, which is known as *gross points*. To make a distinction among mega-stars, some get gross points after the film has reached a certain level in box office sales, while really huge stars like Arnold Schwarzenegger get gross points as soon as the movie opens. These are called gross points *from the first dollar*.

Star deals in television movies are less subject to wild excesses. There is a limited range of salaries and privileges offered to a television movie star. However, as in any other human endeavor, even though the status symbols are limited, there are no limits on individual egos and competitive drives. A television producer often finds himself soothing conflicts by doling out billing, perks and money to stars, albeit from a small pot.

The casting director is given a budget for casting all the roles, including the lead, so casting a film is like dividing a pie. If the star is expensive, then the other actors are by definition cheap, unless extra money can be found. In television, if a star is particularly expensive, then the network agrees to pay *cast breakage*, which is money spent on the production in excess of the negotiated license fee for the purpose of casting a star.

The casting of co-stars is similar to the casting of stars, though usually with less fanfare and heartache. Scripts are sent to agents and creative meetings are sometimes required, but the agents have less negotiating leverage, so the deals are easier to make. In some cases, the star will want to interview the potential co-star.

For secondary roles, the casting director either approaches actors he already knows, or submits the scripts to *Breakdown Services*, a company that prepares descriptions of available roles in many films, and releases the information to theatrical agencies every day. The agents in turn submit photographs and resumes for their clients to the casting director.

The casting director reviews the submissions for each role and determines which actors he wants to *read* for the part. Readings are like auditions. Actors are given some description of the role by their agents. They may or may not be given scenes, also known as *sides*, to prepare in advance. When they come in to the casting director's office, they act out the scene. Readings go in several rounds. In the final round, the director and producer also evaluate the actor. A casting director might look at hundreds of photographs and read dozens of actors in the process of casting a few roles. It is a time-consuming process.

For a series or pilot, the casting director often makes what is known as a *test option deal* with the actor. In this case, the producer negotiates the terms of the actor's contract before the actor has his final reading at the network. If the network approves the actor, then the actor's deal is already in place. This precludes a situation where the actor may ask for more money once he knows that the network wants him.

In a *pay-or-play deal*, the actor is promised to be paid completely, whether or not his services are actually required. That way, if the movie is never made, the actor can still get paid. Directors and producers also make pay-or-play deals. Pay-or-play deals protect the talent (actor, director, producer) from being tied up indefinitely on a project that doesn't happen.

Directors and stars often ask for terms that are on *favored nations* with other people on the production. Favored nations means that a term in one person's deal will match a term of another person's deal, even if the specifics are still unknown. For example, a director might ask for a share of net profits on the basis of favored nations with the star. That means that whatever net profit terms the star receives will also be enjoyed by the director.

Location Scouting, Boarding and Budgeting

To determine the cost of making a film, a producer must know how many days of shooting there will be, where the shooting will take place, and what the costs of people and materials will be for each of these days. This information is derived by *breaking down* the script into individual scenes and then examining each scene in detail to estimate the cost of its production. The vehicle for this process is a *production board*.

To create the production board, the *unit production manager* or *first assistant director* of the film goes through the script with colored pencils and highlights every detail that will cost money. Props are underlined in one color, costumes in another, and actors yet another. The details of a production, such as the location, names of the actors, and sets required for each scene, are then summarized on thin strips of cardboard. The strips are color-coded to signify a day, night, interior or exterior scene.

The strips are then assembled in a pattern that will become the optimal shooting schedule for the film. All the day scenes requiring a certain location are grouped together, for example. Since films are shot out of sequence, all the shooting at one location will be shot at once. This reduces the number of times the production unit has to move. Even if, in the final version of a film, the characters visit a place more than one time, all the scenes at that location will have filmed back to back. The scenes are then recombined in editing.

Concurrent with boarding is *location scouting*, which is the process of identifying, and negotiating for the right to shoot on, a location. Until the advent of portable, battery-powered cameras and sophisticated sound recording technology, films were shot mostly indoors on sound stages, which are really just enormous, dark, soundproof rooms. Today's films are shot partly on stages and partly out in the real world, in houses and buildings that are known as *practical locations*. The person who finds these places is the *location scout*. Location scouts are usually people who are familiar with a whole range of locations in an area. They know people who like to rent out their houses to film crews and they know the regulations and negotiations involved in getting permission to film on locations.

The location scout works with the *art director* and/or *production designer* of the film to find locations that have the right look. The art director is responsible for the look of the film, so location is a critical aspect of his trade. The location scout is also responsible for finding interesting outdoor places and vistas, in addition to interior rooms and spaces. In some instances, the location scout will take the director and producer on scouting trips to inspect various places, even if they are halfway around the world. Most of the time, though, location scouts photograph a place in detail and then present the director and art director with composite photographs for evaluation.

The production board is modular, and its scene strips can and will be moved around a great deal before the schedule is set. A production manager must sort out many different variables in boarding a film. For example, the various unions involved each have their own work rules concerning the amount of time allocated between periods of day and night shooting. The unions exact overtime penalties if the work rules are violated. The production manager has to choose what alternative will be the least costly.

The basic factor of film scheduling is the number of script pages that will be shot in a day. When the production manager breaks down the script, he notes the length of each scene in eighths of pages. Shooting days are grouped together on the production board to reflect the number of *pages per day* that the director wants to shoot, and for which the production has committed funds. Each mode of film production has a standard rate of pages per day. Feature films generally shoot two or three pages per day, so forty to sixty days is average for a feature film. Television movies are shot at about six pages per day, and television series at about seven to eight pages per day or one episodic-length script per six-day week.

Generally, the more pages per day being filmed, the less time the director and crew have to set up each shot, and the lower the *production values* will be. However, a talented director working quickly is better than a hack taking his time.

Pages per day is a rough guide to the speed with which a film will be produced, and a good production manager always looks at the content of the scene to determine the amount of time it will take to shoot. A three-page dialogue scene can be shot in a matter of hours, while some short but complex scenes can take a whole day, or even longer. According to legend, the longest one-eighth page scene in history was in the movie BEN HUR. The description simply said, "Chariot Race."

When the board reaches a state of satisfactory completion, the production manager creates a *shooting schedule* that reflects the contents of the board, but in a more readable form than the board. At this point, the production manager can draft a realistic budget for the film. Until now, the budget figure has been theoretical. Now the producers can know with some precision how much the film will cost, because they know how long it will take to shoot. The number of shooting days is the prime determinant of cost in most films. Everyone on the film works freelance, and their rate is based on the number of days they have to work. Non-personnel costs such as car and prop rentals, hotel and meals, and location fees are all based on length of utilization.

The *below-the-line costs*, all the expenses of making a film except fees paid to talent, are estimated by multiplying the daily cost of an item by the number of days the item is needed. When the production manager adds in extra costs such as insurance, he arrives at a figure for the complete below-the-line cost of the film. Then he adds in the *above-the-line* costs, which include the salaries for the director and actors, and reaches the first total budget figure for the film.

This total figure is usually too high at first. The producer, writer, director and production manager then begin to examine where the money in the budget is going, and decide where to cut back without damaging the quality of the film. For example, a scene where two people have a conversation on the deck of an aircraft carrier might be changed so that they now have the conversation in a backyard. Gone are the high costs of renting a ship and hiring extras. This forms the basis for the production rewrite.

(For more information on production scheduling and budgeting, there are two excellent books on the subject. *Film Scheduling* by Ralph Singleton [*Lone Eagle Publishing*] is a step-by-step guide to boarding and scheduling a film. The book *Film and Video Budgets*, by Michael Wiese [*Michael Wiese Productions, Studio City, California*], describes the ins and outs of budgeting many productions varying in cost.)

Production Rewrite

As the film nears production, the script undergoes scrutiny from a number of different perspectives. The director will have suggestions for how he would interpret certain scenes. The star wants her part adjusted to reflect her individual abilities and character. Then there is the whole process of fitting a fictional script to the practical and economic realities of film production. All these inputs will change the makeup of the script. Sometimes the revisions will be superficial. Other times the script may arrive at the start of principal photography a totally different piece of material. In either case, there is always some sort of production rewrite on a film.

The original writer may or may not do the production rewrite. A television movie production rewrite is almost always done by the original writer. In features, the opposite is true. Production rewrites are not always a friendly process. Directors or stars can bring in their own writers to "fix" problems in the script and end up with a radically different story. Some films are rewritten as they are shot, a process that, though commonplace, can lead to disaster.

In a production rewrite, the writer hands in loose pages with each set of changes instead of an entirely new draft of the script. Your job is to track the comments, notes, and rewritten pages that are generated in script meetings with the director and star. The pages have to be dated. That way, as successive rewrites of the same scene come in, anyone looking at the script can tell how recent the rewrite is. The changed passages have to be marked in the margin with an asterisk, as shown below. If the writer does his job properly, this will already have been done.

However, given the crush of production activity, this dating and marking may fall on you. There are several computer programs available that allow you to create a screenplay format with ease. (See Appendix G for a list.)

The following is an example of a scene before and after it has been revised in a production rewrite:

As originally written:

                    BILL
          I won't have it. I'm leaving you.
          Don't bother to write.

                    DIANE
          That's fine with me...

The rewritten scene now reads as follows.

Revised 1/1/93
                    BILL
          How could you sleep with my best   *
          friend? I'm leaving you, and I   *
          want the kids.   *

                    DIANE
          That's fine with me...

To help everyone keep track of what's changed, put the date on top of the page, as shown above. Place asterisks in the right margin where the text has changed. Make copies of the new pages and insert them into all existing copies of the script in the office. (If you don't have time to insert them, just hand out the pages to everyone.) Be sure to insert new pages in the master script file.

You have to keep track of these page changes until the script supervisor (also known as a *continuity person*) is hired and takes over this job. The script supervisor is in charge of keeping track of the changes made in the script. As changes come in, the production office color-codes the new pages and distributes them to all members of the production, along with a new colored title page that indicates the date of revision and the corresponding color. The changes go in an industry-standard sequence of colors. The Original script is white, followed by blue, pink, yellow, green and goldenrod pages. The title page of a production script might be goldenrod, and have a legend that reads as follows:

3rd draft	1/1/93	White
Revision	1/15/93	Blue
Revision	1/17/93	Pink
Revision	2/14/93	Yellow
Revision	2/20/93	Green
Revision	2/22/93	Goldenrod

I mention color-coding in case you ever have to perform this task. In addition, you have to maintain a perfect copy of the script for your boss at all times. Your boss should have a script at the office and at home. The production office will give you two sets of colored page changes and you will have to insert them into your boss's shooting scripts at the office and at home.

Insurance

Every film production has insurance. Since a film is really a one-shot multi-million dollar business venture, the backers require that the production be insured against accidents or "Acts of God," just like any other business. There are several companies that specialize in insuring motion picture companies. (Appendix G again.) As the assistant to the producer, you have to track and file all correspondence relating to insurance matters.

Errors and omissions insurance (usually referred to as *E&O*) covers the producer in case of any libel suits, copyright infringements, or misrepresentations. E&O is especially relevant for true story adaptations. Before an insurance broker sells E&O, he must receive proof that the film has been checked for potential problems. If a real person is being portrayed in a film, the insurance company would need to see the rights agreement and the release, which states that the producer has the permission of the person to dramatize some aspect of his life. Otherwise, the person being depicted could sue, claiming the producer had no right to use his name or likeness. Even with the signed release, there could still be a lawsuit. That's why producers and production companies always buy E&O.

Your boss might send scripts to the insurance agents well before production, just to verify that the script is insurable. To show the insurance company that a true story script is authentic, and thus insurable, the writer prepares an *annotated script*. The annotated script shows the source for each scene in the movie, whether it came from a book, an interview, or a court transcript.

In addition to the annotated script, most producers also pay a company such as DeForest Research, a Los Angeles-based research firm, to study the script and analyze any potential errors and omissions problems. The resulting report is submitted to the insurance company to clear the script for E&O insurance.

Negative Insurance covers any damage to the actual film negative. Since all the value of the production, from star salaries to sets and props, is contained in the fragile film stock that runs through the camera, the production must insure against any accidental loss of this negative. If fire, lab damage, or a faulty camera destroys the negative for a scene, the company will have to reshoot the entire scene, paying the actors and crew all over again. Negative insurance provides for this situation, though the lab or equipment rental house's insurance policy may cover the loss. (These policies usually have very high deductibles, however, which the production company has to absorb.)

Key Person Insurance covers the production for the loss, due to illness or death, of the star, director, or any other person deemed "indispensable" to the film. Stars do fall ill, or worse, during the making of films, and if they become unable to complete the film, the financial backer can be out millions of dollars with no way of recouping its investment. To get insurance, the star has to undergo a physical examination by a doctor.

Besides these basic types of production insurance, most productions are insured for general liability and equipment damage. A production cannot rent equipment without insurance. A fully equipped 35mm camera can cost as much as $250,000. It is impossible to rent one without proof that it will be repaired or replaced if it is damaged.

A *Completion Bond* is a type of insurance that provides funds to complete the film in case the production goes over budget. There is a joke in Hollywood that goes, "What's worse than a bad picture? Half a bad picture." The financial backer must have a completed film to realize any value from his investment. An incomplete film is worthless. Completion bond companies take money from production companies in return for a guarantee to bail out the film and fund its completion if the budget is exhausted. In reality, a completion bond company is likely to come in and finish the film as quickly and cheaply as possible. The film will be completed, but the quality might suffer.

Hiring Department Heads

After the director has been hired, the production searches for and hires *department heads* to run the functional areas of the production. The designation of department heads varies with each shoot, but generally this title is bestowed on the *Production Designer, Wardrobe Person, Cinematographer,* and *Hair and Makeup Person.* (More on these specific jobs below.) On some films, special effects is a major department.

Before production, your boss and the director will interview candidates for department head positions. Before or after the interviews, your boss might want to see samples of their work. If their agents don't have a sample reel or cassette copies, rent them from the local video store. The director gets virtual *carte blanche* in hiring department heads. In most cases, the director is given first choice with little interference, unless the department head selected is seen as completely inappropriate or too expensive.

When the team has been assembled, the department heads begin a series of discussions with the director and producer to finalize the look and style of the film. These "nuts and bolts" discussions also involve the writer, location scout(s) and production manager. No longer are the ideas vague and general. These pre-production meetings deal in specifics. Will this location do? How will the production make this costume for this actor? Pre-production discussions translate into budget negotiations, as each department head asks for the special resources needed for certain effects and scenes. Unless your production is CLEOPATRA or TERMINATOR 2, a series of compromises will have to be worked out. The production designer gets to build his restaurant set, but not the colonial mansion. The wardrobe department gets to build suits of armor for the one scene, but will have to make do with rented costumes for another scene, and so on. If the negotiations turn into conflicts, your boss might be the adjudicator of these disputes.

The ideas, rewrites, conflicts and negotiations of the preproduction period are not always resolved by the first day of shooting, but normally by that time the film will have a shooting schedule and a detailed budget. As the film gets closer to the production start date, many other crew members come aboard. A film crew can have as many as seventy or eighty specialized people working at one time. The production crew is so big that it requires a separate, temporary *production office* to manage the shoot. A *production coordinator* supervises the day-to-day administrative workings of a film shoot, shipping film to the laboratory, filing production reports, and making travel arrangements, just to name a few of this person's tasks.

6.2   PRODUCTION
The Making of a Single Shot

A single shot in a film begins with either an empty sound stage or an unembellished practical location. The director and production designer evaluate the visual effect they want to achieve. If the idea is a complex one, the designer will make sketches and blueprints, to be approved by the director and production staff before construction. For a regular location, the production designer usually just describes how he will redo what is already there, and lets the director make suggested changes. In either case, the end result is a film set.

The *prop person* and the *set decorator* must now make the set perfect for the scene. In recreating reality, these two people (or teams of people) search for the objects that will make the picture look absolutely real. The prop people and set decorators scan the script for mention of specific items that need to be in a scene. The decorating of a set involves intense attention to detail. In a period movie, this requires research into the minutiae of the past. If the scene takes place in a restaurant, how much food should be on the table? What kind of food? If the set decorating is perfect, it will be invisible, because it will appear so real that nobody notices.

The departments of wardrobe, makeup and hair then prepare the actors for the scene. Like the set, the look of the actors has to be perfect, and the wardrobe and makeup departments agonize over details of how an actor will look on camera. If there are extras in the scene, they too must look just right. The process is labor intensive and time-consuming. The job of makeup and wardrobe is not over once the shoot begins. They must watch the actors as the scene is shot in case anyone needs adjustment during the day. The director may pronounce the look of the actor unsuitable as a scene is being rehearsed. Wardrobe and makeup people have to be resourceful, and able to respond to such challenges immediately. The crew cannot wait all day while an alternate costume is found.

After the set is decorated, the *cinematographer* (also known as the *Director of Photography*, or *DP*) begins to light the scene. The director works with the cinematographer to establish how the scene will be photographed, where the camera will be placed, how it will move, and what visual effect he wants to achieve. Since the lighting takes place while the actors are being made up, the cinematographer employs *stand-ins*. Stand-ins are the same size as the actors who will be in the scene. They have the same skin tone and wear clothing similar to the actors'. That way, when the actors actually get to the set, the cinematographer only has to fine-tune the lighting.

In most feature films and hour-long television shows, there is usually just one camera filming. A second camera is used if it can be placed without being filmed by the first camera. In action scenes, crowd scenes, special effects scenes, or scenes where expensive props are destroyed, there may be half a dozen cameras filming all at once.

As the camera crews practice their moves, the sound person determines the optimal way to record the dialogue in a scene. He will usually place several microphones around the set to capture ambient sound as well as dialogue. In addition, a microphone mounted on a boom (a long fiberglass pole) is positioned near the actors during the scene. As the actors move, the boom operator follows them, pointing the microphone towards them. The boom operator must practice his moves with the camera crew, as the boom can block lights or cast a shadow if it's moved the wrong way. Each microphone feeds into a mixing board and synchronous-sound tape recorder.

When everyone is ready, the whole unit runs through the shot. The actors practice their dialogue and movements. If they deviate from the rehearsed pattern, they will foul up the camera and sound crews. An experienced film actor can repeat the same scene over and over again identically, except for desired changes in tone or performance dictated by the director.

When the scene is ready to be shot, the *first assistant director* yells for everyone on the set to be quiet. At this point, everyone on the set who is not involved in shooting the scene should freeze and be absolutely quiet. The first assistant director then tells the camera and sound to roll. Sound and camera acknowledge by saying "rolling," and then "speed," which means that the camera and sound recorder are running at synchronous speed. The camera operator then calls "mark it." This prompts a camera assistant to run out and clap the *clapper board*, or *slate,* in front of the camera. This act, which you have doubtless seen in many movies, is done to mark the point of synchronization between sound and picture. At this point, the director yells, "Action!"

As rehearsed, the actors, camera crews and sound crew go through their moves and film the scene. At the end, the director says "Cut," and everyone stands down for a moment, but then promptly gets ready for the next take. Once the setup has been completed, the director will do several takes in a short time. Most directors like to prepare for the next take immediately, to preserve the concentration that has been mustered for the performance. When the director finally gets a take he likes, he says "Print it," and the designated take is marked "print" on the shot list. The film negative will be developed for every take, but the lab will print only the selected takes. This saves money, since the lab charges for developing and printing by the foot, and it would be quite expensive and confusing to print every take.

The *Continuity Director* observes the scene and takes notes on the precise action. The continuity director's job is to ensure that the final version of the film will have perfect visual continuity. That means if an actor opens a door with his left hand in one scene, he must have his left hand on the door knob when he is filmed coming through the other side of the door in the next scene. Problem is, that next scene where he comes through the other side of the door might be shot two weeks later, or two weeks earlier, since films are shot out of sequence. An audience can always see a bad continuity error. The continuity director has to take in all the details of a scene and write them down on her script. To aid in this observation, the continuity director will often snap a Polaroid photo right after the director yells "Cut," to record the exact location and detail of a scene in retakes and subsequent scenes. (For an excellent description of this process, see *Script Supervising and Film Continuity* by Pat Miller [*Focal Press, 1986*].)

At the end of the day or at lunch, the director and producer retire to a screening room to watch the *dailies*, which are synchronized scenes filmed the day before. Dailies are also known as *rushes*, since they are rushed to and from the lab. While the crew shoots during the day, the editing team is synchronizing the footage from the day before. The director and producer determine if the previous day's shots are satisfactory and decide whether to reshoot anything. The studio or network executives also watch the dailies, so they can voice their comments. The camera picks up details that elude the human eye, so dailies are a critical confirmation that everything went all right in the shoot. Camera or sound problems are also invisible until the film is developed and examined. A spot on the lens or a blurred shot will not show up until dailies are screened.

The operation described above applies to feature films, television movies and dramatic television series. Situation comedies are filmed under different circumstances, though. Sitcoms are also referred to as *Three-Camera Comedies*, since they are normally shot in sequence in front of live audiences with three (sometimes four) cameras filming at once. The set is fixed, changing little from episode to episode. The show is rehearsed and rewritten for a week. On Friday or Saturday afternoon, the technical crew runs through the whole show with the cast. In the evening, the show is filmed in front of a live audience in real time, with short breaks between scenes for the cameras to be reset. In this respect, situation comedies are much more like live theater than films.

6.3 THE ASSISTANT'S ROLE IN PRODUCTION

Production is a tense time. Many things can go wrong, and they often do, at great expense. An assistant in a production must be prepared for disaster lurking around every corner. Your goal, then, is to provide information and service in quick response to the needs of your boss. This means continuously updating files and materials, at the office and wherever else your boss might go.

Production Files

When a movie goes into production, you should designate an area in the filing cabinet as space for production files. All the folders should be clearly marked for easy identification. The documents you will file there include the following:

Contracts

All legal agreements for the director, writer and stars should be accessible at the office. Deal letters and memoranda are also to be filed with the contract.

Page changes

As each set of revisions is added to the script, the old pages should be filed away, in case it is ever necessary to trace the evolution of a written scene.

Day out of Days.

This chart lists how many days each actor has to work during the shoot, which is important in determining actors' salaries.

Budgets.

As the film is rewritten and rescheduled, the budget will change. Old versions of the budget are useful to retain, because arguments often revolve around individuals' expectations of payment based on an obsolete budget.

Production reports

At the end of each day, the production office sends around a production report. This report lists the scenes that were filmed during the day, and matches the results of the day with the schedule, indicating if the film is behind schedule. These have to be filed in case it is necessary to track the progress of the production, or the director.

Correspondence

Letters sent or received, which are specific to the production, should be kept with the production files.

Crew Resumés and Contact Lists

The contact list contains the name, home address and home phone number of every person on the production. This information is useful for future productions.

Script Notes and Edit Notes

The notes that dictate the successive rewrites and recuts of the film are filed for possible reference in case of any kind of dispute with the director or writer.

The Production Folder

The President of the United States has the "Football," a briefcase that contains launch codes for nuclear missiles. Your boss has a *production folder*, the showbiz equivalent of the Football. The production folder contains everything your boss needs to know about the production at a glance. The idea behind the production folder is that your boss should be able to find out what he needs to know without having to consult an assistant, since he might be alone at some remote location. Handy in either a notebook or a manila folder, the production folder should hold the following:

1) The most up-to-date shooting schedule.
2) The most recent version of the budget.
3) Cast and crew lists with all home telephone numbers on them.
4) A phone number list which contains the work, fax, car and home phone numbers of all individuals associated with the production:
    a) The network/studio executives.
    b) The agents for the stars and director.
    c) The production's law firm.
5) The Day out of Days.
6) A special phone sheet detailing all production-related calls your boss needs to make.
7) The up-to-date shooting script

As the production department of the film distributes new copies of each of these items, you have to make sure that the production folder is properly updated. You can reduce the bulk of materials you carry around by creating a miniature production folder on a photocopier. You can easily reduce the script, schedule, and crew lists to 6"x 9" or smaller.

Dailies

If your boss is not on the location and he has to watch dailies, then it's up to you to make sure that he gets them, wherever he is. On most productions, the dailies are transferred onto videotape and duplicated for the people who have to watch them. The production department will drop off a copy for your boss. You will have to schedule an hour or so in the day for your boss to watch the dailies and make any necessary phone calls to discuss them. (Lunch is a great time for dailies. Keep your boss's lunches free and order food in, so she can watch dailies and eat without leaving the office.) Dailies, like any production-related matters, take precedence over less urgent development or personal meetings and calls.

Rules of the Set

A film set is a tightly controlled environment, so if you visit, you are well advised to observe certain rules of courtesy. A film crew that works together for several months becomes a close-knit group, almost like a family. The director sets the tone, and encourages the crew to feel as if they are creating a unique work of art. As an outsider, then, you have to act on a movie set as if you were a guest in someone's home. Basically, that just means behaving properly, but there are a couple of subtleties that are worthy of mention.

1) Don't talk to people unless necessary. There is no need to be unfriendly, but people on film crews are quite busy, and they don't need to be bothered by you.
2) Be quiet in general, but don't move or make any noise when the director is talking to the actors. When the camera is rolling, don't even breathe.
3) When lunch is served, don't rush to the front of the line to be served first. Let the crew eat before you.
4) Cameras are forbidden on sets.
5) Be conscious of where you are standing. Anticipate having to move out of the way of cranes, dollies, and grips moving the sets around.

6) Avoid touching props and sets. You don't want to be responsible for disrupting the continuity of a scene, breaking something, or making noise by knocking something over.

7) Don't wear something that calls attention to you.

8) Don't get in an actor's "eyeline."

9) Don't look at the video monitor unless asked to. (Too many people already need to look at this.)

10) Turn your beeper and/or cellular phone off.

These rules may seem excessive to you, but they stem from the well-defined political milieu of the film set. If you work for the producer, or worse, the studio, you are a complete outsider—one of "them." You are an enemy of the creative clan that has assembled to produce the work of art. Whatever your personal feelings, you stand for crass commercialism and the forces that destroy creativity. As an enemy of art, you have to be doubly well-behaved.

6.4 POST-PRODUCTION

As its name denotes, *post-production* refers to all the activities on a film that occur after the completion of principal photography. It is a bit of a misnomer, though, because some of the post-production occurs while the film is being shot. The three phases of post-production are editing, sound rerecording, and final finishing of the film.

When the shot film negative comes out of the camera, it goes to a lab where it is developed. Motion picture film negative looks a lot like the 35-millimeter color negative you get from a photo lab. In fact, it's identical, except that motion picture stock is a little thicker. The lab prints the selected takes and ships them to the editing room of the production. The prints of selected takes are referred to as *work print,* meaning that they are for cutting only. They are never shown to anyone outside the production, except for test audience screenings. (The print is made by exposing a fresh piece of film to the negative, thus reversing the image, much like a contact print in still photography.) The negative is then stored in the lab's vault, a dust-free, fireproof, climate-controlled area.

The film editor synchronizes the selected takes with the corresponding sound track, which has been dubbed onto a special magnetic tape of the same width as the work print. The editing table rolls the picture and sound track simultaneously through a lens and a magnetic playback head.

The flatbed, or KEM editing table, has a small screen and a loudspeaker, so the sound and picture track moving together create the effect of synchronous sound.

Since videotape is faster and cheaper to edit than film, many television productions are shot on film but edited on tape. (Shooting on film preserves the richer image quality of film.) When a production is shot on film but edited on tape, the lab develops the film negative, but instead of printing the selected takes on work print film, transfers the negative to videotape (electronically reversing the image) and then dubs in the sound track. The editor receives videotape with which to work. Tape is cheaper than film, and various effects for television are far less expensive to accomplish on tape than with film.

As soon as there's enough footage, the editor begins to assemble scenes. By the time the shooting is completed, the film might be at least partly edited. After production, however, the director comes into the editing room and supervises the editing full time. Shots are trimmed and recombined in any number of ways. Editing is a complex and fascinating art that deserves far more space than I am going to give it here. A good editor is an artist, a technician, and a "film doctor." He fixes mistakes made by every other department.

The first stage of editing yields an intermediate product known as the *director's cut* of the film. The director's cut is a full-length version of the film exactly as the director would like it to be. If the director has been granted the right of *final cut*, the director's cut is the version of the film that will be released; the studio must abide by the director's decisions regarding the final composition and length of the film.

After the director has turned in his cut, unless his is the final cut, the producer and financing entity get to evaluate it and make changes. The director may or may not stay involved after this point. It depends on his relationship to the producer and his experience with the film. If the relationship is collaborative, then the director will stay on and fight for scenes he wants to keep intact. Otherwise, after the director turns in his cut, the film is re-edited.

Editing is followed by screenings of rough cuts of the film and notes given by the producer and production executives, in a process similar to the development of the script. After several rounds of screening and recutting, an acceptable cut of the film begins to take shape. When everyone is satisfied, the picture is *locked*. Locking a picture means that no more changes to the visual content can be made.

The *on-screen credits* for the film are finalized around this time. A list circulates which contains the name and billing of every participant in the film. It might be your job to verify the contents of this list. You hope you won't get that honor, but it happens. Every name has to be checked for correct spelling, and every credit has to verified. Then, billing has to be checked. Each contract with talent dictates the type of billing. The credits list will show whether the credit will appear on its own card, or in a shared card. All this has to be perfect.

A titles company designs the title sequence. Titles companies are usually animation and/or graphic design firms that specialize in creating memorable title sequences for films. Their demo reels and work samples will find their way into your office. The titles company prepares sketches of how they envision the title sequence. Your boss will probably have the ability to suggest changes, or at least comment on the style of the proposed title sequence. Once a title company has been given the go-ahead, they create the title sequence using the approved and corrected titles list. Once they have completed their job, someone has to check to see that they transferred all the names and credits correctly.

Until now the movie has only had its raw sound track, which was recorded on the set. Before a movie can be shown, extensive work has to be done to improve the quality of the sound track. In addition, music and sound effects have to be added to the sound track.

For scenes that don't sound right, the actors are brought into a studio where they re-record the dialogue from the scene. This process is known as *looping*, so named because the picture of the scene is threaded in a loop through the projector in the studio. The actor watches the scene repeatedly to time the re-recording of dialogue perfectly. Actors' contracts all provide a guarantee that the actor will be available for a given number of days to loop scenes.

When the picture is locked, the *composer* and *music editor* get ready to create the musical soundtrack of the film. The producer, editor, composer and music editor (and perhaps director) screen the movie in a *spotting session*, where they determine which scenes will require musical underscoring. The composer then writes the music and hires an orchestra. The composer leads the orchestra in scoring the film in a specially designed recording studio that contains a movie screen and sophisticated playback equipment. Composers today also use synthesizers to score films.

To add sound effects that were not recorded properly during shooting, the production uses a special sound studio called a *foley stage*. In the foley process, sound effects actors watch a scene on a screen and recreate the scene's sounds using special props. For example, the sound of footsteps rarely sounds right when it is recorded on location. On the foley stage, an actor watches the character walking in the film and walks around the stage with the same gait in heavy shoes, all while a technician aims a microphone at his feet.

Finally, there is the *sound mix,* when all the elements of the sound track are combined onto one track. The *sound mixer* (different from the mixer on the set) controls dozens of different inputs, ranging from looped scenes to music to sound effects. On each input, he can modify volume and pitch, as well as other acoustic properties of the sound. The result of this blending is the high-quality sound you hear in the theater. The director, producer, composer and editor usually attend the sound mix, which can last several days. Scenes are mixed one at a time, and there are frequent modifications to the mix of a scene before everyone is satisfied with the sound.

When everything has been performed to the satisfaction of the producer and the financing entity, the lab releases the negative from the vault to the *negative cutter.* The negative cutter matches the cuts made on the work print by the editor. The result is a cut negative in the exact sequence of the work print. This cut negative is used to make prints of the film for distribution (give or take a few steps that are excessively detailed for our purposes).

The first clean print of the film made from the cut negative is called the first *answer print.* The producer, editor, financing entity, and sometimes the cinematographer evaluate the answer print for its color correctness and image quality. The lab changes the answer print's color and picture characteristics each time it makes a new one. Finally, everyone agrees, and the lab is ready to make *release prints* of the film.

In television editing, the equivalent to negative cutting is the *on-line edit session.* The rough cutting of a video tape takes place in a relatively low-tech room, known as an *off-line suite,* using copies of the original tapes in case the tape is damaged in the process. When everything is perfect, the original tapes (or masters) are placed in a sophisticated and very expensive editing suite (the on-line suite) where they are copied to a fresh tape in conformation with the rough cut. Successive color corrections then follow. An on-line suite can cost upwards of $600 per hour to rent, so editors try to minimize the time spent in on-line. All creative decisions are made beforehand. The on-line is merely a matching process.

6.5   RELEASE/AIRING

When a nearly complete version of the film is ready, the studio sometimes conducts *test screenings* to gauge audience reactions. The movie is now the property of the *marketing and distribution* arm of the studio. The marketing department recruits audiences for test screenings. While the test audience watches the film, the producers and studio executives watch the audience, trying to evaluate different reactions. Did this joke work? Was this scene scary? An enormous amount of effort is expended in trying to understand the moviegoer. After the screening, the audience rates the film on survey cards. The results of test screenings can dictate changes in the content of the film, even to the point of requiring reshoots.

The distribution and marketing department of the studio then delivers a proposed advertising campaign and trailers for the film. This they often do in conjunction with a specialized film advertising agency. The producer normally has a consultation right on the advertising campaign and trailers. This means that he cannot flatly refuse to accept it, but his opinion might be valued. At the very least he was consulted, if not listened to. The advertising and releasing of films is a sore subject for many producers. A good film can be rendered ridiculous, given a misdirected advertising campaign.

The network handles all aspects of advertising for a television movie, and the producer has some consultation right, but limited ability to sway the network The network is more of a machine in the way it puts shows on the air every night, so there is less room to monkey around with the schedules and contents of promotion.

The network tests series pilots the same way the studio tests feature films. The testing is usually done by airing the pilot on a small local station or cable system, and contacting viewers by phone to judge their reactions. These tests are one of the criteria the network uses in determining which shows warrant more episodes.

The studio or network prepares a *press kit* for the film. A press kit is a folder that contains information about the movie, its story, and the people who made it. The press kit also contains still photos from the production. The point of the press kit is to enable a reviewer to write a good review of the film. Your office will undoubtedly receive requests for press kits, so you should make sure to have a supply on hand. Keeping a copy for your boss's scrapbook is also a nice idea.

Close to the release date or air date, the studio or network may hold a premiere. For television films, premieres are usually simple affairs where the stars and major participants, as well as friends and other guests, can watch the completed work. For features, premieres can be enormous, front-page spectaculars. You might have to play a role in organizing such an event, though that job usually falls into the hands of the distribution department or a specialized firm that throws premieres. At the very least, you will probably have to monitor your boss's guest list and make sure that everyone who is supposed to receive an invitation has. This is accomplished by thinking ahead and drafting an initial list several weeks before the invitations are mailed out. Then you can add names to the list as you think of them. If you wait until the last minute, you are guaranteed to forget some people. Then save the list for the next premiere, since your boss's A-list probably won't change that much over time.

* William Goldman, *Adventures in the Screen Trade* (New York. Warner Books, 1983) p. 206

Chapter 7
Travel

Murphy was the assistant to a top movie producer...

7.0 THE PHILOSOPHY OF TRAVEL FOR THE ENTERTAINMENT EXECUTIVE

Entertainment people are demanding travelers. They expect the best, so everything on a business trip or visit to a location has to be perfect. Your job is to assure total ease of travel and a minimum of anxiety and confusion. Your goal is to allow your boss to work as effectively while traveling as he would in the office.

Murphy's Law was probably coined to describe entertainment executive travel. Events conspire against even the most organized and dedicated assistants who plan trips for their bosses. You have to prepare for the worst whenever your boss travels, and be ready with contingency plans when the inevitable problems occur.

7.1 ARRANGING A TRIP FOR YOUR BOSS

There are two types of trips. One is a carefully planned business trip with meetings scheduled far in advance. For this type of trip you can easily develop a coordinated itinerary and make the most logical reservations. The other kind of trip is when your boss gets an urgent phone call from somewhere and says, "I have to be on a plane in an hour." The problem is that both types of trips have to be equally well-organized, even if there is no time to plan the second one.

For a routine trip, the first step is to determine the length of the trip and the destination(s). The appointment schedule will dictate necessary travel dates for the trip, if there are important meetings that cannot be changed. If the schedule is wide open, there are theoretically no limits on how long your boss can be out of town. However, you want to keep trips limited to a reasonable length, since time spent out of Los Angeles is usually less productive for your boss. He may sometimes tell you exactly when he wants to leave and return, but you may also have to make that decision.

Let's assume your boss wants to go to New York to meet with a screenwriter. You call the writer's agent and announce that you want to schedule such a meeting. They will get back to you with a series of possible dates, or perhaps they will even let you deal with the writer directly. Next you play a matching game between your boss's schedule, the ideal travel dates, and the writer's schedule. Bear in mind that you want to avoid scheduling your boss to fly in and out of New York at bad travel times like Thanksgiving, or bringing him back to L.A. on a late night flight the day before a major meeting.

Once you have set a tentative meeting with the writer, try to figure out if there is anyone else your boss would like to see while in New York. It turns out there are several agents and friends he would like to see on his trip. Find out if these people are available and set tentative meeting times. Keep a list that contains the names of certain people your boss wants to see whenever he goes to New York, London, or wherever. That way, when a trip is planned, you know right away whom your boss wants to see.

The schedule of the trip is beginning to take shape. If you are not familiar with the layout of New York City, then you have to find out if you are scheduling meetings in an order that makes sense. You don't want your boss to have to jump into taxis to go all over New York if you can avoid it. Always try to get the people to come to see your boss, not the other way around.

As soon as the general shape of the trip becomes evident, you can make reservations for the plane, limousine or rental car, and hotel. If your boss does not have a favorite travel agent, you can use one of the travel agencies in Los Angeles that specialize in entertainment clientele. (See Appendix G for a list.) You have to check and see if your company has a volume discount arrangement with any airlines or hotels. Your boss is the decision-maker, however. He selects the airline, hotel and amenities.

When you have established the criteria for travel, based either on your boss's preference or on company policy, order the tickets and make the hotel reservations. Some companies will mandate a certain type of travel, i.e., Business Class for all executives. One thing almost certain is that the reservations will change at least once before your boss takes the trip, so you cannot order non-refundable tickets. You have to be able to make changes, no matter how much more expensive the fare might be.

Next you map out the full itinerary of the trip on a blank piece of paper. The itinerary should avoid wasting your boss's time, and it should flow in a logical manner. Some meetings may be predicated on prior meetings having taken place. Mapping out the itinerary is also a check that the appointments do not overlap anywhere. With all the detail and changes, you might accidentally schedule two events at the same time.

Some assistants make the cardinal mistake of ignoring the needs and desires of the boss's spouse, or whatever partner with whom he travels. The boss's wife or husband is an important stakeholder in your travel arrangements, and may have strong views on the best times to travel or places to stay. To be safe, you have to double-check all travel plans with your boss and his traveling companion.

After showing the rough itinerary to your boss to verify its appropriateness, you write the fully detailed itinerary. A well-made itinerary should contain every piece of relevant information for every hour of the trip. At every step of the way, your boss should know what he is supposed to be doing, and whom to call if he has any problems or questions. Here is an example of an itinerary:

Monday, October 12th

7:00 AM — *XYZ Limousine will pick you up at your house.*
XYZ's Phone: 213-555-1111

7:45 AM — *Arrive LAX, TWA Terminal. Check in at Ambassador Class window for Flight #23 to New York.*
Booked through Apex Travel. 1-800-555-1000

8:30 AM — *TWA Flight #23 Departs for New York.*

4:00 PM — *TWA Flight #23 Arrives at Kennedy Airport in New York.*

4:15 PM — *You will be met by ZYX Limousines.*
ZYX's Phone: 212-555-0000

5:00 PM — *Arrive Plaza Hotel. Reservation Confirmation #234555.*
Plaza Hotel Phone: 212-555-9887

Tuesday, October 13th

8-10:00 AM — *Breakfast meeting with Chuck Bird, screenwriter*
Oak Room of the Plaza Hotel. Reservations for breakfast made in your name with Pierre, the Maitre D'. Oak Room
Phone # 212-555-3344

- *Chuck Bird's Home Phone: 212-555-3445*
- *Chuck Bird's Agent—Abe Troglodyte Creative Talent Agency, 310-555-1234*

And so on....Every inch of the way, your boss knows what he's supposed to do, and whom he can call if something does not go as planned.

The itinerary is part of the *Travel Folder* that you make for your boss. The travel folder contains every possible piece of information your boss might need while he's out of town. It should hold the current phone list, with all the outstanding phone calls he has to make. (See Chapter 3 for this.) It should also list the direct extensions and home phone numbers of anyone from your company he might need to talk to while he's out of town, including you. The travel agent's phone number should also be prominently displayed. Also include maps of the area and background information on the people he will be meeting. The actual airplane tickets should be placed in their own envelope along with a duplicate copy of the itinerary in case the travel folder gets lost.

An optional addition to the travel folder is a travel reading list. Many executives like to use their time on airplanes and in hotels for reading scripts. Often, they have more peaceful work time while traveling than at home. However, don't give your boss anything irreplaceable to take on a trip. Give him duplicate copies. Scripts are heavy, and quite likely to get lost after they have been read.

When your boss is traveling, he should know where you are at all times. You are the person he will call if there is a problem, so you can't drop out of sight while your boss is away. Since people can now make phone calls from airplanes, you are never safe. An assistant I know answered his phone at 7:30 on a Saturday morning to a tirade from his boss, who was in New York. Such happenings are commonplace. Your best preparation for such events is to keep a copy of the travel folder and phone lists with you when your boss is out of town.

If the trip is a long one, then you will probably need to send a pouch every day or so to your boss, wherever he is. A pouch is an express mail envelope or box containing any important documents or materials that your boss needs. To save money, just send one pouch at the end of each day. Solicit materials for the pouch from each person in the office, in case they need to send something to your boss. At the end of the day, seal the pouch and send it off. Sending one pouch avoids the expense of duplicate packages being sent by a variety of people in the office.

As you run the office in your boss's absence, you will log phone calls and inquiries for appointments. If you fax him the phone list, you can function more or less as if your boss were in the next room. He then calls you and tells you which calls he has returned or placed. If you cannot fax the phone list, or if your boss is too busy to absorb the entire list, then you have to prioritize the calls and only tell him about pressing calls. He may ask you to place a three-way call to connect him to the person to whom he wants to talk, just as if he were placing the call in the office. Conversely, you might want to connect an important call directly to your boss. You should know how to use this three-way feature of your office phone before your boss travels.

Planning a pleasure trip for your boss and his or her partner is a special challenge. Though the details and paperwork are less burdensome, the stakes are higher. Your boss wants to go away somewhere and rest. There cannot be *any* problems. Before your boss goes away, you have to establish who can know where he is, and what calls, if any, can go through to him while he is away. When your boss is on vacation, you have to monitor activity in the office carefully and use your judgment about contacting him. If a situation arises which is serious, you have to decide whether it warrants disturbing your boss.

As your boss jet-sets, he will accumulate healthy frequent flyer mileage bonuses. Your job is to keep all the statements, coupons and newsletters straight. A file folder will do nicely for maintaining all the information in one place, but you have to stay on top of the mileage account as well. Confusing as the systems are, you have to master them, and know which airline will offer upgrades and free tickets for a given amount of miles.

When your boss returns from a business trip, you are likely to be presented with a wad of receipts and restaurant checks. Depending on your company's accounting system, you will probably have to categorize these receipts into some sort of expense account. Be clear on what kinds of expenses are allowable for reimbursement. The company will probably not reimburse your boss for personal expenses. You will be expected to account for expenses according to specific projects. If your boss has breakfast with Chuck Bird to discuss *A Killer in the Snow*, then the lunch should get charged to *A Killer in the Snow*.

7.2   ARRANGING A VISIT BY AN OUT-OF-TOWN GUEST

On a production, or in a development deal where the writer lives in another city, you will have to arrange travel and accommodations for a visitor from out of town. In the case of a development deal, the network or studio pays for the writer to come in for a notes meeting. Or your company might foot the bill for a writer or director to come in to discuss a potential project. Let's assume that a writer is being flown in to attend a notes meeting at the network. Like a business trip for your boss, a visit from an out-of-town writer or director requires that you aspire to perfection in travel arrangements. The visit has to be completely effortless and problem-free for the writer.

The first challenge is to match the schedules of several people. In a simple scenario, where just your boss and the writer are having a meeting, it is easy to align the appointment dates. In the case of a large meeting between your boss, the network, and one or two outside elements, you are in for a scheduling nightmare. As the grand coordinator of all of this, you have to lay down the ground rules. A workable approach is to establish the rough availability of each party in advance, as a first step. Then, once you know that everyone can meet on a certain set of days, you pin down the busiest, or most important person involved, who is usually the network or studio executive. Everyone else then has to conform to that appointment, once it is set. This way, the discomfort of the network executive is minimized, since he will not have to change his calendar unless something drastic happens. For the other parties, there is a minimum of confusion about where they will have to be. If you do not take this approach, you will invariably reschedule the meeting at least a dozen times as everybody changes their plans.

Since a network is paying for the visit, they have a say in how much they are willing to spend. The Writer's Guild agreement dictates that a writer traveling on a project has to be flown first class. That is a given, and everyone abides by it. (For other Guilds, check before you book anyone's plane ticket.) Everything else is negotiable, with certain conventions in place. The discussion of the reimbursement terms for a visit might be handled completely by your company's Business Affairs Department, but it could also be up to you to secure the details. At issue is the number of days the visitor will stay in town, the amount of money the network or studio will pay for a hotel, and whether the visitor is entitled to a rental car and per diem for meals and expenses.

The networks have certain standard figures which they use as a baseline for reimbursing these trips. Let's assume that the Business Affairs person at your company calls the Business Affairs Department at the network and secures the following terms for the writer's visit: First class airfare, $125 per night for two nights in a hotel and $50 per diem, but no rental car. Business Affairs will keep the writer's agent informed of the terms of the visit, since agents take an active interest in such things.

After you receive this information, you can begin to budget the visit. Your travel agent will tell you the price of first-class tickets, and you can probably go ahead and order them, as long as they are changeable and refundable. That locks you into a price for the airfare, which might go up if you delay making the reservation. At this point you can create a *travel work-sheet* for the visit.

Visiting Guest Travel Worksheet					
Day 1	Day 2	Day 3	Day 4	Day 5	Day 6
11:00 Arrive TWA #20	9:00 meet at office / 12:00 meet at NBC	4:00 depart TWA #89			

		Unit Price	Number of Days	Total Cost
Arriving Flight	TWA #20	$ 500.	—	$ 500.
Departing Flight	TWA #89	$ 500.	—	500.
Airline Phone	1-800-221-2000			
Hotel	Beverly Hills Hotel	$ 125.	2	250
Hotel Phone				
Writer's Name	Fred Samson			
Writer's Phone Number	212-555-4000			
Writer's Agent	ICM			
Agent's Phone Number	310 555 4000			
Car		N/A		
Per Diem		$ 50.	3	150.
Extras				
	LIMO	$100.	—	100.
Total Cost				$1500.

Figure 7.1 Travel Work Sheet for an out-of-town guest

The travel work-sheet holds all the information about the visit at a glance. The top of the sheet is a rough schedule of the trip. The lower half of the form is a running total on the anticipated expense of the trip and a list of all relevant phone numbers. By filling in the form with a pencil and updating it each time it changes (and it will change many times), you can be on top of the details of the writer's visit at a moment's notice. The work-sheet contains at least fifty bits of information. It is easy for so much information to get mixed up, especially if you are planning two or three visits at the same time. The form helps you keep it all straight.

Ego is the complicating factor in booking an out-of-town guest. Obviously, for big-name talent, few expenses are spared. For other people, companies try to be more economical. If the visitor does not consider himself to be a small-timer, you can be put in a delicate situation. For example, the writer in this case might request to stay at a more expensive hotel, and insist on having a rental car. Your boss must decide if he wants to appease the ego of the writer, and have the company pay the extra costs and charge them to the budget of the picture. In the current cost-conscious environment, your boss might simply tell the writer that the network spending limits will have to do. The writer's agent often gets involved at this point, arguing that his client deserves the best, etc. You have to be able to present your boss with accurate cost information on a timely basis. He has to know how much the extras will cost, and you have to be right.

When the writer arrives in town, you are responsible for his comfort and safe conduct. Make sure he knows who you are and where he can find you in case there's a problem. If you cannot be located, the writer might call his agent to complain. The agent will call your boss, and you will then have a bigger problem on your hands.

If your guest is unfamiliar with Los Angeles, you might want to prepare an information packet that contains maps, guidebooks, and other materials that will help your guest get around town. Information packets are especially helpful if your guest will be spending a substantial amount of time in Los Angeles, or if you are expecting many guests. The Los Angeles Visitors and Convention Bureau (see Appendix G for their address and phone number) has maps and information for out-of-town guests.

Chapter 8
Information

8.0 "I DON'T KNOW" IS NEVER A GOOD ANSWER

The ability to find accurate information quickly is one of the key skills that differentiate a good assistant from an average one. It is also the skill you are least likely to have developed by the time you start working, since it's dependent on a knowledge of the industry and a network of contacts. Every day, entertainment executives ask their assistants to "find out who did this picture," "find out what the number three bestseller in April was," or "get me a copy of this script...I can't remember who wrote it." So, in the initial period of working on a job, when you have to prove your competence, your information-gathering skills will be one of the first things evaluated. You cannot afford to disappoint people. "I don't know" or "I couldn't find out" are never good answers to an information question.

You will also be judged on your speed in finding information. For example, while your boss is on the phone, she might tell you to find out the name of the writer on a certain film. She needs that information before she hangs up on her present phone call. If it takes you twenty-four hours to find out what she needs to know, you've failed.

This chapter gives you general guidelines and suggestions for finding information. Since they are subject to frequent change, the specific names, addresses and phone numbers of information sources are listed in Appendix G, which will be updated every time this book goes to press, so it will always be as accurate as possible.

8.1 THE GUILD INFORMATION LINES

The guilds maintain information on their members and readily make it available to people in the industry. They provide this service to facilitate employment for their members. The *Writers Guild of America (WGA), The Director's Guild of America (DGA)* and *The Screen Actors Guild (SAG)* each operate an *agency information line.* Anyone can call the agency line and find out which agency represents a guild member. When you call, you are connected to an operator who sits in front of a computer that lists all the guild members and their agents. The operator can tell you the agent for a member within seconds. You can even ask for agency information on more than one member, though each guild sets a limit on the number of inquiries they will field on a single call. (See Appendix G for phone numbers.)

8.2 AGENCIES

The agency lines will refer you to the agency that represents a guild member, but they seldom list the specific agent responsible for a client. So if you call the Directors Guild to find out about a certain director, they may tell you that he is represented by William Morris. That narrows the field to about a hundred agents. You have to connect your boss with the responsible agent for the artist you are seeking.

When you call William Morris, ask for client information. The client information person can tell you who the responsible agent is for the director you want. So, with two phone calls you have the information you need for your boss.

8.3 REFERENCE BOOKS

Reference books form the basis of your information resources. A number of books published each year list and index the vital information on titles, credits, and talent contacts. While you may not need all of these books on your office bookshelf, it's worth spending the money to have up-to-date versions of the ones you consult frequently.

In addition to the standard reference books listed in Appendix G, many states publish their own specialized production guide. These books provide complete information for producing a movie on location in the given state. They list hotels, restaurants, equipment rental services, support services, local technical people, soundstages, photocopying shops, and much more. There are also reference books available for foreign countries. For example, the book *Who's Who—Qui Est Qui* lists production people in

Canada. Depending on the production and development activities of your company, you may want to have a set of these books in your library. (See Appendix G for a thorough list of reference books and their publishers.)

8.4 INFORMATION SERVICES

Several commercial information services cater to the entertainment industry. These companies are in the business of selling information. Though they are often quite expensive, you will find that they are usually the only providers of instant, high-quality information. (See Appendix G for detailed listings of information services.)

These services are at the leading edge of what is sure to be a revolution in information services over the next few years. For example, the computer technology of Compact Disc Read-Only-Memory (CD-ROM) holds tremendous promise for the delivery of information to users in the entertainment industry. A CD-ROM is a compact disc that contains data instead of music. It is readable using a special CD player attached to a personal computer. A single CD can hold the equivalent of about six hundred floppy disks, or hundreds of thousands of pages of data and images!

8.5 LIBRARIES

The public and university libraries of Los Angeles are a terrific resource in your quest for information on the entertainment industry and other subjects. Familiarity with libraries will come in handy when your boss needs historical research or not-so-recent true story research done in a hurry. Appendix G contains a list of general and entertainment industry libraries.

8.6 BOOKSTORES, BOOKFINDERS, AND VIDEO STORES

East Coast snobs always complain that there are no bookstores in Los Angeles. Now, while LA isn't quite like New York or Cambridge, it has a lot to offer in terms of bookstores, if one knows where to look. Several stores offer a computerized Books-in-Print to search for titles. With a little work, you can assemble a network of bookstores that can find you any book you need with a minimum of delay.

If you cannot find the book you need through regular bookstores, you can hire a *bookfinder* to search for you. A bookfinder is a person whose job is to locate rare or out-of-print books. They use contacts and databases to track down everything, from priceless antique manuscripts to obscure works of fiction that time forgot. Though they are expensive, bookfinders usually deliver.

Video stores are another source of information for the assistant. You will often be asked to rent movies for your boss. Some of these films are hard to find, but there are dozens of good video stores in Los Angeles, probably minutes away from your office. You will want to become a member at several of these stores. Certain stores specialize in hard-to-find tapes. (See Appendix G for their particulars.)

8.7 STUDIOS AND NETWORKS

The studios and networks provide information about films that have been produced but not yet released. They can also provide obscure trivia about old films that is not in the reference books. However, studios and networks should be your information source of last resort. Since they are not in the business of giving out information, you will be asking someone to take time away from their job to help you.

The publicity department of the studio has the greatest capacity to answer your questions. They maintain a file of cast and crew lists that they can consult if you need credit information. And the publicity department is ostensibly set up to deal with reporters, so they are more predisposed to answer questions than other departments of the studio.

The network publicity department is similar to the one at the studio. They can answer questions about upcoming shows. However, because of the enormous volume of programming, the network publicity department is less likely to have information on old shows. If you strike out with publicity, you can try either the network library or their research department. The library is where the network keeps a tape of almost every show aired in recent years. The library might be able to verify or find some title and credit information for you, but it is difficult to borrow a tape without the permission of an executive.

The network research department keeps records of ratings. Research can find ratings for old or recent programs. It might take several days to get the information you need, however.

8.8 THE TRADE AND POPULAR PRESS

The trade and popular press publishes almost everything you would ever want to know about the entertainment industry. The two essential daily trade publications are *Variety* and *The Hollywood Reporter*. *Variety* also publishes a weekly edition. These two cover all important news regarding movies, television, cable, home video and music. *Billboard* is the music industry magazine. *Electronic Media* is a weekly magazine that covers broadcast and cable television. *Entertainment Law and Finance* is a monthly publication dealing with legal and financial issues in the business. Popular magazines such as *Entertainment Weekly, TV Guide, Premiere, US* and *People* can all contribute additional information about what is going on in Hollywood.

However, the entertainment press is poorly indexed. It is difficult to find information in a systematic way. How do you use the trades to find out what you need to know? A photographic memory helps, but if you are not so blessed, your best alternative is to create your own customized index of trade articles that are of interest to your boss.

One assistant created an index for feature film development deals. The assistant read through trade and popular magazines and marked down any mention of feature film development. This information is contained in announcements of development deals, studio development press releases (which catalogue numerous projects in development), as well as in interviews with stars and directors. All these articles are sources of information about development deals.

The assistant then entered the information into a database that was organized by project title. He tried to get the name of the writer, producer, stars attached, and director, as well as a plot summary. The assistant found that, over a period of weeks, more information on each project became available through different sources. His job was to update and enhance the database as he saw the same projects mentioned in different contexts. Then, by studying the weekly film production chart in the trades, he was able to determine which of his development deals were headed into production. He could deliver lists of development deals sorted by studio, producer or subject.

The work of reading the trades and cutting out articles on development and then entering them into the computer took the assistant about five hours a week. That's a huge chunk of time, which might not be justified if the information isn't going to be used effectively by the company. The key is selectivity. Indexing information is extraordinarily time-consuming, so it has to be limited to matters of real interest. Attempting to index all the information in just one trade paper would take all day every day.

8.9   NOT EVERYONE WANTS TO HELP YOU

The expression "knowledge is power" would be a cliché if only it weren't so vitally true in the entertainment industry today. In your search for information, you have to be careful about whom you ask for help. Not everyone wants to help you, and there can be serious repercussions to asking the wrong person for information.

One hapless and inexperienced assistant was asked to find out where a major star was shooting a film. The producer wanted to find out where the star was staying so he could sneak him a look at a script. The assistant called the actor's agent and asked the secretary if she knew where the star was shooting his movie. The secretary put the assistant on hold. The agent himself then picked up the phone and began a ten-minute tirade along the lines of, "Who the hell does he think he is, going behind my back like this..." The agent then called the producer directly and continued his tirade. Needless to say, the producer never got to send the script. Luckily, the assistant got to keep his job (and write a book about it).

This anecdote underscores the sensitive nature of information. The assistant should have known to read the Feature Film Production Chart in Tuesday's trades. The agent's office was probably the last place he should have called. At the very least the assistant should have been ready with some harmless reason for wanting to know the whereabouts of the star, if he had been asked. The physical production department of the studio could have told the assistant where the film was being shot, or at least given the name of the film's line producer. From this information, the assistant could have tracked down the star without consulting the agent, the one person who has a vested interest in keeping people out of direct contact with the star.

Much information in the entertainment field is confidential. Agencies never publish their client lists, for example. Most production companies keep their development activities secret until the projects are well on their way to being produced. You cannot always expect to get an enthusiastic and helpful answer to a question about development when you call a production company or studio. In fact, the quest for information about development is fraught with danger. Looking for development information usually involves calling either a competitor or a customer and prying into their important business. Even if you are very nice, you will probably be turned away.

8.10   CREATING YOUR OWN INFORMATION NETWORK

Most of the difficulties described above disappear if you know people who work inside these companies. You probably have the makings of an information network already, even if you didn't think you were that well connected. How many of your friends or college classmates work in the business? An information network is a collection of people who are at your level. They can all help you find information, and you can help them.

Information network etiquette requires that you return favors and never push a friend to do something he doesn't want to do. You have to respond to other people's information needs as long as they fall within your comfort zone. For example, an agent's assistant can help you by tapping into a wide range of expensive and hard-to-find information about the workings of the industry, but he can be fired for leaking copies of the client list. You don't want to press an agent's assistant for a client list. You won't get the list, and by pushing too hard you might damage the relationship.

If you don't know anyone who works at the company where you need to find information, you can try for a referral, provided your reputation is solid. Perhaps a friend can introduce you to someone who works at the company. If you don't know anyone, try calling up and turning on the charm. You'd be surprised what you can accomplish with pure pleasantness and respect. Before you know it, you've added another person to your information network.

Information networks between assistants and other workers form the basis for future relationships in the industry. A close look at certain relationships and partnerships between senior people in the industry reveals that many of the friendships began in something that resembled an information network.

8.11 TYPICAL INFORMATION GATHERING SITUATIONS

It would be impossible to list the hundreds of situations where you will have to find information while serving as an assistant. Instead, I have described several typical difficult information requests as examples.

Tracking down film rights to a book when you don't know the author or title:
1) Call a bookstore that has Books In Print on-line and describe whatever you know about the book. They might know the title.
2) *If that fails*, search for the book using an on-line library card catalogue.
3) *If the book is too recent for that*, call someone you know who is familiar with the publishing world and get their help. If you still cannot get the information you need, you may be out of luck for the time being.
4) Assuming you get the correct title and author, find out the name of the book's publisher.
5) Call the subsidiary rights department of the publisher. Ask who

represents the film rights. They usually refer you to the author's agent.

6) The author's agent can tell you the status of the film rights.

Tracking down an actor, writer or director who does not belong to guilds:

1) Get the person's latest film credits using an on-line information service or one of the reference books.
2) Identify the name of the producer of one of the films.
3) Locate the producer using the *Producers, Studios, Agents and Casting Directors Guide.* (See Appendix G.)
4) If the producer isn't listed, call the studio that released the film. They may have a contact number or address for the producer.
5) Call the producer's office and ask if they have a contact number or address for the person in question. Chances are, they do.

Finding a film which is not available on videotape:

Many films are not available on home video, and the studios will not lend tapes for fear of piracy. If your boss needs to see the film, you have two alternatives:

1) You can arrange for a screening of a print of the film at the studio, a service for which the studio charges.
2) Some films are available in the form of 16mm prints through a rental company if they are not available on tape.

Finding a tape of a film that was not released by a major studio:

1) Locate the film's producer and ask to borrow a copy of the film. If you cannot locate the producer,
2) Try a video store which specializes in foreign and classic films.

Getting episodes of a recent show:

1) The show's producer might be willing to lend your boss a copy of the tape. You will probably have to explain what your reasons are for wanting to see the tape. For example, your boss might want to see the work of a particular actor or director.
2) If the producer is unable or unwilling to lend you the tape, you can try the agency of the episode's director. They might lend you the tape.
3) The network will lend you tapes if you have clout.
4) If all else fails, Radio and Television Reports will sell you a copy of the show.
5) Whatever you do, remember to return the tape!

Chapter 9
Putting It All Together

9.0 ROUTINES AND GOALS

Now is the time to put all your skills and knowledge together and get down to the hard work of being an assistant. You are already an expert (or on your way to becoming one) at industry structure, office basics, script reading, story development, production, travel, and information gathering. The challenge now is to integrate all that skill and knowledge into an effective work routine.

Because no two bosses are alike, every assistant has his or her own special work routine. After putting a cup of coffee on her boss's desk, Karen Swallow, assistant to Largo's Michael Barnathan, checks the phone messages, opens the mail, and sorts out the faxes. Karen types a new phone list for the day, highlights any outstanding calls from the previous day, as well as important "want-to-calls," and places it on Michael's desk before he gets in. Karen also puts an up-to-date list of outstanding literary submissions next to the phone list. "I read the trades, and I highlight anything that's important for Michael."

For Karina Downs, assistant to a studio executive, a typical day begins with retrieving phone messages at nine in the morning. "I put them on his chair," she says. "His chair is the emergency in-box. The regular in-box is for things which can wait a week. Then we have what's called a tickler, which is a folder with tabs for the days of the month. Something might be tickled for December 1st. I go through that and pull the stuff I ticked for myself and for him."

Jennifer Mintz, assistant to agent David Kanter, spends from eight to nine-thirty every morning copying the phone sheet from the previous day and preparing a fresh, accurate phone sheet. David arrives at nine-thirty and gives her a few instructions, such as sending out a script to a particular studio. They then place calls together until lunch. While David drives to lunch, Jennifer connects calls to him in his car. On her lunch break, Jennifer catches up on typing dictated letters and orders copies of scripts from the agency library to be sent out to studios. Jennifer has to have all the outgoing material ready for the agency's six o'clock messenger run.

Whatever your routine, your goals in developing a working relationship with your boss are personal education and maximum effectiveness on the job. The two are linked, in the sense that you begin to learn only when you can cope with a chaotic office. Your tools for the job are the basic skills, the information management techniques, your growing industry knowledge, and your own imagination.

This chapter will review procedures and reports discussed earlier, and attempt to integrate them into a model work routine on which you can base your routine. These procedures have proven effective in the demanding work environment of Edgar J. Scherick Associates. However, it's up to you to refine and adapt these suggestions to perfect your working relationship with your boss.

9.1 DAILY/WEEKLY/MONTHLY/ANNUALLY

Most assistants have trouble defining an average day. Though there are some basic routines, the job is seldom the same on any two days because flexibility is the key to success. The workday at an entertainment company is a free-flowing and frenzied time of phone calls, conversation, letters, filing and odd jobs. The only mandate is to move every project forward a little bit every day. That can encompass hundreds of different activities.

Beyond the day-to-day improvisation of the office, you will find that a number of tasks need to be performed on a regular basis. These are the various status reports and information updates essential to the smooth running of an office. Depending on your boss's work cycle, you might want to take care of these tasks on a weekly, monthly, or quarterly basis. A few jobs need to be done only once a year.

Edgar J. Scherick Associates has developed the following basic work routine:

Daily

Phone Calls—Assistants place phone calls at any free moment.

Scheduling—Setting meetings, lunches and personal appointments.

Preparing Phone Sheet—A new phone list is prepared first thing in the morning to list phone calls which need to be returned. Assistants compile a second list at the end of the day for executives to take home in the evening.

Responding to Submissions—In addition to regular meetings to review submissions, assistants can discuss submissions at any time. Submissions are returned to agents throughout the week.

Writing Letters and Memos—Assistants prepare dictated letters for signature.

Opening and Sorting Mail and Faxes—Assistants open all mail unless it is marked "confidential" or "personal," and sort it in order of importance, placing opened mail visibly on the boss's desk.

Filing—Letters, contracts and project-related paperwork are filed whenever time permits. Assistants maintain the filing system perpetually.

Photocopying—Assistants copy any scripts, books, letters, etc.

Reading List—Lists scripts, books and video tapes that the boss has to review at home.

Schedule Card—A pocket-sized schedule of the following day that the boss takes home every night. The schedule card includes all names, addresses, phone numbers and projects of people who are scheduled for meetings.

Meeting Agenda—A pocket-sized card that encapsulates the boss's ideas for an upcoming meeting. For example, the meeting agenda might contain two or three projects that the boss wants to pitch, or a list of edits he wants to perform in a cutting session.

Maps—For any appointment to which the boss has to drive, the assistant prepares a map that traces the route.

Weekly

Submission Report—Lists literary submissions that need to be answered. Used daily as a reference for phone calls and letters.

Outgoing Report—Lists destinations of development projects that have been sent to other companies or talent. Used daily for follow-up and phone calls.

Development Status Report—Gives up-to-date status on all development projects. Highlights actions that need to be taken on each project.

Review of Mail—Mail piles up during the week, so it is often more easily handled at one focused sitting over the weekend or in the evening. A weekly mail review can clear the boss's desk, removing the daunting pileup.

Review of Schedule for Upcoming Week—Gives the boss a view of his schedule for the next week, allowing for changes to be made.

Monthly

Ratings/Boxoffice Report and Review Summary—Encapsulation of subject matter and performance of various films and industry activity compiled from the trades.

Expense Accounts—Normally a monthly activity. Boss's business-related expenses are tabulated and submitted for reimbursement. Keep all receipts!

Annual Reports

Annual Submission Report—A list of every literary submission received by the company during the year.

Annual Outgoing Report—A list of every piece of material that was sent out during the year.

Annual Project Summary—A complete list of all projects that were developed during the year.

Permanent Reference Reports, Updated Annually

Complete Outgoing—Lists every piece of material ever sent out by company. Useful for getting development histories of projects.

Complete Development and Research Report—Lists every project that has ever been developed or researched by the company.

Backlist Report—Lists projects that are no longer active, but can still be sold.

Rolodex Printout—Corrected paper version of the address database.

Writer/Director Directory Update—Corrected, augmented printout of the writer and director credits database.

Figure 9-1 charts a typical work week for an assistant. It is simplified but generally accurate. Note the long hours. The schedule illustrates how the key times of the day, when the boss is in the office and free to work, are quite limited. There are probably only about twenty hours per week when your boss is free to interact with you. If you subtract time that she is on the phone, you are left with about four or five hours a week.

	Mon	Tues	Wed	Thur	Fri	Sat	Sun
8AM 9	Prep for Story Mtg.	Write Cov.	Write Cov.	Write Cov.	Write Cov.	Script Reading/ Library Research/ Write Coverage or Presentation	Script Reading/ Library Research/ Write Coverage or Presentation
10 11 12	Story Mtg.	Phones/ letters/ meetings	Phones/ letters/ meetings	Phones/ letters/ meetings	Phones/ letters/ meetings		
1PM 2	Boss to Lunch	Boss to Lunch	Boss to Lunch	Boss to Lunch	Boss to Lunch		
3 4 5 6 7	Phones/ Letters	Phones/ Letters	Phones/ Letters	Devel- opment meeting	Prepare boss's for weekend/ Print weekly reports	Free Time	Free Time
8 9 10 11 12	Get Home Read Script(s)	Get Home Read Script(s)	Get Home Read Script(s)	Get Home Read Script(s)			

Figure 9.1   Typical work week for an assistant

Your goal during these crucial few hours is to get her to do as much important work as possible. You have to manage your boss's time minute by minute, always thinking ahead to the next task. When she is on a phone call, look to see whom she should call next. When she arrives in the morning, you should be ready with a work agenda that complements her scheduled meetings.

The challenge to you during the day is to maintain constant priorities among the tasks that you and your boss must perform. Only a few of the phone calls, letters and faxes that your boss receives will be urgent. You have to direct her to those priorities first, while keeping track of less pressing matters at the same time. After the urgent situations have been considered, then you can move on to the other work. The trick is to avoid ignoring the non-urgent tasks.

As new information comes in during the day, place it somewhere on the scale of priority. This is where flexibility and knowledge of the business are essential. You have to know if something is important. Then, if it's an important matter, you have to be able to switch everything over to handling it. For example, let's say that while you are typing some form rejection letters, your office receives a fax stating that the crew on location is about to go on strike. Since this is an emergency, it takes precedence over the form letters. In fact, until the potential strike has been averted, all secondary tasks have to be sidelined. It might be days before you can complete the letters, but that is of little consequence. Most issues are more subtle than this, but the task of triage remains the same.

9.2 CULMINATION—THE "TO DO" SHEET

The culmination of your work routine is a focused, concise *To Do Sheet*. At a certain point you will be familiar with the major spheres of your boss's job, and the status of the relevant projects going on. When you reach this stage you can skim the most important items off the top of each category and create this short list, which will focus your boss's attention on the most urgent matters he must see to on any given day.

The idea is to keep your boss fixed on important business. The first part of the To Do Sheet should be a section that reiterates pieces of information about which your boss wants to be reminded. This section is an "echo" of his voice, and it serves the valuable purpose of assuring him that his words of wisdom do not get lost in the chaos of the office. Whether he acts upon them is up to him. You have done your job by reminding him.

Next, you survey the key status reports to look for items that require action. Look over the development status report. Which projects require meetings, phone calls, or letters? Those should go on the To Do list. Look at the Incoming Submissions Report. Are there any submissions that require immediate answers? Scan the Outgoing Submissions Report from the previous week or two. Which outgoing pieces of material require follow-up phone calls? Those go on the list.

When you are done, you will have about ten or fifteen items requiring attention. You can break the list into sections for quick reference, or you can prioritize and mix the items. You can place maximum emphasis on the one or two most important things your boss has to do. If he only glances at the list for ten seconds, he will see the highest-priority tasks at the top. The decision on how to format the list will also depend on your boss's preference.

The key factor in making a good To Do list is having total familiarity with what is going on in the office. If you don't understand what your boss does, or what he's putting most of his time into, then you won't be able to make a useful list for him. You may want to wait a few weeks after starting a job to make a list. Making a To Do list during your first week might even

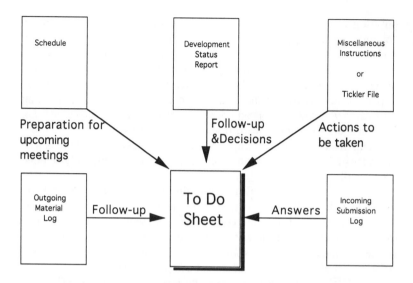

Figure 9.2 Selective flow of information from reports and notes onto the To Do sheet

seem presumptuous. As time goes on, though, the list will become evidence that you have a firm grasp on the business of the office and that you are ready to move up.

It helps to print the To Do Sheet on one eye-catching color of paper every time. Your boss will then know that the To Do Sheet is always the orange sheet, for example. He can ignore everything else except the orange sheet. And he can always find it on his messy desk.

9.3   DIAGNOSING AND SOLVING PROBLEMS WITH YOUR WORK ROUTINE

Have you become a firefighter? That is, do you spend all your time fixing problems that spring up from nowhere, leaving you no time to do anything constructive? Firefighting is a syndrome in which assistants become overwhelmed with problems that are too numerous to be solved all at once. The result is a cold panic that can doom assistants.

Firefighting can be the result of a disorganized work routine that allows you to be taken by surprise. Your system fails to catch important information before it becomes dangerously relevant. For example, if you only log in submissions once a week, you run the risk of missing an "overnight read" script until it becomes a crisis. If your system has several such holes in it, you will spend most of your time reacting to crisis situations.

If you feel that your firefighting is caused by an enormous volume of work, the problem probably stems from your inability to distinguish important matters from routine tasks. Did you spend an entire morning organizing your boss's frequent flyer bonus statements while an urgent fax from an agent went unattended? If you process work sequentially, in order of receipt instead of order of importance, you will always feel there is way too much to do. The reality is that some unimportant jobs can only be done occasionally, if at all.

A slow work pace also leads to firefighting. You might work too slowly to address all the relevant issues of the work day. If that is the case, you will have to improve your basic skills. Tasks with too many steps can slow you down. You may have to "carbon copy" ten people on every letter you send, for example. The wrong tools for the job can add time to routine tasks. An unreliable copier or computer can put you behind.

It takes diligence to overcome the firefighting trap. Your first step is to work longer hours and not leave until all the work has been done. You then have to take a firefighting situation, dissect it, and figure out where the problem originated. Where did the critical element come from? Are your problems caused by a blind system in the office, your own disorganization, a slow work pace, or a faulty piece of equipment? Can you fix the problem yourself, or does it concern someone else? You may be relieved to find out that you are, in fact, perfect, and some other person in the office is making your life hell. While that will do your ego some favors, it is much harder to solve someone else's problems.

Poor information sharing between employees creates firefighting conditions. Disaster will strike an office in which one assistant pays attention to details, and the other assistant has an easy-going, "ignorance is bliss" attitude. The easy-going assistant will sit on problems until they burst into flames, and the other assistant is forced to fight the fires. This situation is also known as "justifiable homicide."

Information might be flowing around you. If your boss makes appointments with people and then forgets to tell you, it's not your fault when you schedule a conflicting appointment at the same time. Your boss might hand someone a script at a lunch meeting and then not tell you about it. You have no record that he gave the script out, so you cannot arrange for any follow-up.

If you find yourself in this predicament, the solution is to canvas people in the office for relevant information once or twice a day. By asking everyone what is going on, you will be able to ferret out potential problems before they get too far along. You have to make it easy for people to share information with you. The alternative solution, exhorting people to change their ways, is usually less effective.

Bureaucracy is firefighting's evil twin. The symptoms of a too bureaucratic office include crises, excessive attention to paperwork, and an inflexible work routine. If you find yourself spending so much time on reports and files that you can't meet the moment-to-moment needs of your boss, you work in a bureaucratic environment.

A typical bureaucratic situation is where every literary submission is treated in exactly the same way, regardless of origin or purpose. Every script is sent out for reading and full-length coverage. Every script is discussed for a certain amount of time in a meeting and then returned with a customized letter that is filed in two places. Not only is this a waste of time and money, it's a terrible way to run a story department. Coping with a large volume of written material demands flexibility and resourcefulness. Some scripts require half a page of coverage or a thirty-second discussion. Rigidity forces the office to waste its energy following the "rules." In most entertainment offices, however, you have the power to change the rules.

The two problems of firefighting and bureaucracy can be related. They can both can be caused by inefficient and unnecessary tasks. The full work routine described in this chapter is based on an office with four assistants and three executives. It would be impossible for you alone to generate all these reports and written documents, and even if you could, it would be redundant. The information needs of an office with three executives are much greater than a those of a stand-alone office with one boss. If you find yourself firefighting or burdened with bureaucracy, the first step is to examine the number of tasks you routinely perform. Prune the unnecessary ones.

Keeping your boss's immediate needs in sight, take a hard look at exactly what information he requires to do his job, and jettison everything else. For example, generating a development status report every week might be overkill if your boss only looks at it once in a while. Try switching to a monthly report and see if any problems arise. You have to identify the core tasks that cannot be pruned and then concentrate on increasing your efficiency in those critical areas.

Efficiency is doing more work in less time. Time is your greatest constraint on the job. You will always have less time than you need to get your work done. To become more efficient, you have to become a master of scheduling and streamlining, the two tools that provide control over time constraints.

Scheduling in this case means managing your time during the day. Scheduling yourself for greater efficiency requires pushing non-critical jobs to the periphery, or even taking some work home with you. When you start work on a task, ask yourself if it's the most critical activity you could be performing at the time. Is anything more important? If so, why aren't you doing it? Can the task you are performing wait until later in the day, or tomorrow? Can you take it home with you? You will work longer hours if you follow this practice, but the time spent in contact with your boss will be more productive.

Streamlining means performing a task in fewer steps. This shortens the performance time. Fewer steps also mean less chance of making a mistake. As you perform routine tasks, count the steps and look at them objectively. Is anything being done repetitively? Can a simplification be made? Streamlining can also involve batching similar work together. For example, the process of writing a pass letter and mailing back a rejected script requires several steps. Each step involves a setup, such as turning on the word processor, and an action, such as typing a letter. It's more efficient to perform a series of like actions after you've done the initial setup than to repeat the setup and action numerous times. It takes less time to turn on the word processor once and type ten letters than it does to turn the word processor on and off ten separate times for ten separate letters.

As your work efficiency increases, you will have more time to devote to advanced assignments and to increasing your knowledge. You want your boss to feel that he can rely on you for challenging tasks. He will only trust you with an important assignment if he's completely confident that you can handle it. You can build that confidence by demonstrating that you can perform routine tasks with ease and efficiency. If you cannot handle the routine tasks, you will not get to do any advanced work.

The more efficiently you work, the more your boss gets done. The better he does, the better you do. The goal of the entry level, then, is to accelerate your boss's rate of work, as well as to improve its quality. This acceleration takes attention to detail, a constant focus on the most pressing task at hand, and a vigilant awareness of time.

9.4 OBSERVING MEETINGS AND LISTENING TO PHONE CALLS

Many assistants sit in on meetings to observe and learn. Some take notes for later use. The invitation to observe a meeting generally indicates that a level of trust has been reached between assistant and boss. If she thinks that you will embarrass her in a meeting, she will not ask you to observe. Meetings are an excellent opportunity to learn, and to become deeply involved in the business activities of your boss.

As an assistant in a meeting, your attitude has to be "don't speak unless spoken to." Observing a meeting is a privilege. In some cases you might be invited to participate, but in general your purpose is to absorb the happenings at the meeting and perform any subsequent tasks necessitated by it. Reasons for remaining silent include the chance that you will either say something damaging to the project, make a fool of yourself without doing any specific damage to the project, or appear to be usurping your boss's authority. An assistant once walked into a development notes meeting and began to give his thoughts on the script before anyone else could speak. That was a bad faux pas.

You should prepare for a meeting as if you were going to run it, even if you will not say a word while the meeting is in progress. If the meeting is about a script, then you will want to have read the latest draft beforehand. If the meeting is about casting, you will want to have thought about your own top choices for the part. Thinking through the demands of a meeting ahead of time will begin to give you a feel for doing a more advanced job. After the meeting, compare your expectations for the meeting with what actually transpired. Can the discrepancies tell you anything? This is how you learn.

Unless specifically asked not to, you should take notes on any meeting you attend. Your notes do not have to be a precise transcript, but they should record any relevant ideas or decisions. If you can take good notes, your boss will learn that he doesn't have to bother writing things down in a meeting. That freedom will allow him to concentrate more on thinking and deal-making. You may have to type a transcript of your notes after a meeting, but if that is not requested, you should just keep the meeting notes on file. Some assistants keep all meeting notes in a spiral notebook.

It is your job to make sure that ideas and tasks arising from meetings wind up on the To Do Sheet. In a creative bull session between a writer and a producer, for example, half a dozen ideas for movies might emerge during the meeting. These ideas will get lost unless you write them down and bring them back to your boss for action later.

In some offices, assistants have to listen in on their boss's phone conversations with an earpiece. This practice is more common at talent agencies than at other types of companies. The value to the boss is that any tasks for the assistant that get mentioned on the phone are automatically performed. The boss never has to think twice about reminding his assistant to do something. The assistant will already have heard about it. Listening to conversation also teaches the assistant the language of the industry and the nuances of deal-making and discussion.

Even if you don't listen to phone conversations with an earpiece, you should always cock an ear toward your boss's phone conversations. He may call for you during a phone conversation, or ask you to bring in some document or script. Know whom he is talking to and pay careful attention. Your boss's phone calls are not leisure time for you.

Some executives tape their phone calls and expect their assistants either to transcribe the conversations for the files, or to listen to the tapes for detailed instructions. One executive used to tape all his car phone calls for his assistant, so that when the assistant would hear him say, "I'll send you that script," it was as good as done.

9.5   LEARNING TO ANTICIPATE

Developing a strong instinct for anticipating your boss's needs will be your ultimate accomplishment as a top assistant. Anticipation requires a thorough understanding of the industry, of your company's current projects, of the procedures used in your office, and of your boss's idiosyncrasies. The anticipation phase is when you become truly valuable to your boss and your education on the job intensifies. When you can anticipate well, you have moved well beyond the basics.

Jennifer Mintz spends much of her day sitting in on phone calls with her boss, David Kanter. With a special headset, she can listen to the conversation without being heard. As she hears the conversation end, she has to know whom David will want to call next. She may even place the next call as the previous one finishes, so there will be no delay. To know whom her boss wants to call next, Jennifer must have a comprehensive understanding of current deals and client needs.

You begin to anticipate by keeping the time horizon of all your boss's projects in your head. When you know the project milestones, you can help your boss push projects along by suggesting meetings and phone calls. For example, if you know that a writer is due to turn in a draft of a script, you can ask your boss if he wants to call the writer to see how things are going. You have anticipated that he will need to call the writer. If you hadn't anticipated that phone call, your boss would have had to remember it himself.

If you anticipate properly, you will be able to provide instant gratification to your boss's every professional need. Your ability to anticipate will demonstrate to your boss that you know his business as well as he does. Your boss will trust you more, and look to you to find out what's pending. That trust will grow into a view that you are ready for more responsible work.

Chapter 10
Looking Ahead:
Issues and Perspectives

This concluding chapter is about surviving on the job and preparing to move up. It is intended to give you some perspective on the difficulties of your entry-level work experience by addressing several important, subjective issues that you will undoubtedly face.

10.1   GRACE PERIODS

How long do you have to prove yourself in a job? When will your boss expect you to be perfect? The grace period depends on your boss, but entertainment generally offers very little of the standard honeymoon that new employees enjoy in other industries.

Chip Diggins of Hollywood Pictures believes that it takes an innate sense of judgment to do the job correctly. Diggins defines judgment as an understanding of how to work with people and knowing what is important and what's not, regardless of specific industry knowledge. If you don't have good judgment, you wouldn't work out as his assistant. "There are two issues," says Diggins. "One is judgment and the other is mere competence — the ability to get things done." He gives his assistants about six weeks to gain enough knowledge to get things done. At the end of six weeks, according to Diggins, you ought to know the studio lot backwards and forwards.

"There's usually a two- to six-month adjustment period," says David Kanter. "We're both going through it together. It's a process of mutual accommodation. I'm nice at first, then I can get kind of harsh." Like any successful agent, Kanter is sufficiently busy that he needs an assistant who can learn quickly and get up to speed. "If it works out, then humanity breaks out again," says Kanter. "Otherwise, I've learned to pull the plug quickly."

Plan for a minimal grace period in your new job, and don't be afraid to ask how you are doing. You may be able to pick up on subtle hints that people are not happy with you (a friend once had an ashtray hurled at him), but in most cases your boss will be too busy to give you a review. If your boss gives you some constructive criticism, act on it. It may be your only chance to improve.

10.2 DEALING WITH EGOS

You hardly need to be an insider in the business to know that some entertainment people have outrageous egos. As an aspiring mogul, you probably have one yourself. One of the great challenges to you as an assistant, then, is to understand how to handle the range of megalomaniacs, paranoids, meddlers, passive-aggressives and crybabies who populate the industry.

Handling big egos and weird personalities with grace demonstrates that you are well-adjusted enough to become an executive in the business. The ego qualities of certain major actors and directors are legendary. Great films get made by managing these colossal egos and driving them to artistic achievement. You can't appear to be the type who loses his cool when dealing with such a personality.

Most assistants make an effort to be polite to senior people regardless of how unpleasant their behavior may be. "I try to bite my tongue," says Karina Downs. "My boss doesn't call an agent back, and the agent's pissed off. They're bothered that they can't get in touch with him. I spend half my time calming people down, or apologizing for other people's faux pas, trying to make a situation easier to deal with. Half the time I call myself a psychologist. It's a whole matter of diplomacy, because people's egos are so fragile."

"I just keep my mouth shut," is Karen Swallow's approach to handling egos. "It depends," she qualifies. "If someone is above me and I respect them, I just keep my mouth shut and say 'You know—that's life.' What can I do? If they're [someone at my level] talking down to me, I certainly wouldn't stand for that."

While you may not want to take any grief from other assistants, it is important to maintain cordial relations with other people on the office staff. Executives work together most of the time, and your job is to facilitate. If you conduct a feud with the assistant of someone who is important to your boss, that can cause problems for your boss. The assistant to the studio president may theoretically be at the same level as you, but you had better be sure that you are on his or her good side. You boss's career might depend on it.

What about your own ego? Your self-esteem may wilt during your tenure as an assistant. However, that you can survive at all proves you have a strong ego. Only a strong person can withstand constant abuse and not talk back. The good news is that most assistantships turn into higher-level jobs at some point, and you will no longer be at the bottom of the pecking order. Until then, you can only make an occasional stand.

Karen Swallow once had to contend with an important person in her organization who repeatedly called her "babe," which she considered patronizing and sexist. "He kept calling me 'babe,' and I told him, 'Please don't call me that anymore.' I said, 'I don't like being called babe or baby.' And finally Michael [her boss] got on the phone after that and said, 'I would appreciate it if you didn't call Karen that.'"

As Karen's story illustrates, you don't always have to suffer in silence. What's important to note, though, is that she did not lose her temper with this man. Rather, she asked him not to call her by a name she didn't like, and when he continued, she asked her boss to intercede. It was a reasonable request, and many bosses will back their assistants up in this type of situation.

One executive in the industry was known for treating her staff like dirt. She routinely yelled and screamed at all the people in the office. Yet if anyone outside the firm mistreated one of her people, she would react with extreme indignation. She would call the person up and say, "How dare you treat my people like that? You have no right."

In auto insurance, there is the concept of "No Fault," which places no blame for an accident on either party. In the entertainment industry we have the doctrine of "Your Fault." "Your Fault" means that anything that goes wrong in your jurisdiction is your responsibility. You can get blamed for everyone else's errors. It will be hard for you to adjust to the world of "Your Fault," because we live in a world where people are expected to take responsibility for their actions. Entertainment is not like the rest of the world. If your boss's housekeeper throws away a script, that is **your fault**!

There is no perfect solution to the problem of difficult personalities and egos. The optimum approach is to develop what I call the *Attitude-Free Lifestyle*. The attitude-free lifestyle is simply a process of not letting anything bother you. You become the Teflon assistant. Nothing sticks.

Nothing sinks in. Nothing hurts you. Whatever people do to you, it doesn't matter. You are not shaken. No matter how outrageously people treat you, you never display any attitude. This is not an easy thing to accomplish, but it can be done, even by people who habitually talk back. The trick is to convince yourself that a petty "tit for tat" attitude is far beneath you.

10.3 OFFICE POLITICS

Power struggles between executives are endemic to the industry. Rightly or wrongly, most executives perceive politics to be a zero-sum game. That is, one person's gain is automatically someone else's loss. Executives fight bitterly to acquire power, and defend it vigorously. While the zero-sum theory is deeply flawed, it is nonetheless prevalent in the minds of executives. It is a fact of life in most entertainment companies that executives will maintain, at best, a tense truce among themselves. At its worst, politics will involve outright plots to destroy rival executives.

Ugly politics will affect your working life. Let's say that you work for a production executive at a studio. While it is not explicitly stated, the executives compete to be assigned the best projects, and jockey for promotion to the next level. One day while your boss is out, an executive approaches you and asks if a certain agent has called your boss. Without thinking, you tell the executive that the agent has called, and you mention that the call concerned a specific script. The executive asks if your boss has returned the call, and you answer "no."

Did you do anything wrong? The answer is yes and no. Depending on your working relationship with your boss and the environment of the office, you might have either passed along useful information or set off a time bomb. In the best-case scenario, the other executive was just trying to clarify some detail of his work, and the inquiry meant nothing. However, if the other executive was plotting against your boss, he could call the agent in question and steal the script away from your boss.

"I expect everything that I say to my assistant to be held in confidence," says Diggins. "But, of course, I don't do certain things. I don't plot against other executives within my company, so I don't know how to deal with all that. But I do believe that my assistant will know everything about my life, both professional and personal, and I can't afford to have that trust betrayed."

Your primary loyalty is to your boss. Was telling the other executive about the phone call a simple slipup, just doing your job, or a calculated attempt on your part to sabotage your boss's career? If you are new, you can honestly claim that you didn't realize you weren't supposed to tell other executives detailed information about your boss's work. The unwritten rule is that the specifics of your boss's work are confidential. Obviously, if the head of production wants to know who called, you have to tell him. When other people want to know what's going on, play dumb. An experienced assistant would have confirmed that the agent had called, but he would not have given the reason for the call. If pressed, the assistant would have pretended not to know. The danger of appearing disloyal, or the fear of giving valuable information to a potential enemy, would keep a good assistant's mouth shut.

Assistants who work for more than one person often find that they have to make a concerted effort to share all information equally. This is the only way they know to be fair and avoid favoring one executive over another. The appearance of favoring one person can jeopardize working relationships and trust. Since it is difficult to predict who will be promoted, the smartest approach is to avoid alienating anyone.

People may ask you to take sides, but you should avoid doing so if you possibly can. For example, an executive says to you, "Your boss told me such and such. Don't you think he's wrong?" Though it may seem innocent, you are being asked to take a side. Since gossip and rumor can be destructive to your boss's reputation, you have to weigh your position carefully. Unless you are preparing to abandon your job, you are best served by an outward posture of fixed loyalty to your boss.

There is no ideal way to deal with politics, so most assistants try to be perceived as hard-working noncombatants who got caught in the middle of a bad situation, rather than as active participants. If you do participate in politics, you accept the rewards and punishments that come with it. Your boss may triumph, and rise through the ranks, taking you with him. Just as easily, your boss could self-destruct, and you will both be unemployed. Ideally, you will want to find an apolitical boss, if such people exist.

10.4 KNOWING WHEN TO MOVE UP

How do you know you're ready to advance in the business? Most people who have progressed from assistant positions to executive jobs describe a moment when they just knew they were ready. In some cases, it was an instance where they recognized they could do their boss's job, or the job of someone senior to them. The moment to move up is unpredictable. It can happen a few months after you start, or a few years. Everyone moves at their own pace. There is no standard gestation period.

Some opportunities for promotion appear prematurely. After Michael Barnathan had worked as an assistant to film producer Scott Rudin for a few months, he was offered the job of assistant to Gillian Armstrong, who was then directing MRS. SOFFEL for Rudin and Edgar Scherick. The job would have taken Barnathan closer to physical production, which was of great interest to him. He turned the job down, however, because Scherick told him he would be passing up a big opportunity. According to Barnathan, Scherick said to him, "If you go, you'll have a good time...but you won't be any closer to your goal of getting a strong foothold in the movie business."

If you are presented with an opportunity to take what looks like a better job after a short time as an assistant, you have to ask yourself if you have learned enough to make the new job a stepping stone to something even better. As Michael Barnathan was able to determine, the immediate step of working for Gillian Armstrong would have been a promotion, but it would have left him out of circulation when the film shoot was over.

Bill Todman takes the opposite view. He doesn't think you ever know the right time to move up. "Your hand is forced. I think either an opportunity presents itself, or you get fired, or your boss ends up moving on." Diggins also insists that you should be ready to move up on your first day as an assistant. "In my opinion you should be ready for that moment [to move up] right off the bat," says Diggins. "The reason you're an assistant, probably, is because that's the only job you can get. Once you get it, you should use it to learn everything you can. Read everything you can get your hands on. Read nights. Read weekends. If you want to be an executive, you've got to work like an executive." It is worth noting that Diggins is the rare executive who never had to work as an assistant. His first job in the industry was as a creative executive.

Diggins does not ask his assistants for a specific time commitment. "I say I'd like them to stay for a certain amount of time, but I always assume — and most bosses don't — that if on their second day they get offered a job as an executive, they'd be moronic not to take it." However, he qualifies that by saying, "What I ask them not to do, is go interview for those jobs. If they're asked to go interview that's fine. If they...actively research those jobs immediately, I find that some form of betrayal."

Seeking a new job right after starting an assistant's position does not sit well with most bosses, as Diggins' comment illustrates. If you leave a job too early, you risk alienating your boss. You may need that boss for a recommendation later on. Most bosses will help you find a better job if you serve them well for a respectable amount of time.

10.5   TROUBLESHOOTING IN AN ESTABLISHED OFFICE

Though this book outlines a complete and systematic way to run an entertainment office, most companies are not clean slates. You may be ready to install the operating procedures described in this book, but you will have to be patient. People have come before you, and their systems may still be in place when you begin working. In a large office, there will be other people who have worked there for a long time. They will have their own way of doing things. Just because you have read this book on how to run the office, doesn't mean they will automatically give you carte blanche to redesign their entire routine.

Dealing with entrenched people is one of the great challenges of entry-level work. The other people in the office will be your companions twelve hours a day, so it pays to achieve harmonious relations with them if you can. That means handling people with care, and respecting that they have been there longer than you. They might even be able to teach you a thing or two.

When you begin work, gauge the landscape. Who seems nice? Does anyone seem to be out to get you? You can assume that most people are neutral about you, but you never know. They might have recommended someone to do your job, but you got it instead of their friend. If anyone seems potentially troublesome, make an extra effort to be friendly to him or her.

The trick to fitting in at the office and effecting changes in systems, is to do nothing without gaining other people's acceptance first. Nothing goes over worse than a fait accompli. Think how you would feel if after a year on the job, some newcomer said to you "Guess what, I just trashed your filing system and installed a computerized one that you will absolutely love." You would probably kill that person.

As management journals recommend, you want to make changes in working systems based on a consensus. By allowing each person to offer his or her views on how a system should be run, you create "buy-in" for the changes you are proposing. If one person is particularly opposed to change, the consensus method is democratic. The lone opponent to your idea will have to make his case to the whole group, not just to you.

The way to achieve consensus is to show that your idea will save people time. You have to give people an incentive to approve your ideas. The computerized script log described in Chapter 4 of this book, for example, took several months to implement. The old script log was a notebook that was updated by a busy secretary. The log book was just one of her many tasks, and she did not like having to update it every week. I offered to take over the job of maintaining the script log because I was responsible for knowing the whereabouts of different scripts. Gradually, I changed the log to a computerized form. However, at each stage of the changeover, I made sure that the secretary was happy with the format. There were no surprises for her in the process of computerization. The net effect for her was that she had more time to devote to other important work.

10.6   DO YOU OWN YOUR OWN IDEAS?

The question of whether you, as an assistant, have any claim to your creative ideas, is one of the stickiest and most explosive issues you face. If you work for a producer or a production executive, part of your job is to think of ideas for movies. In this context, you do not own your ideas. Some companies even force employees to sign a contract dictating that your original ideas during your time of employment are the property of the firm. Even if there is no contract, it's an understood principle that your company takes credit for your ideas. If you think about it, that's the only way a production company can operate. To do otherwise would be to invite an intellectual property lawsuit by every former employee.

It is an unfortunate situation for many assistants. If you say to your boss, "Let's make a movie about an extraterrestrial who befriends a child," your boss is free to develop the idea as a company project, and he doesn't owe you a thing. If Steven Spielberg walks in the door and says, "Let's make a movie about an extraterrestrial who befriends a child," he has just sold your company E.T., and is entitled to millions of dollars.

Is there any reason for you to express creative ideas on the job? The answer is yes, because you will be rewarded for creativity. For example, if you show a creative streak, you might be promoted to a development position. You might get first crack at writing a treatment for one of your own ideas, which is a great experience to have if you are interested in becoming a writer or a producer. You probably won't get to put your name on it, but your boss will know who wrote it.

If you expect little, you will be okay. Since many film ideas are formed in collaboration, your boss will also play a role in shaping the concept. As a result, the idea will not be one hundred percent yours when it is finished. Outlandish expectations, such as wanting to write the screenplay for the idea, will only lead to disappointment.

If you want to create your own ideas for your personal career, then the best advice is to keep them entirely separate from your work. Don't even talk about these personal ideas in the office. One generally accepted principle is that if you write a full-length script or novel on your own time, it is yours. You would have to consult a lawyer to get a detailed interpretation of this, but most bosses will accept such a large piece of personal work as falling outside your role as an assistant.

10.7   GROOMING A SUCCESSOR

When you are finally ready to move, your boss might ask you to find a replacement for yourself. In some instances, finding a good replacement is a precondition to promotion. You want to find someone who will do the job as well as, or better than, you did. That means finding a person who is as perfect as you. Now, while that may be downright impossible, there are ways of attempting it.

During your tenure as an assistant, you will be contacted by people who are interested in working in the business. They are just like you a year ago. To them, you are an informational contact—a college alum or a friend of a friend. If you take the time to meet the more promising individuals, you will be able to keep a file of possible successors for you when it comes time to move up. If they get other jobs in the meantime, they will become part of your network in the business.

You can recruit a successor through an internship program at your company. Internships offer you the chance to evaluate a person over a long enough time to judge whether they could do your job. And, like the people who come to see you for information, the interns will go on to become part of your network later on.

You may be working with talented potential successors and not know it. Many people who work in non-assistant support functions at your company may want to move up to a job like yours. Many mailroom clerks, messengers and receptionists want to become assistants to executives. One way to gauge these people's interest is to ask them to read scripts for you. A highly motivated person will read for free, just for the experience of writing coverage. This will save everyone a lot of reading and coverage time. You can offer them critiques on their coverage, and help them put their resumé and coverage portfolio together. If they are really promising, they can be potential successors for your job when you move up.

10.8   GROW UP WITH YOUR FRIENDS

"Grow up with your friends in the industry" is one of the greatest pieces of advice that anyone ever gave to me. It is also one of the truest. The people whom you know now in the business will very likely be the power brokers of tomorrow. Since the business is so relationship-based, the people you know at the entry level will be your oldest and most trusted friends when you ascend to positions of power.

The strategic objective of the entry level is to build your network for use later in your career. People your own age will have similar experiences in the business at roughly the same time. You may be able to help someone one month, and next month they will be able to help you. Most executive positions are filled through a discreet, narrow search which people conduct through their own network. An agent, producer or executive calls someone looking to change jobs, and an interview is set. You want to be the person who receives that phone call.

Appendix A
Glossary of Entertainment Terms
for the Job-Hunter

A

A.K.A. List

Gives alternative titles to current film projects, which may change title from time to time.

Above-the-Line Costs

Costs of film production associated with the "talent" involved. Refers to star salaries, director fees, producer fees, and writer/rights payments.

Above the Title Billing

Positioning one's name in advance of the film's title in the credits sequence and above the title on posters and advertising. Reserved for major actors who have the power to negotiate it into their contract.

Academy of Motion Picture Arts and Sciences

Organization in Beverly Hills which sponsors the Academy Awards, screens movies and holds movie-related functions, debates current issues in the industry, and maintains a Motion Picture Library.

Academy of Television Arts and Sciences

Organization which runs the Emmy Awards, the Television Academy Hall of Fame, the College Awards, and the Academy Internship Program.

Acquisition

The process wherein a distributor buys the right to release a film which has been produced by another company. Studios frequently acquire foreign films for domestic release or remakes.

Acquisition Executive

A person at a studio who is responsible for overseeing the purchasing of films for distribution.

Affiliate Station

An independent television station which broadcasts network programming in exchange for a fee and slots where it can air its own local commercials.

Aftermarket

Venues for distribution of films after the primary market has been exhausted. e.g., home video, television syndication.

Agency Line

A phone line at each of the major guilds which gives callers agency information on its members.

Agent Track

Refers to entry-level employees at a talent agency who have expressed an interest in becoming agents, and are hired into a specific training program to learn how to become agents, beginning in the mailroom.

Agent Trainee

An entry-level employee at a talent agency who is selected to train for the role of agent.

Amtel

A machine which transmits written messages between two desks using keypads and display screens.

Analysis

See "Coverage"

Annotated Script

In the industry it refers to a screenplay of a true story which contains references to sources of each scene, whether they are from interviews, books, or newspapers. Used in assessing script for insurance purposes.

Aspect Ratio

The ratio of a movie frame's height to its width.

Assistant Directors Training Program

A program which trains young people to become second assistant directors. Sponsored by the Directors Guild of America and the Alliance of Motion Picture and Television Producers.

Availability

A writer, actor, or director's theoretical freedom to work on a project. If there is no other project scheduled, the talent is said to be available to do something else.

B

Back End

Profits participation paid when a movie is in distribution, in contrast to fees paid in advance—the "front" end of a deal.

Backdoor Pilot

See "Movie Pilot"

Backlist

A set of projects which are unproduced, but which can be brought back to life if so desired.

Barter Market

Syndication practice where a syndicator accepts commercial slots from independent stations instead of cash, in exchange for licensing rights to a syndicated show. The syndicator then sells the commercial slots to advertisers.

Basic Cable

A cable programming service or channel which is provided to a subscriber as part of the monthly cable subscription price. Examples include TNT, CNN, and Lifetime Television.

Below-the-Line Costs

The costs of physical production. The expenses of a film production excluding star salaries, director's salary, producer's fees, and writer/rights payments.

Billing

The position of a person's credit in a film.

Blind Commitment

A promise to give a talent an assignment at some later date, specific content unknown; e.g., if a series is canceled, the star may get a blind commitment from the network to star in a new series next season.

Book Agency

A specialized literary agency which represents authors to the publishing industry and the film industry.

Bookfinder

A person or company which specializes in finding rare or out-of-print books for a fee.

Books-in-Print

A publication which lists all books currently being sold by publishers in the United States. Available electronically. (Published by Cahners. Also available through CompuServe.)

Boutique Agency

A small agency with a selective clientele.

Breakdown
1) A list of characters in a movie.
2) A detailed but concise description of each scene in a movie.
3) A reader's report on a script. See "Coverage."

Breakdown Service
A company which breaks down scripts and distributes information to actor's agents about the parts being cast in a script.

Business Affairs
A legal department of a studio, network, agency, or production company which negotiates deals for all current projects.

Buyout
A deal in which a person sells in advance his opportunity to earn royalties, residuals, or profits off a movie in return for one lump sum of money.

Byte
Computer storage equivalent of one character or number. The basic unit of computer memory. A "Kilobyte" equals 1,024 bytes. A "Megabyte" equals roughly one million bytes.

C

Cable Feature
A feature-length movie made originally for cable television. For example, HBO Pictures' original movies.

Cable Operator
Company which manages a local cable television system after having acquired the rights to provide cable service to the community by negotiating with local government.

Cable Programming Service
A company which produces programming and distributes it via cable television. Can be either basic or pay.

Cast-Contingent Order
A production order subject to the casting of a certain star.

Casting Director
Person in charge of filling major and minor roles in a film and making the necessary deals.

Casting Lists
Lists of available actors to fill each major role in a film.

Chronological File
A file of outgoing letters arranged in chronological order, usually by the month. (Also known as the "chron.")

Cinematographer

The person responsible for lighting and photographing the movie.

Client Information

The person at a large talent agency who can give out information about the agency's clients.

Clipping File

A folder of newspaper and magazine articles clipped out for use in research or publicity.

Closed Deal

A deal which has been negotiated to everyone's satisfaction and is ready for signature.

Co-Production

A movie which is financed by more than one entity. Normally applies to a television program which is financed by American and European networks.

Comments Section

The end section of coverage, where the reader tells whether or not he thinks the script would make a good, commercial movie. Ends with a one word recommendation such as "PASS" or "CONSIDER."

Comp Ticket

A ticket to a play or performance provided for free (complimentary) by the play's producer to a person in the entertainment industry. Also known as a "comp" for short.

Completion Bond

A type of insurance policy which guarantees that the financing for finishing a film in production will be provided. Used on independent films. If the production runs out of money, the completion bond company then takes over control of the picture.

Completion Funds

Money spent to finish a film which has already begun production.

Conditional Offer

An offer made by a production company, network or studio which depends on some condition which has not yet been met; i.e., an offer to play a role conditional on network approval, or an offer to purchase a spec script conditional on a creative meeting between the writer and the director.

Consideration List

See "Submission Report"

Contact List

A list of phone numbers for every person (cast and crew) involved in a film production.

Continuity Person

    See "Script Supervisor."

Core Memory

    The computer's capacity to store programs and data within its own circuitry, as opposed to the memory capacity of floppy or hard disks. Also known as Random Access Memory (RAM). Measured in Kilobytes and Megabytes.

Corporate Sponsors

    Advertisers which fund production of television programming directly instead of just buying commercials. Examples include AT&T Presents and Hallmark Hall of Fame.

Counterprogramming

    The practice of broadcasting programming which is aimed at a different audience from that of what's being aired on competing stations. For example, while station A shows sports, station B counterprograms with reruns of *The Flying Nun*.

Cover Letter

    A letter or note which accompanies a submission.

Coverage

    A short synopsis of a piece of written material, including a one-sentence log line and a set of critical comments.

Creative Executive

    Lower-level studio executive who supervises script development under the authority of production executives.

Creative Meeting

    A meeting between a writer and any configuration of producers, executives, stars and directors to discuss the contents and possible rewrite of a script.

Creative Track

    See "Development Track."

D

Dailies

    Footage filmed the day before on the set, synchronized, and projected for the producers and production executives. (Also known as "Rushes.")

Daisy Wheel Printer

    A computer printer which creates an image on paper using a plastic ring embossed with the letters of the alphabet.

Database

A computerized set of information created with a database program. The database allows the user to sort, search, and index information in a wide array of categories based on need. A computerized Rolodex® is an example of a database.

Day out of Days

A chart which shows which days of a film shoot each actor has to work.

Deal Memo

A short, concise summary of a deal, usually considered binding until formal contracts are drawn. (Sometimes contracts are not finalized until after the film is already in production.)

Deficit

The difference between the network license fee and the actual cost of producing the program. The deficit, which is usually about 15 percent of the production budget, is normally paid by the distributor.

Deficiting

The practice in television of paying more money for a writer or option (or some other element) than the network will reimburse, and adding it to the program's deficit.

DeForest Report

See "Research Report"

Delivery Log

A form of outgoing material log which tracks the dates on which official drafts of screenplays in development are delivered to the networks and studios. Used in tracking writer payments.

Department Heads

The key members of the production unit — the costume designer, the makeup and hair people, the cinematographer, the production designer.

Desktop Computer

A personal computer which is not portable. It sits atop a desk.

Detailing

A thorough hand-cleaning and waxing of a car. Can cost upwards of $100.

Development

The process of creating screenplays from books, plays, original ideas, true stories, and other screenplays.

Development Hell

A term used to describe the occasionally lengthy and tortuous process of developing screenplays.

Development Status Report

A weekly or monthly report which tracks the progress of each of a company's script development projects.

Development Track

Series of jobs which take one toward becoming a producer, production executive or agent. For example, script reader or assistant to producer. (Also known as the "Creative Track.")

DGA

Directors Guild of America. See Appendix H for address and phone number.

Direct Satellite Broadcasting

See "Satellite Broadcasting"

Director List

A list of directors who are available to fill a directing assignment. Includes credits and agent information.

Director of Development

1) Lower-level studio executive who coordinates development projects
2) Network executive who works under a vice president in a given department.

Director of Photography (DP)

See "Cinematographer"

Director's Cut

The version of a film edited to the director's liking. May not be the version of the film actually released.

Director's Reel

A sample of work by a director, contained on a reel of film or, more frequently today, a videocassette.

Directors Guild of America (DGA)

The Director's Union. See Appendix H for address and phone number.

Dispatch

The task of delivering packages to clients from an agency mailroom, usually in one's own personal car.

Distributor

A company which sells or licenses entertainment product to exhibitors or broadcasters.

Domestic Box Office

The total amount of money spent on movie tickets for a film in its theatrical run in the United States.

Dot Matrix Printer

A computer printer which creates an image on paper using metal pins and a ribbon. Considered slow, but good for multiple-part form printouts.

DP

Director of Photography. See "Cinematographer."

DSB

Direct Satellite Broadcasting. See "Satellite Broadcasting."

E

Episodic Television

Refers to television series produced in episodes, as opposed to movies or specials.

Errors and Omissions Insurance (E&O)

Insurance policy which protects a film producer from liability in the event of libel, copyright infringement, or misrepresentation.

Executive/Senior Vice Presidents of Programming

Senior network executives who work with the head of programming in determining the content and schedule of the primetime lineup.

Exhibitors

1) Movie theaters

2) Movie theater owners

F

Favored Nations

A deal point which is negotiated to be on the same terms as the deal for another person on the show. Example: The Star negotiates profit participation on Favored Nations with the producer. He receives the same profit participation as the producer.

Fax Modem

An electronic device which allows a computer to send and receive facsimiles.

Film to Tape Transfer

The process of reproducing on videotape footage which was shot on film.

Final Cut

1) The final edited version of a film, which is locked for release.

2) The contractual issue of whether a director has the right to insist on releasing the film in the version he or she dictates.

Financial Interest and Syndication Rule

Federal law which restricts television network activities in production and syndication of the programming which they broadcast.

FinSyn

> Shorthand for "Financial Interest and Syndication Rule."

First Look Deal

> A deal in which a producer is obligated to show any new projects or ideas to a specific studio before he takes them elsewhere.

First Revision

> The rewriting of a script after the first draft has been completed and discussed.

First-Run Syndication

> A method of programming where a company signs up a large number of independent stations to broadcast a show—a sort of ad hoc network. Examples include *The Arsenio Hall Show* and *Star Trek: The Next Generation.*

Floppy Disk

> A magnetic storage device for a computer. Made of material similar to that of a cassette tape, a floppy disk can store up to 1.4 million characters of information.

Foley

> The process of rerecording sound effects such as footsteps or face slaps, created by a "Foley Artist" on a "Foley Stage," to be added to the final soundtrack of the film during the sound mix.

Foreign Box Office

> Gross revenues from ticket sales of a movie in foreign countries.

Free Option

> An option deal in which the initial period costs the producer or studio no money.

Freelance Reader

> A script reader who works independently, reading material and writing coverage for different clients on a fee-for-service basis.

G

Getting on a Desk

> Refers to promotion to assisting an agent, producer, or executive after a stint with the mailroom or reading staff.

Greenlight

> The go-ahead to make a movie. The studio "greenlights" a film when it decides to spend money on its production.

Gross

> The total amount of money generated by a film at the box office during its theatrical run. Also known as Gross Revenues, or Box Office Gross.

Gross Points

> A deal in which a person (usually a star) receives a percentage (points) of a film's gross revenues.

H

Handshake Deal

> Any deal where two parties agree to work together without a formal contract, trusting each other to act in good faith in the event of a development deal or film production.

Hard Disk

> A high-capacity disk used for storing large amounts of data. Can be installed internally in the computer or purchased separately as a peripheral device. Range from 20 to 1,000 Megabytes — a Gigabyte.

Head of Affiliate Relations

> Executive at the network who is responsible for maintaining relations with affiliate stations.

Head of Production

> Top executive at a movie studio, who has the power to put a movie into production. (May be called "President of Production," "Chairman of Film Group," or "Studio Chairman," among other titles.)

Head of Programming

> Network executive ultimately responsible for the content and scheduling of the primetime lineup. (Also known as "President of Programming," or "President of the Entertainment Division.")

Home Reading List

> An ongoing list of written material that an executive has to read. The executive may have to take this material home. See "Weekend Reading List."

Hot Read

> Any piece of material which a lot of companies are interested in buying. A piece of material which must be read quickly.

Hot Script

> A screenplay, usually written by a popular or talented writer, which has the prospect of becoming a major film—often at great expense to the acquirer. A hot script must be read quickly.

Housekeeping Deal

Deal between a studio and producer, or between a large production company and a small one, where the producer gets an office and secretary in exchange for promising the parent company first look at any projects he creates.

I

IBM Clone

See "IBM Compatible Computer"

IBM Compatible Computer

A personal computer which has a microprocessor (Intel 286, 386 or 486) identical to that of an IBM PC, so it can run the same software as an IBM. The output of an IBM Compatible computer can be shared with an IBM PC or another brand of compatible.

Independent

1) A company which finances production of films without studio backing.

2) A producer who works without studio support.

3) A producer who does not have a deal with a studio.

Informational Interview

A meeting between an aspiring assistant and an established person for the purpose of learning about how to get a job in the industry.

Institutional Market

The market for films in schools, airlines, prisons, the military, etc.

Internship

A type of short-term, unpaid employment which offers one the chance to work inside a movie company and gain experience and contacts.

L

LAN

Local Area Network. A computer network which spans a small area such as a building or office. See "Network (Computer)."

Laser Printer

A computer printer which creates images using a laser beam and a charged metal drum similar to that in a photocopier.

Legal Files

Folders containing executed versions of all legal agreements on current projects.

Letter of Intent

General term to describe a letter from one party to another which expresses the desire to make a business deal of some kind. A non-binding prelude to a formal agreement.

Letter of Transmittal

A letter which accompanies a piece of written material. Also known as a "cover letter" or "covering note." See "Cover Letter."

License Fee

Money spent by the network on programming, which guarantees the network a fixed number of exclusive broadcasts (usually two) over a given period of time (usually four years).

Licensing

1) A deal in which one entity pays for right to use a copyrighted piece of material such as a computer program, book, television program, or film, under a contract which specifies limitations and payments for use.

2) The sale of merchandising rights to third parties. For example, an American studio might enter into a licensing agreement with a video game company to market a video game based on a movie. The studio would receive royalties on the sale of the video game as part of the licensing agreement.

Line Producer

A production person hired to supervise the physical logistics of actual film production.

Literary Agent

An agent who represents writers and authors.

Location Scouting

The process of finding locations which would be suitable to make a movie. Performed by a location scout.

Log Line

A one-sentence description of a piece of written material.

Long Form Agreement

A full-length contract, completely written out with all subclauses included. The official contract between two parties. See "Deal Memo."

Long Form Television

Term referring to television movies and miniseries.

Looping

The rerecording of actors' dialogue using a special recording studio/film projection system. Used when the original recording is not usable due to poor conditions (noise, airplanes overhead, etc.) Also used to record "TV version" dialogue.

M

Made-for-Video

A feature-length film produced for the home-video market only. Often low-budget action or exploitation films. (Also known as "Direct-to-video" production.)

Mailroom

The department of the agency or studio which is responsible for mail, photocopying, receipt and delivery of packages, and general servitude.

Majors

The major films studios: Warner Bros., Disney, Columbia Pictures and TriStar (known collectively as Sony Pictures Entertainment), Twentieth Century Fox, MGM, Universal, and Paramount.

Master Script file

A set of folders containing the master copies of screenplays currently in development, for ease of photocopying and safe storage.

Merchandising

The creation and sale of toys, clothing, and gadgets based on concepts from a film.

Miniseries

A television movie with a length of four hours or greater.

Modem

An electronic device which allows a computer to transmit or receive data over phone lines to another computer or a fax machine. (Stands for "Modulator-Demodulator.")

Montage

1) A fancy word for editing.

2) A sequence of several brief scenes in quick succession, which creates a time-lapse effect.

3) A video editing system utilizing a set of video decks and a computerized controller that allows the editor to insert shots and recut scenes within a sequence of shots, which was previously impossible using traditional tape-to-tape video editing.

Movie Pilot

A two-hour television movie which is not developed as a pilot but which is considered to have potential as an eventual series. Also known as a "Backdoor Pilot."

MSO

See "Multiple System Operator."

Multiple System Operator (MSO)

A cable operating company which runs more than one cable system. Some MSOs provide cable to millions of subscribers.

N

Negative

1) The film stock which runs through the movie camera. Similar to photographic negative film used in popular photography. Can be 16, 35, or 65 millimeters in width.

2) The master copy of a film, used to make prints of a film for release.

Negative Insurance

Insurance policy which covers any damage to the film negative.

Negative Pickup

A deal wherein a major studio guarantees that it will pay to release a movie produced by an independent, based on the cost of completing the finished film and producing a "negative." The independent uses the studio distribution guarantee to borrow production funds from a bank.

Net Profits

The profit of a film after all expenses have been deducted. Broadly, that means boxoffice gross minus exhibitor share, house costs, prints and advertising, distribution costs, negative cost, interest, etc.

Network

A broadcasting company which produces and licenses programming which it airs nationwide over a system of stations. The network owns several stations in major cities, but broadcasts nationally through 200+ affiliate stations in other cities.

Network (Computer)

A system of software and wires or telephone lines that allows many computer users to share files, send messages, or utilize central pieces of equipment such as laser printers or mainframe computers.

Network Acceptable

See "Network Approved"

Network Approved

A writer, actor, or director whom the networks are willing to employ.

Network Entertainment Division

Department of the network responsible for the creation of primetime programming. (As distinct from News, Sports, Radio Stations, and other corporate units of the network.)

Network Share

The percentage of the television audience on any given night which is watching ABC, CBS, NBC, and Fox. (Since the advent of cable, this share has gone down.)

Newton

A hand-held personal address and note system made by Apple Computer. It has a no keyboard, but recognizes handwriting. Can communicate with desktop computers by infrared (similar to a TV remote control).

Notebook Computer

A lightweight battery-powered personal computer which is roughly the size of a notebook.

Notes

A meeting, report or memo that identifies a script's problems and makes suggestions for changes.

Notes Meeting

Meeting between a network or studio executive and the writer and producer of a movie to critique the latest draft of a script and determine future changes to be made.

Novelization

A novel written based on a screenplay.

O

O&O

Abbreviation for a television station which is "Owned and Operated" by one of the four networks.

Off-Line Edit

Video editing which takes place in a relatively low-tech edit suite. Used for rough-cutting video tape.

Off-Network

Refers to a series or TV movie which has completed its network run and can be syndicated.

Offer

A formal proposal by a production company, network, or studio to engage the services of a creative talent (actor, writer, director) for a specific sum of money, i.e., an "offer" of a job.

On Hold

A submission which has been evaluated, but for which the accept/reject decision is delayed for any reason.

On-Line

Term referring to a computer service or function which allows you to access information from a remote location over your personal computer. Example: Baseline is an On-Line information service.

On-Line Edit

Final videotape edit using broadcast quality 1" video tape equipment. Used to make the network's broadcast version of a program.

One-Camera Comedy

>   A half-hour comedy program filmed without a live audience in sets and on locations, i.e., *The Wonder Years* or *Doogie Howser, M.D.*

One-Sheet

>   1) A one-page advertisement for a movie.
>
>   2) A poster for a movie.
>
>   3) A one-page description of an entire movie concept used in internal selling of ideas within a company.

Open Assignment

>   A job as writer or director, currently unfilled.

Open Point

>   A piece of a contractual negotiation which has not been settled to everyone's satisfaction, and is still open to discussion.

Operating System

>   A computer program which tells the computer how to run itself. All other software works off the operating system software.

Option

>   A deal in which a small amount of money is paid by a producer or studio to a rights holder in exchange for a limited period of exclusivity in which a script may be developed. The option can be exercised by paying the rights purchase price. For example, a book may be optioned for one year for $5,000 against a purchase price of $75,000.

Option Renewal

>   Payment of a second option for another limited period of exclusivity.

Option Rewrite Deal

>   A deal in which a producer or studio options a script under the condition that it be rewritten. The option fee includes the rewrite fee, and the option period may commence with the delivery of the rewrite.

Outgoing Material Log

>   A book or computer database which tracks the date and destination of written material sent out by an entertainment office.

Overall Deal

>   A producing deal that encompasses both film and television.

P

P&A

>   Prints and Advertising. Refers to money spent by the studio on copies of a film (prints) for theaters, and advertising in the release of a feature film.

PA

See "Production Assistant"

Package

A deal in which the major elements of a film, usually star, director and writer, are supplied by one talent agency. The agency collects a packaging fee, often a fixed percentage of the film's budget, for delivering the elements.

Packaging Agent

An agent who specializes in putting together package deals.

Pages Per Day

The rate at which a film is produced, as measured by the number of script pages shot in a day. Ranges from 1 or 2 for a feature film to 8 for an hour-long television episode.

Pass Letter

Letter accompanying a piece of material which has been rejected and is being returned to the author or agent.

Pay Cable

Cable channel for which the subscriber has to pay extra to receive. For example, HBO.

Pay or Play

A deal in which a studio or network guarantees paying a person's salary regardless of whether the movie is produced or not.

Pay Per View

A form of broadcasting where individuals pay to receive a specific program in their homes.

Personal Management Firm

Company which manages talent for a commission. Personal managers work in conjunction with agencies and law firms to find the best work for their clients.

Petty Cash

Cash on hand to pay for small daily expenses such as lunch or books. Records of petty cash transactions are logged on a "petty cash voucher" or "petty cash envelope."

Phone Log

The notebook which records all incoming and outgoing phone calls.

Phone Sheet

The list of people who have called, and to whom calls are to be placed.

Physical Production Department

Staff of a studio or independent which is responsible for the actual logistics of producing films in the field.

Pilot

Prototype episode of a television series, produced to determine the audience appeal of the series concept.

Piracy

The illegal duplication and sale of copywritten material (e.g. films, tapes, record albums) by unlicensed companies.

Pitch

1) The presentation, usually verbal, of a film idea to a producer or studio to make them want to buy the idea. The film's sales pitch.

2) The act of presenting a film idea. As in, "I pitched them an idea."

POC

See "Production Office Coordinator"

Polish

A minor rewrite which addresses superficial problems with the script, perhaps making some jokes funnier or adding detail to certain scenes.

Post-Production

The phase of production following principal photography, which includes editing, sound recording and mixing, and rough cuts.

Practical Location

A real place, such as a house or school, used to film a movie.

Preemption

Refers to situation where a network affiliate broadcasts programming other than the network's primetime lineup. The affiliate preempts the network broadcast.

Premium Channel

See "Pay Cable"

Press Kit

A folder containing information about a movie for use by a critic or reporter. Might include photographs from the production, a synopsis of the movie's plot, and biographies of the film's cast and crew.

Principal Photography

The physical production of a film, when the major scenes are photographed. The "Production" period of a film, preceded by development and casting, and followed by "Post-production".

Print

A copy of a movie, printed from the film's negative. Also known as a "Release Print."

Prints and Advertising

See "P&A"

Producer

The person who initiates, facilitates, and usually oversees the making of a movie.

Product

General term for any film or television program: the film is the end "product" of the production process.

Production Assistant

An assistant who works on a film set, helping the producer, the director, the star, or whoever needs help. (Also known as a "PA.")

Production Board

A schedule for a film shoot where each scene is described on a detachable strip of cardboard for flexibility in production planning.

Production Bonus

A contractually-guaranteed payment made to a writer or some other person involved with a film, upon commencement of principal photography.

Production Office Coordinator (POC)

Person who oversees the day-to-day workings of a film set at the administrative level. Involved in shipping, equipment rentals, transportation, and numerous other production logistics. Works with the Unit Production Manager (UPM)

Production Designer

The person who is ultimately responsible for the look of the film. He or she designs the sets, oversees the set decor, and helps choose locations.

Production Executive

An executive at a movie studio who oversees the development and production of feature films. Production executives run the gamut from highly placed Executive Vice Presidents to ordinary Vice Presidents.

Production Folder

A file folder containing contact lists, budgets, schedule, shooting script, and day out of days on a production.

Production Manager (UPM)

Person responsible for coordinating and supervising all administrative, financial and technical details of the production, and overseeing the activities of the entire unit.

Production Office

A temporary office set up to administer a film production, often on location.

Production Order

The network or studio commissioning production of a movie or program.

Production Rewrite

A rewrite of a script done at the time of production to adapt the script to changes in location or actors, or to other last-minute issues.

Production Track

The set of jobs which will take one on a career path towards becoming a line producer or craft specialist. For example, production assistant, assistant cameraman, assistant editor, etc.

Production values

Loosely—the end effect of the amount of money spent per minute of finished film. The overall visual and performance quality of a film. (Not necessarily a function of money, but it often is.)

Profit Participation

A deal in which a person receives a share of a film's profits (subject to some definition of net or gross profits).

Project Files

File folders for development projects, containing all relevant materials, letters, and contracts.

Purchase Price

See "Rights Purchase Price"

Q

Quote

The salary which a piece of talent was paid on his last project. Can be verified by calling the producer of that project.

R

RAM

See "Core Memory"

Reader's Report

See "Coverage"

Reading Offer

An offer to an actor made before the actor has read the script.

Release Form

1) A contract which permits the producer to portray a real person in a film.
2) A contract wherein an unrepresented writer allows his script to be read by a producer, generally by signing away his right to claim that the idea contained in the script is similar to a script currently in development.

Rent-a-studio

Distribution practice whereby a substantial independent funds production of a feature film and then arranges for distribution through a major studio.

Research Report

A report prepared by a research firm to guarantee that the details of a script are authentic and that an Errors and Omissions insurance policy can be written.

Residuals

Payments made to certain talent upon rebroadcast or re-release of a film.

Rights Holder

The person who owns the rights to a book, script, or true story.

Rights Hustler

A person who acquires rights to a true story and resells them to a legitimate producer.

Rights Purchase Price

The amount of money paid to the rights holder in exchange for control of the rights. Usually paid upon commencement of production, though in some cases prior to that.

Rolodex®

A specialized card filing system for addresses and phone numbers. Also known as an address card file.

Rough Cut

The editor's first viewable version of the complete film.

Rushes

See "Dailies"

S

SAG

See "Screen Actors Guild"

Satellite Broadcasting

System in which a company broadcasts programming via satellite to those subscribers who own a satellite receiving dish and a decoder. (Also known as "Direct Satellite Broadcasting", or "DSB.")

Screen Actors Guild (SAG)

The actor's union, which sets the basic contract for actors, and handles health and other benefits.

Screenplay

A work written in a standardized format which contains the story, scenic descriptions, characters, and dialogue of a film.

Script

See Screenplay

Script Notes

See "Notes"

Script Supervisor

The person responsible for assuring that the film matches the script in terms of detail and continuity, and that everyone in the production unit has the same revision of the script. (Also known as the "Continuity Person.")

Sell-Through

Refers to home video tapes which are bought, not rented, by retail customers. They "sell through" the store to the final customer.

Selling Coverage

Coverage written to show a piece of material in the best possible light to sell it to someone.

Shopping (an Idea) Around

The practice of selling a piece of material not owned. A producer might take a book for which he does not control the rights and submit it to studios, thus "shopping" it to them.

Showrunner

A writer-producer who is capable of producing a television series.

Sides

Pages of a script given to actors to read during the audition process.

Sneak Preview

See "Test Screening"

Software

Computer programs which allow the user to perform functions such as word-processing, calculation, or database management.

Sound Mix

The process of creating the final soundtrack for the film from multiple inputs such as music, sound effects, and rerecorded dialogue in a sophisticated electronic studio.

Spec Script

An original script written by a writer on his own time. Sold to the highest bidder.

Spreadsheet

A computer program which allows the user to arrange numbers on a large grid for any number of calculations. Applications include budgeting, expenses, or financial projections.

Staff Reader

A script reader who works full time for a studio or production company.

Star Insurance

Insurance policy which covers sickness, injury, or death of the star of a film. Also known as "Cast Insurance."

Station Group

A collection of independent television stations owned by the same parent company, such as Westinghouse's Group W stations. If large enough, a station group can buy programming at a discount, or even produce its own shows.

Step Outline

1) An outline of the plot of a book, with a short paragraph describing each chapter.
2) An outline of a movie script, with one sentence describing each scene.

Stepup

A clause in an entertainment contract which calls for an increased payment in the event of certain circumstances; e.g., if a script is produced as a feature instead of a TV movie, the writer is entitled to extra money as a stepup.

Story Editor

1) A junior executive at a studio or production company who coordinates story development and reading.
2) A person on the staff of a television series who is responsible for overseeing the continuity of stories through a season of episodes.

Story Meeting

1) A meeting of executives to decide which submissions to acquire and which to reject.
2) A meeting between writer and executive(s) to discuss the story of a script under development and any possible changes.

Story Report

See "Coverage"

Strip

A television show, usually in syndication, which runs five weekdays in a row. A show in this category is said to be "stripped."

Studio System

Pre-1948 structure of Hollywood, in which the major studios owned their own movie theaters, and held virtually all talent under exclusive contract. A 1948 antitrust suit broke up the studio system.

Submission

A piece of written material sent in to an entertainment office by an agent, executive or writer. Can also apply to other types of material, such as newspaper articles or videotapes.

Submission Log Card

An index card used to track incoming submissions. It contains the title, author, agent information, date of receipt, log line, and decision which was taken on the material.

Submission Report

A list of submissions which have been read and are ready for evaluation and discussion.

Submission Log

> A notebook or computer database which chronicles the material submitted to an entertainment office. The log contains the title, author, agent, and log line of the material.

Syndication

> Can refer to first run syndication, or the licensing of old television programs which have completed their network run. A series which has been broadcast on the network to the end of its licensing agreement and is being aired on independent stations, is said to be "in syndication."

Syndication mark

> The number of episodes of a series required to make syndication feasible. Roughly 100 episodes, or five seasons.

Syndicator

> A company which arranges for programs to be broadcast through first-run syndication.

Synopsis

> A concise, non-editorial description of the plot and characters of a movie.

T

Talent Agent

> An agent who represents actors and directors.

Technical Advisor

> An expert in some field who advises the filmmakers on how to make the film as realistic as possible in his field of expertise, e.g., a police officer who instructs the actors in how to speak like police officers.

Telefilm

> A movie made for television.

Telephone Pass

> Situation where an executive or producer rejects a piece of written material in a phone conversation with the agent or writer.

Telepicture

> A movie made for television. (Also known as a "Telepic", "Movie of the Week" or "M.O.W.")

Teleplay

> A screenplay written for a television program.

Test Option Deal

> A deal made between an actor and a production company prior to an audition at the network. If the network approves the actor, his deal is already in place.

Test Screenings
>   Screening of a film arranged by the studio's marketing department at a regular movie theater for the purpose of evaluating audience reactions.

Theatrical Agency
>   An agency which specializes in representing actors.

Thomas Guide
>   A highly detailed book of street maps of Los Angeles and vicinity, with a grid and index which enable the user to pinpoint virtually any street in the city.

Three-Act Structure
>   The dramatic structure of most films. The first act, which sets the stage and identifies the characters, ends with a decisive event which propels the characters into action. The second act has the characters doing whatever it is they do—solving the mystery, etc. Act three is the resolution.

Three-Camera Comedy
>   A situation comedy performed in front of a live audience on a sound stage with three (or four) camera filming simultaneously.

Tickler File
>   A file folder specially designed to hold information until a later date, when it reappears to "tickle" or remind an assistant to do something.

To Do Sheet
>   A list of things an executive or producer has to do. Separate from the phone sheet, which is exclusively for phone calls.

Top Billing
>   Positioning one's title first in the credits, after the film's title.

Trade Press
>   Newspapers and magazines devoted to the entertainment industry, including Daily and Weekly Variety, The Hollywood Reporter, and Billboard. Known as "Trades" for short.

Travel Work Sheet
>   A form designed to ease the planning of a visit by an out of town guest. Contains flight, hotel, car, budget, and scheduling information.

Treatment
>   A short, prose description of a movie story that includes setting, characters and story structure. Usually around 5 to 10 pages in length.

U

Underlying Rights
>   The rights to the material which are the basis for the screenplay. For example, the person depicted in a true story controls the underlying rights to his story.

Unit Production Manager (UPM)
>
> See "Production Manager."

Unsolicited Submission
>
> A script or other submission which arrives from an unknown, unrepresented writer without invitation.

UPM
>
> Unit Production Manager. See "Production Manager."

V

Vice President of Creative Affairs
>
> An executive at a studio or production company who has responsibility for story selection and project development.

Vice President of Comedy Development
>
> Network executive responsible for the development of comedy pilots.

Vice President of Current Programming
>
> Network executive responsible for the content and quality of the current primetime programs.

Vice President of Drama Development
>
> Network executive responsible for creation of dramatic series pilots.

Vice President of Motion Pictures for Television
>
> Network executive responsible for the creation of movies of the week and miniseries.

Vice President of Physical Production
>
> Studio or production company executive in charge of supervising the actual production of films.

Vice President of Production
>
> A studio executive who has responsibility for choosing projects, developing scripts, and overseeing the production of feature films.

W

Want-to-Calls
>
> Subsection of the phone sheet containing names and numbers of people an executive wants to call.

Weekend Reading List
>
> A list of material that an executive or producer has to read over the weekend. Should be listed in order of priority and contain agent information for each piece of material.

Word Processing Program

A computer program which allows the user to type text into the computer and edit it on screen before printing it out.

Worldwide Gross

Total theatrical gross revenue of a film from every country in the world, including the United States.

Writer List

A list of writers who are available for an assignment, and their credits and agent information.

Writers Guild of America (WGA)

The writer's union, which dictates standard contractual terms in the hiring of writers and arbitrates credits issues. Also handles residuals owed to member writers.

Writing Sample

A screenplay, either produced or unproduced, used by a writer to show off his talent.

Appendix B
Sample Coverages

Screenplay
Coverage Report

Title: The Storm	**Submitted by:** Nan Blitman—WMA
Author: Larry Brothers	**Submitted to:** Story Department
Material/Pp: Screenplay - 104pp	**Circa**: Present
Analyst: HBT **Date**: 9/5/92	**Location**: Western USA **Genre**: Psychological thriller

---

LOGLINE: A serial killer attempts to define his terrifying world to his prisoner, a psychiatrist who is an expert on his condition.

SUMMARY

SYNOPSIS: CARROLL closes a sale on a home. He's a successful real estate broker. After the office Christmas party he spends an erotic evening with his girlfriend, who is a police officer.

Alone again later, we see a change come over Carroll. He talks to himself, using the name "Billy," and he eats ravenously while listening to loud rock music.

Carroll picks up a drunk couple in a bar and takes them to his barn where he murders them gruesomely after torturing and raping them for hours. Though he has never met the couple before, he repeatedly tells them, "This is what you two deserve."

Cut to a tabloid-TV, "Morton Downey"-type show. The host presents the subject of serial killers and introduces MARTIN, a psychiatrist who is a leading expert on the subject. Martin tells the audience that the serial killer has a specific kind of mental illness, often brought about by incest or other traumas in childhood. The rabble-rousing host of the show makes short work of such sissy liberal sentiments.

The next day Martin is consoled by his brother, who invites him over for dinner so his wife can introduce Martin to "someone new" since his divorce. Martin never makes it to dinner. He is kidnapped by Carroll.

In his barn, Carroll tells Martin that he wants a biographer, since he is the greatest serial killer of all time. Carroll says he has killed seventy-six couples. He beats and terrorizes Martin, toying with him until Martin finally stands his ground. The two begin to talk.

Carroll tells his story. His mother was an alcoholic who molested him and made him wear dresses. His stepfather beat him and raped him while his stepbrothers watched. At a certain point in his teens, Carroll meets Billy, his aggressive alter ego, and the killing begins. Now he just kills couples who remind him of his mother and stepfather.

Martin tries to run away but Carroll catches him and punishes him by locking him in a small room. Carroll has researched Martin and knows a lot about him, including the fact that he is claustrophobic.

Carroll abducts another couple and brings them

into the barn. Martin has been left alone untied all the time Carroll was out. Why didn't he leave when he could? (He's too afraid/fascinated to move.) Carroll orders Martin to help him handcuff the couple and Martin complies.

Carroll murders the couple while Martin hides in the corner. He then helps Carroll bury the bodies in what is obviously a mass grave. He flees, and Carroll catches up with him. They struggle, but Martin succeeds in killing Carroll. He does it to save his own life, but also out of revulsion at what he has been forced to witness.

COMMENTS: Larry Brothers's talent is in detail, timing and dialogue. He is masterful at terrorizing his reader, and this script has plenty of raw energy. This is a disturbing yet compelling portrait of madness. Though intensely violent, this could make a powerful film.

CONSIDER

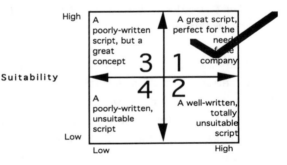

Novel
Coverage Report

Title: City of the Dead

Author: Herbert Lieberman

Material/Pp: Book

Analyst: HBT

Date: 9/5/92

Submitted by:

Submitted to:
Story Department

Circa: 1970s

Location: New York

Genre: Medical Mystery

LOGLINE: Dr. Paul Konig, the Chief Medical Examiner of New York for forty years, solves a grisly double murder while anguishing over his kidnapped daughter.

SUMMARY

SYNOPSIS: DR. PAUL KONIG, 64, is the preeminent forensic pathologist in the world. He is the Chief Medical Examiner for New York City, a job he has held through six mayoral administrations. He is a fixture at the criminal courts and Gracie Mansion. Doctors and police departments from all over the world seek his expertise in forensic matters.

Police Sergeant EDWARD FLYNN sends a car around to pick up Konig on Monday morning for a tour of weekend murders in Harlem. Konig is taken to see the untouched bodies of a junkie who lies stabbed in a bathtub and a prostitute garroted in a hallway. Only after Konig has noted the scene of the crime and the exact condition of the bodies does he give the command to wrap them up and take them downtown to the morgue.

Back at his office, Konig is greeted by an anxious call from his friend, Deputy Mayor MAURY BENJAMIN. The District Attorney's office is pressuring the Mayor to re-examine a suicide at the Tombs prison in the Bronx. There is new evidence to suggest that Robinson, the young man in question, was beaten to death by prison guards, who strung him up to make it look as if he had hung himself. The DA's office wants to exhume the body to look for signs of fatal skull fractures inflicted prior to death—a detail which Konig's department had missed. Benjamin pressures Konig to reveal the name of the Deputy Examiner who performed the autopsy, but as a matter of policy Paul will not identify which of his staff made the mistake.

The phone rings in Konig's office and he picks it up. There is no sound at the other end, but he knows it is his daughter LOLLY, who vanished five months before. After a few seconds, Konig starts to talk to Lolly, though she doesn't answer him. He pleads with her to come home. Then the phone goes dead.

FRANCIS HAGGARD is the detective working on locating Konig's daughter. Though Lolly is 22, too old to be a missing child officially, her case is being treated as one because of Konig's clout on the police force. Haggard assures Konig that every man in blue is looking for her, since they are pretty sure she is in Manhattan. A bugging device on Konig's phone has traced her calls locally. Though they don't have much to go on, Haggard feels he may have a good new lead. He will call Konig later.

Nervous from Lolly's call, Konig heads out to dinner at his favorite Italian restaurant. A young girl sits down at his table and propositions him. She seems desperate, so Konig buys her dinner and sneaks a peak at her pocketbook to get her real name. He goes back to her apartment house to find out where she lives. He tells her to get off dope. Later he calls her family in Kansas to tell them that he has seen their daughter. They tell him they have no interest in hearing from her. He is shocked.

Konig agonizes over the fate of his daughter. He sees her as a fawn among leopards. She disappeared after Konig's wife Ida died of cancer. She blamed her father for letting her mother die. Ida had not wanted the painful treatments and amputations, and Konig had supported his wife in that decision.

Haggard goes to a loft in Soho where neighbors had complained about a violent struggle in a nearby apartment. The area matches the traced phone calls to Konig. Haggard is astounded at the level of destruction visited upon the loft. There are shredded remains of paintings covering the place. The neighbors recognize the photograph of Konig's daughter Lolly, though she had gone by a different name. She was an artist, according to the neighbors, who had been having some luck selling her paintings. The man in her life, say the neighbors, was a revolutionist, or so he claimed. The neighbors are sure that the guy, whose name they don't know, was just a con man who suckered vulnerable young women out of their money. To Haggard, though, the apartment looks like the aftermath of a violent abduction.

Konig is called to a crime scene on the banks of the East River. Chunks of dismembered bodies are washing up on the beach. They have been mutilated beyond recognition and there are no heads. At first glance it is impossible to tell how many separate victims they represent. A nearby shack with blood on the floor is the presumed murder site. Several members of Konig's staff are now assigned exclusively to putting together this grisly jigsaw puzzle of over forty chunks of flesh.

Using a piece of one of the paintings found in the loft in Soho, Haggard tracks down the gallery which sold Lolly Konig's paintings. The owner of the gallery identifies Lolly from her photograph. He has not seen her lately.

Konig gets a phone call at home. A voice tells him they have Lolly. A girl screams in the background. The phone goes dead. Konig is in a frenzy. His worst fear has been confirmed. While he had thought she was just off on her own in the city, he now knows she is in the hands of kidnappers.

The body of the Robinson boy is exhumed, and another pathologist finds the telltale evidence of skull fractures, which prove that Robinson was beaten to death before he was hanged in his cell. This has all the makings of a big scandal, and Konig knows he is in trouble.

To make matters worse, a second scandal is brewing at the Medical Examiner's office. Someone has been assigning John Doe bodies for unmarked burial by local morticians, which costs the city $500. Someone in Konig's department is sending unclaimed bodies out for burial and receiving a kickback from the morticians. Konig has known about this for some time, but he has not done anything about it. Konig suspects that his ambitious heir apparent, DR. CARL STRANG, is behind the sudden wave of scandals. Konig is certain Strang wants him out so bad that he has been running to the newspapers and the DA's office and leaking damaging information.

Haggard goes to an abandoned apartment in the South Bronx which has been destroyed like the loft in Soho. There is evidence of explosives everywhere, and the same slogans spraypainted on the walls which were seen in Lolly's wrecked loft. Haggard now believes that Lolly is in the hands of violent radicals who will use her to get a huge ransom out of Konig.

After hours of work, Konig's staff has come to the tentative hypothesis that the dismembered parts found on the riverbank represent two people, one male, the other female. Working alone, Konig goes over the evidence, especially a lone hand with nail polish, and concludes that both bodies were men.

Konig finds the man who has been taking kickbacks for the John Doe bodies. He tells the man, a middle-aged Italian immigrant security guard, to resign before he gets in real trouble. No one need know the truth.

Konig gets another terrifying call at work. Lolly can be heard screaming in the background.

Haggard tells Konig about the gallery where Lolly's paintings have been sold. Konig sees the canvases and recognizes views of his summer house that Lolly must have painted from memory. He becomes agitated and buys up all of her paintings at full price, dropping $5,000 in two minutes. The gallery owner is baffled at first, but finally realizes that Konig must be the father of the artist.

Witnesses near the river say they saw a man wearing a Salvation Army uniform going in and out of the shack several times. Flynn goes to the abandoned Salvation army station near where the bodies were found and finds evidence that someone has been living there.

At Konig's urging, Flynn's men rip open the floor of the shack on the river and find an old suitcase with the two heads belonging to the bodies. They are wrapped in newspapers and badly mutilated. Almost all the flesh has been stripped away and many of the teeth have been extracted.

Konig gets a ransom note demanding $300,000 cash in a suitcase inside a Grand Central Station luggage locker for Lolly's safe return. Haggard's men botch the following of the man who picks up the money from the locker.

There is a hearing about the flubbed autopsy of the Robinson boy. An ambitious young DA tries to make a fool out of Konig, but Konig is able to thwart a major scandal while conceding that errors were made by his staff.

The newspapers are still full of screaming front page headlines about "Scandals in the ME's Office!" and "Million-Dollar Body Snatching Ring!" Konig gets confirmation that it was Carl Strang, his presumed successor, who had been leaking the information to the DA in the hopes of getting Konig fired.

Konig pulls Carl Strang into his office and tells him right out that he will never be Chief Medical Examiner. Strang walks out in a huff.

Based on Konig's idea, Detective Flynn tries to track down the distributor of the newspaper in which the severed heads of the bodies were wrapped. It was a local paper, The Clintonian, with a circulation of a few thousand residents of Clinton, a neighborhood on the West Side. After exhausting work, Flynn tracks down a candy store owner who swears that a man in a Salvation Army uniform comes in and buys a paper every day.

Through partial finger prints and dental records, Konig homes in on the identities of the dismembered bodies. It is likely that they belong to two missing soldiers who went AWOL from Fort Bragg after their homosexual relationship was discovered. Konig calls up the ranking doctor on the base, and the identities are confirmed.

Konig gets a threatening call from the kidnappers. He just has to follow a white car from the Brooklyn Bridge at 3:00 A.M. the following Sunday and drop off the money where they tell him. The caller tells Konig to look out his window. At that exact moment, a car pulls up and Lolly is shown to be alive. The car then speeds off.

Konig is summoned to Gracie Mansion, where the mayor advises him to take early retirement. Konig expected as much in the wake of the scandals.

Flynn closes in on the man suspected of the riverside killings.

At 3:00 Sunday morning Konig does as he was instructed and drops off the ransom money.

Haggard gets a tip from the superintendent of the building in the South Bronx that the freaks who were in the wrecked apartment are back. Haggard goes out and arrests the men, who are the suspects in Lolly's kidnapping.

Konig sits alone in his office at 5:00 on Sunday morning. Haggard calls to tell him that they have found Lolly, and that she is dead. They never intended to give her back alive. Haggard brings the body down to the morgue and Konig examines his dead daughter's body on one of his own autopsy tables.

Flynn calls and tells Konig that he has found the riverside killer. It was an old guy, he says, who had been in the Salvation Army. The old guy has confessed to the killings. Flynn tells Konig there are some new murders he wants Konig to come out and look at. Flynn has no idea that Lolly is dead. Konig tries to bow out of doing anything, but Flynn talks him into coming out to the crime scenes.

COMMENT: This is good material for a four hour miniseries with a major male star. The ending is a bit of a downer, but that could be fixed.

CONSIDER

Short Form
"Pass Script"
Coverage Report

Title: Memoirs of Henry VIII	**Submitted by**: Abe Troglodyte, CTA
Author: Peter MacMillan	**Submitted to**: Stan Blockbuster
Material/Pp: Screenplay—142pp	**Circa**: 1500s
Analyst: Joe Wannabee	**Location**: England
Date: 9/5/92	**Genre**: Historical

LOGLINE: Henry VIII reflects on his life and his six wives.

SUMMARY

SYNOPSIS: As King Henry VIII of England lies on his deathbed, he is visited by the ghosts of the people he has killed or ruined. All the ghosts lament their fates to Henry, who argues that, as King, he had no choice but to do what he did to them. Thomas More then leads Henry through a nightmarish tour of the England he has created.

COMMENT: Too obscure and artsy to be a viable movie, especially given the period costs.

PASS

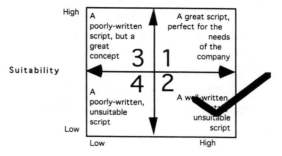

High

A poorly-written script, but a great concept **3**

A great script, perfect for the needs of the company **1**

Suitability

4 **2**

A poorly-written, unsuitable script

A well-written + unsuitable script

Low

Low

High

Quality

Research Assignment

The Army-McCarthy Hearings

IN BRIEF: The seminal event of the cold war - Senator Joe McCarthy's epoch-making encounter with the US Army and the battle with the greatly respected lawyer Joseph Welch, which lead to McCarthy's demise.

Claiming to be the sole crusader against an "immense" Communist conspiracy in the government, Wisconsin Senator Joseph McCarthy built a whirlwind political career and a huge popular following from uncovering alleged Communists in positions of power. In the aftermath of the loss of China to the Communists in 1949 and the leaking of atomic bomb secrets to the Soviets, McCarthy found that he had hit upon the ultimate formula for power and press recognition. The time was ripe for a Red scapegoat.

With the help of boy genius lawyer Roy Cohn as special counsel to his Senate Investigative Committee, McCarthy enjoyed a white hot spotlight as he pointed his finger at important government figures. The careers of brilliant and established men and women were ruined by McCarthy's spectacular charges and relentless attacks. His power went unchecked until he made the mistake of taking on the US Army, announcing that it was riddled with Communists who were destroying the security of the nation. The Army chose to do battle with McCarthy, a unique experience for the Senator, and the Senator lost.

It all began when G. David Shine, a young

Harvard graduate and close friend of Cohn's, was appointed as a special unpaid counsel to McCarthy's committee. The two went on a "fact-finding" tour of American installations in Europe, searching Army bases and embassy libraries for communist literature. The press labeled them "junketeering gumshoes." The following year Shine was drafted, and Cohn, from his position of power on the Committee, immediately started badgering the Army at the highest levels to get special privileges for the young private.

After many unsuccessful attempts to get an officer's commission for Shine, or at least a pass for every weekend so he could work with the committee, Cohn threatened to "wreck the Army" with the power of the committee. McCarthy and Cohn began to focus their attention on Communist infiltration of the Armed Forces, especially at the secret laboratories of Fort Monmouth, New Jersey. The conflict escalated until a special Senate subcommittee was formed to look into the allegations made by both the Army and McCarthy.

Joseph Welch, an old-fashioned Boston lawyer, was named special counsel to the Army. Welch was the antithesis of Cohn and McCarthy. At sixty-three, he was the epitome of integrity and class, while Cohn, his prime adversary, was the ultimate symbol of crass lust for power and disregard for propriety.

With battle lines drawn, the army filed charges against Cohn and McCarthy of severe interference by their committee into Army affairs and even personal abuse of ranking officers. In return, McCarthy railed against an immense Communist conspiracy and cover-up at Fort Monmouth. The Army accused McCarthy and Cohn of exerting extraordinary pressure to get special privileges for G. David Shine. The Army contended that its unwillingness to fold under Cohn's pressure on behalf of Shine was at the heart of the dispute.

For ten weeks the hearings went on. All America watched with fascination as the flamboyant McCarthy attacked and the reasoned Welch parried. Issue after issue in the conflict was contended, but always present was the subtext of who would survive this death struggle politically.

Using tactics of the past that had obliterated individuals too weak to fight back, McCarthy and Cohn introduced a doctored photograph of Army Secretary Stevens standing with G. David Shine as evidence that Stevens had lied about ever knowing Shine. If authentic, the photo would have proved that the Secretary had tried to cultivate Shine's friendship in an effort to placate McCarthy—destroying the Army's case against the committee. Welch, however, was able to prove that it was a fake, and McCarthy suffered his first major setback.

Later, McCarthy produced a letter from J. Edgar Hoover of the FBI to a Fort Monmouth general warning him of severe security leaks at the Fort. On a leap of faith, Welch countercharged that the letter was a forgery, and J. Edgar Hoover was then asked if he had actually written and mailed it. Hoover denied having written the letter, and McCarthy received the second serious blow to his credibility.

In a last-ditch effort to save his reputation, McCarthy publicly urged all government and military personnel to report directly to him on Communist activity in their areas. Eisenhower, who until then had stayed above the fray, believing the Presidency to be above doing battle with a character assassin, now publicly blasted McCarthy for the first time. He accused the Senator of tactics worse than Hitler's and asserted that any person caught reporting directly to McCarthy would be fired immediately for committing an act disloyal to the United States.

As the hearings went on, McCarthy leveled a charge of Communist affiliation against a former member of Welch's team, a young lawyer who had returned to Boston before the hearings began. McCarthy accused the lawyer, before the nation, of involvement early in his career with the left-leaning American Lawyer's Guild. It was true but irrelevant to the hearings. Welch turned to McCarthy and asked "At long last, Senator, have you no sense of decency?" McCarthy wilted under Welch's measured yet emotional attack, and at that moment, the American people, as if reacting to a single stimulus, saw McCarthy for what he was. McCarthy himself, sensing impending disaster, sat silently while the TV cameras projected his deflated image from coast to coast.

McCarthy did not survive the hearings politically. He was censured by the Senate. Never a totally well man, he died a short time later. Joseph Welch returned to private practice in Boston, the Army-McCarthy hearings a brief but spectacular interruption in a well-ordered and prosperous life. Despite his modesty, Joseph Welch in a moment in time left his imprint on American political history.

Appendix C
Where to find it all

STUDIOS
PRODUCTION COMPANIES
HOTELS
RESTAURANTS

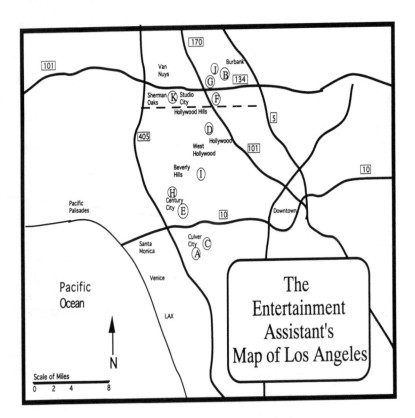

A **Sony Pictures Entertainment Lot**
Columbia Pictures
TriStar Pictures

B **Disney Lot**
Walt Disney Pictures
Hollywood Pictures
Touchstone Pictures

C **MGM- Pathe**

D **Paramount Pictures Lot**

E **20th Century Fox Lot**
20th Century Fox Film Corp.
Fox Broadcasting Company
Largo Entertainment

F **Universal Studios Lot**
MCA World Headquarters

G **Warner Bros. Lot**
Warner Bros. Pictures
Lorimar Telepictures

H **ABC Entertainment**

I **CBS Television City**

J **NBC Entertainment**

K **MTM Lot**

WHERE THE COMPANIES ARE

Beverly Hills Area
Broder, Kurland, Webb, Uffner Agency
Camden-ITG
Castle Rock Entertainment
Contemporary Artists
Creative Artists Agency
Gersh Agency
ICM
Metropolitan Talent Agency
New Line Cinema
Irv Schechter Company
Susan Smith & Associates
United Talent Agency
William Morris Agency

Beverly-Fairfax Area
CBS Entertainment

Burbank Area
Buena Vista Pictures Distribution
DIC Entertainment
Disney Channel
Disney Studios
Group W Productions
Harry Gold Agency
Hollywood Pictures
Lorimar-Telepictures
NBC
NBC Productions
Saban Entertainment
Touchstone Pictures
Warner Bros.

Century City Area
ABC
ABC Productions
The Agency
The Artists Agency

Cooper Agency
Fox Broadcasting Company
Gores-Fields Agency
Harris and Goldberg
Home Box Office
Imagine Entertainment
Largo Entertainment
Lifetime Television
Morgan Creek Productions
Orion Pictures
Turner Network Television
Twentieth Century Fox

Culver City Area
Columbia Pictures
MGM-Pathe
Sony Pictures Entertainment
Tristar Pictures

Hollywood Area
Stephen J. Cannell Productions
Fox Television Stations
Fries Entertainment
Paramount Pictures
Robinson-Weintraub-Gross
Screen Actors Guild
Sunset-Gower Studios
H.N. Swanson
Warner Hollywood Studios

Studio City/Van-Nuys/
Sherman Oaks Area
ITC Entertainment
MTM Studios
Preferred Artists
David Shapira & Associates

Universal City Area
Amblin Entertainment
The Arthur Company

MCA
Showtime
Universal Studios
Viacom

West Hollywood Area
APA
J. Michael Bloom Agency
Carolco
Directors Guild
Geffen Film Company
Island World, Inc.
Richland-Wunsch-Hohman
        Agency
Shapiro-Lichtman & Associates
Writers Guild

West Los Angeles Area
Hearst Entertainment
Interscope Communications
Writers and Artists Agency

WHERE TO ARRANGE A MEAL
(A sampling of restaurants)

Legend: B=Breakfast, L=Lunch, L*=Also late lunch, D=Dinner

Beverly Hills Area

Asylum	182 N. Robertson Blvd, BH	310-657-8484	L/D
The Bistro	246 Canon Dr., BH	310-273-5633	L/D
Bistro Garden	176 Canon Dr., BH	310-550-3900	L/D
Chasen's	9039 Beverly Blvd., BH	310-271-2168	L/D
Chaya Brasserie	8741 Alden Dr., LA	310-859-8833	L/D
The Grill	9560 Dayton Way, BH	310-276-0615	L/D
The Ivy	113 Robertson Blvd., LA	310-274-8303	L/D
Jimmy's	201 Moreno Dr., BH	310-879-2394	L/D
La Scala	410 N. Canon Dr., BH	310-275-0579	L
Ma Maison	8555 Beverly Blvd., LA	310-655-1991	L/D
Noa Noa	464 N. Bedford Dr., BH	310-278-1904	L/D
Polo Lounge	9641 Sunset Blvd., BH	310-276-2251	B/L/D

Burbank Area

Cafe Du Soleil	4315 Riverside Dr., Burbank	818-954-8734	B/L*
Hampton's	4301 Riverside Dr., Toluca Lk.	818-845-3009	L/D
La Scala Presto	3821 Riverside Dr., Burbank	818-846-6800	L/D
Val's	10130 Riverside Dr., Toluca Lk.	818-508-6644	L/D

Century City

Harry's Bar	2020 Avenue of the Stars, CC	310-277-2333	L/D
Jade West	2040 Avenue of the Stars, CC	310-556-3388	L/D
Tripp's	10131 Constellation Ave, CC	310-553-6000	L/D
Yamato	Century Plaza Hotel, CC	310-277-1840	L/D

Hollywood/West HollywoodArea

Columbia Bar and Grill	1448 N. Gower St., H'wd	213-461-8800	L/D
Hugo's	8401 Santa Monica Blvd, W-H	213-654-3993	B/L/D
Le Dome	8720 Sunset Blvd, H-Wood	213-659-6919	L/D
Morton's	8800 Melrose Ave., W-H	213-276-5205	D
The Palm	9001 Santa Monica Blvd, W-H	213-550-8811	L/D
Spago	1114 Horn Ave., H'wd	213-652-4025	D

Studio City/Universal/Van-Nuys/Sherman Oaks Area

Bistro Garden	12950 Ventura Blvd, Stud. Cty.	818-501-0202	L/D
La Loggia	11814 Ventura Blvd, Stud. Cty.	818-985-9222	L/D
Teru Sushi	11940 Ventura Blvd, Stud. Cty.	818-763-6201	L/D

Bel Air/Beverly Glen

Adriano's	2930 Beverly Glen Crc., Bel Air	310-475-9807	L/D
Shane Hidden on the Glen	2932 Beverly Glen Crc., Bel Air	310-470-6223	L/D

West Los Angeles Area, Culver City

Carioca	10831 Venice Blvd, Culver Cty	310-837-8957	L/D
Ivy at the Shore	1541 Ocean Ave. S.M.	310-393-3113	L/D
La Bruschetta	1621 Westwood Blvd, W-LA	310-477-1052	L/D

WHERE TO ARRANGE A VISIT

Bel Air/Beverly Hills Area

Beverly Hills Hotel	9641 Sunset Blvd., BH	310-276-2251
Beverly Hilton	9876 Wilshire Blvd., BH	310-274-7777
Hotel Bel Air	701 Stone Canyon Road, Bel Air	310-472-1211
Nikko Hotel of Beverly Hills	8929 Wilshire Blvd., BH	310-247-0400
Regent Beverly Wilshire	9500 Wilshire Blvd., BH	310-275-5200

Burbank/Universal City Area

Oakwood Apartments*	3600 Barham Blvd., LA	213-851-3450
Sheraton Universal Universal City	333 Universal Terrace Pkwy, 818-980-1212	
Universal City Hilton Univesal City	555 Universal Terrace Pkwy, 818-506-2500	

Century City

Century City Inn	10330 West Olympic Blvd., LA	310-553-1000
Century Plaza Hotel	2025 Ave. of the Stars, CC	310-277-2000
J.W. Marriott Century City	2151 Ave. of the Stars, CC	310-277-2777

Hollywood/West HollywoodArea

Bel Age	1020 North San Vicente Blvd.	213-854-1111
Chateau Marmont	8221 Sunset Blvd., LA	213-656-1010
Four Seasons	300 South Doheny Dr., LA	213-273-2222
Ma Maison Sofitel	8555 Beverly Blvd., LA	213-278-5444

Santa Monica/West Los Angeles Area

Loews Santa Monica Beach	1700 Ocean Ave., SM	310-458-6700
Beverly Hillcrest	1224 South Beverwil Dr., LA	310-277-2800
Hotel Shangri-La	1301 Ocean Ave., SM	310-394-2791
Westwood Marquis	930 Hilgard Ave., Westwood	310-208-8765

* For Long-term stays of one month or more.

LOCATIONS ALPHABETICALLY

Name	Area
ABC	Century City
ABC Productions	Century City
Adriano's	Beverly Glen
Agency, The	Century City
Amblin Entertainment	Universal City
APA	West Hollywood
Arthur Company	Universal City
Artists Agency, The	Century City
Asylum	Beverly Hills
Bel Age	West Hollywood
Beverly Hillcrest	West Los Angeles
Beverly Hills Hotel	Beverly Hills
Beverly Hilton	Beverly Hills
Bistro Garden	Studio City
Bistro Garden	Beverly Hills
Bistro, The	Beverly Hills
Broder, Kurland, Webb, Uffner Agency	Beverly Hills
Buena Vista Pictures Distribution	Burbank
Cafe du Soleil	Burbank
Camden ITG	Beverly Hills
Carioca	West Los Angeles
Carolco	West Hollywood
Castle Rock Entertainment	Beverly Hills
CBS Entertainment	Beverly-Fairfax/Wilshire
Century City Inn	Century City
Century Plaza Hotel	Century City
Chasen's	Beverly Hills
Chateau Marmont	West Hollywood
Chaya Brasserie	Beverly Hills
Columbia Bar and Grill	Hollywood
Columbia Pictures	Culver City
Contemporary Artists	Beverly Hills
Cooper Agency	Century City
Cooper Agency	Century City
Creative Artists Agency	Beverly Hills
David Shapira & Associates	Sherman Oaks
DIC Entertainment	Burbank
Director's Guild	West Hollywood
Disney Channel	Burbank
Disney Studios	Burbank
Four Seasons	West Hollywood
Fox Broadcasting Company	Century City
Fox Television Stations	Hollywood

Fries Entertainment	Hollywood
Geffen Film Company	West Hollywood
Gersh Agency	Beverly Hills
Gores-Fields Agency	Century City
Grill, The	Beverly Hills
Group W Productions	Burbank
H.N. Swanson	Hollywood
Hamptons	Burbank
Harris and Goldberg	Century City
Harry Gold Agency	Burbank
Harry's Bar	Century City
Hearst Entertainment	West Los Angeles
Hollywood Pictures	Burbank
Home Box Office	Century City
Hotel Bel Air	Beverly Hills
Hotel Shangri-La	West Los Angeles
Hugo's	West Hollywood
ICM	Beverly Hills
Imagine Entertainment	Century City
Interscope Communications	West Los Angeles
Irv Schechter Company	Beverly Hills
Island World, Inc.	West Hollywood
ITC Entertainment	Studio City
Ivy at the Shore	West Los Angeles
Ivy, The	Beverly Hills
J. Michael Bloom Agency	West Hollywood
J.W. Marriot Century City	Century City
Jade West	Century City
Jimmy's	Beverly Hills
La Bruschetta	West Los Angeles
La Loggia	Studio City
La Scala	Beverly Hills
La Scala Presto	Burbank
Largo Entertainment	Century City
Le Dome	West Hollywood
Lifetime Television	Century City
Loews Santa Monica Beach	West Los Angeles
Lorimar Telepictures	Burbank
Ma Maison	Beverly Hills
Ma Maison Sofitel	Beverly-Fairfax/Wilshire
MCA	Universal City
Metropolitan Talent Agency	Beverly Hills
MGM-Pathe	Culver City
Morgan Creek Productions	Century City
Morton's	West Hollywood

MTM Studios	Studio City
NBC	Burbank
NBC Productions	Burbank
New Line Cinema	Beverly Hills
Nikko Hotel of Beverly Hills	Beverly Hills
Noa Noa	Beverly Hills
Oakwood Apartments	Burbank
Orion Pictures	Century City
Palm, The	West Hollywood
Paramount Pictures	Hollywood
Polo Lounge	Beverly Hills
Preferred Artists	Sherman Oaks
Regent Beverly Wilshire	Beverly Hills
Richland-Wunsch-Hohman Agency	West Hollywood
Robinson-Weintraub-Gross	Hollywood
Saban Entertainment	Burbank
Screen Actors Guild	Hollywood
Shane on the Glen	Beverly Glen
Shaprio-Lichtman & Associates	West Hollywood
Sheraton Universal	Universal City
Sony Pictures Entertainment	Culver City
Spago	Hollywood
Stephen J. Cannell Productions	Hollywood
Sunset-Gower Studios	Hollywood
Susan Smith & Associates	Beverly Hills
Teru Sushi	Studio City
Touchstone Pictures	Burbank
Tripp's	Century City
Tristar Pictures	Culver City
Turner Network Television	Century City
Twentieth Century Fox	Century City
United Talent Agency	Beverly Hills
Universal City Hilton	Universal City
Universal Studios	Universal City
Val's	Burbank
Viacom	Universal City
Warner Bros.	Burbank
Warner Hollywood Studios	Hollywood
Westwood Marquis	West Los Angeles
William Morris Agency	Beverly Hills
Writers and Artists Agency	West Los Angeles
Writers Guild	West Hollywood
Yamato	Century City

Appendix D
Frequently Dialed Phone Numbers

Studios & Independents	Main Office	Auxiliary Office
Columbia Pictures	310-280-8000	
Hollywood Pictures	818-560-1000	
Imagine	310-277-1665	
Lorimar	818-954-6000	
MGM - Pathe	310-280-6000	
Miramax Films	212-941-3800	213-969-2000
Morgan Creek Productions	310-284-8884	
New Line Cinema	310-854-5881	212-239-8880
Paramount	213-956-5000	
Touchstone Pictures	818-560-1000	
TriStar	310-280-7700	
Twentieth Century Fox	310-277-2211	
Universal	818-777-1000	
Viacom	818-505-7500	212-258-6000
Walt Disney Pictures	818-560-1000	
Warner Bros.	818-954-6000	

Broadcast Networks		
ABC	310-557-7777	212-456-7777
CBS	213-852-2345	212-975-4321
FBC	310-277-2211	
NBC	818-840-4444	212-664-4444

Cable Networks

HBO	310-201-9200	212-512-1000
Showtime	818-505-7700	
TNT	310-551-6332	404-827-1500
USA Network	212-408-9100	

Agencies

APA	310-273-0744	212-582-1500
CAA	310-288-4545	
Gersh Agency	310-274-6611	212-997-1818
ICM	310-550-4000	212-556-5600
Metropolitan	310-247-5500	
United Talent	310-273-6700	
William Morris	310-274-7451	212-586-5100

Guilds

DGA	310-289-2000	212-581-0370
SAG	213-465-4600	212-944-6797
WGA	213-550-1000	212-245-2180

Appendix E
The Trades

The trade newspapers contain volumes of information and news about the entire entertainment industry. However, finding what you want in the trades can take a little practice. Here are some of the regular features of the trades:

News of the Entertainment Industry
Every day, the trades contain articles that describe spec script sales, producing deals, executive changes, technology, mergers and acquisitions, regulatory legislation, box-office figures, and ratings performance. The trades also publish articles about syndicated programming, home video, and the music industry.

Film Reviews
Reviews of feature films that are being released domestically, as well as films premiering at film festivals.

Television Reviews
Reviews of television pilots, first episodes of the new season, movies of the week, cable programming, miniseries, specials and documentaries.

Legit (Stage) Reviews
Reviews of live theater and opera from both Los Angeles and New York, as well as selected regional theater.

Concert Reviews
Reviews of rock concerts and live musical acts.

Entertainment Industry Financial News
Stock market and financial news of major media companies.

Weekly

Box-Office Figures
Weekend box-office grosses on leading films, ranked in descending order. Usually reported on Tuesdays.

Film Production Chart
Comprehensive list of films which are in pre-production, production, or post-production. Contains major studio releases, as well as direct-to-home-video movies. Gives distributor, production credits, casting, locations, and dates of production for each film.

Television Production Chart
Lists television shows currently in production, including series, movies-of the week, miniseries, and daytime dramas.

Cable Production Chart
Lists production for cable programming services, including movies for cable.

Television Ratings
The ratings chart shows ratings and share figures for the primetime schedule of the previous week for all four networks. Usually reported on Wednesdays.

HOW TO READ THE BOX-OFFICE FIGURES
(Please refer to chart on page 288)

The figure below is an annotated version of the weekly box-office report from the trades. Each number on the chart is significant. In this case, the movie is Paramount's WAYNE'S WORLD. From this entry we can tell that the movie has dropped from being the sixth-highest-grossing movie the previous weekend to being the seventh-highest-grossing movie this weekend. Over the weekend, people spent $3,435,115 on tickets to WAYNE'S WORLD. That is 22% less than they spent the previous weekend. On average, every theater showing WAYNE'S WORLD took in $2,003 for each screen that was showing the movie. This per-screen average is often cited as a barometer of a film's popularity. It measures how full the theaters were. The drop in the weekend gross from last week to this week might be attributable to the fact that WAYNE'S WORLD is playing on 163 fewer screens.

In total, the film has grossed $98,007,901 domestically in 59 days. Though this total boxoffice gross figure is the most often quoted with regard to a movie's commercial success, it can be quite misleading. This figure is the exhibitor's gross—the total amount of money spent at the boxoffice. After deducting the exhibitor's share and house costs, the amount of money reaching the studio may be significantly lower. And this figure is only for the United States. The international boxoffice figures do not appear regularly in the trades.

HOW TO READ THE TELEVISION RATINGS CHART
(Please refer to chart on page 289)

The chart below is similar to the ratings charts published in the trades. It shows the ratings for Thursday, April 9th, 1992. The bold type and shaded areas indicate the highest rating of the timeslot. For example, NBC has the highest ratings from 8:00 to 10:00, but after ten, the lead goes to ABC for the first half of PRIME TIME LIVE, and then to CBS for the second half of KNOTS LANDING. Each half-hour time slot has its own rating.

Overall, NBC "won" the night, as indicated by the bold-face 11.8/20 in the top row. That split figure, the *ratings/share* figure, represents two significant facts. The first number, 11.8, is the rating. Ratings are an absolute measure of television audience. The rating is a percentage of the number of homes with television in the United States. Since there are about ninety million television homes, a rating of 11.8 means that about 10.6 million homes were watching NBC on Thursday night. The second number, 20, is the share figure. That means that of the television *sets in use* on Thursday night, twenty percent were tuned to NBC. Adding across the top row, we can determine the network share of the total television audience. In all, 74% of the audience was watching ABC, CBS, NBC, and Fox. (That's 18% for ABC, 19% for CBS, 20% for NBC, and 17% for Fox.) The other 26% of the audience was watching cable or independent stations, or using VCRs.

BOX-OFFICE FIGURES

Ranking This Week	Last Week	Title (Distributor)	Weekend Boxoffice	% Change	Per Screen ~ Average	No. of Screens This Week	No. of Screens Last Week	Cumulative Boxoffice	No. Days in Release
7	6	Wayne's World(Par)	3,435,115	-22%	2003	1715	1878	98,007,901	59

The film dropped from 6th place to 7th place in terms of total weekend take

The film is Wayne's World, distributed by Paramount Pictures

A total of $3,435115 was spent on tickets to Wayne's World this last weekend.

That is a 22% drop from the previous weekend.

On Average, each movie theater playing Wayne's World grossed $2003 over the weekend.

Wayne's World was playing on 1715 screens this weekend, down from 1878 the previous weekend.

In Total, Wayne's World has brought in $98,007,901 in gross ticket sales in the United States.

The film has been out in theaters for 59 days.

TELEVISION RATINGS CHART

The rating/Share figure for the network for the night

	ABC 10.6/18	CBS 11.1/19	NBC 11.8/20	FOX 10.0/17
	Thursday			
8:00	Columbo (R) 9.1/16	Top Cops 9.0/16	Cosby 11.5/20	Simpsons 11.4/20
8:30	(9.5/16) 9.1/15	(9.5/16) 10.1/17	D'frnt Wrld. 13.2/22	Drexell's Class 7.9/13
9:00	9.7/16	Street Stories 10.5/17	Cheers 15.5/25	Beverly Hills 9.8/16
9:30	(9.5/16) 10.1/16	(10.8/17) 11.0/17	Wings 12.6/20	90210 10.7/17 (10.3/16)
10:00	Prime Time Live 12.8/2?	Knots Landing 12.7/21	LA Law 9.4/16	
10:30	(12.0/21) 11.5/21	(12.9/22) 13.0/23	(9.0/16) 8.6/15	

Prime Time Live was the highest rated show from 10-10:30, but after 10:30, the lead went to Knot's Landing

Fox did not air any network programming after 10PM.

Appendix F
Sample Development Spreadsheet

Project Name: Vegas Kid — **Network: NBC** — **Today's Date 10/2/92**

OPTION

Amount	Date of Commence	Date of Expiration	Reimbursable Amount	Amount Paid	Date Paid (Network)	Amount Billed (NBC)	Date Billed	Amount Collected	Date Collected	Days Outstanding
1st year	8/24/92	8/23/93	$2,500	$2,500	8/24/92	$2,500	8/24/92	$2,500	10/1/92	42
2nd year	8/24/93	8/23/94	$2,500							
Consultant			$5,000	$5,000	8/20/92	$5,000	8/21/92			
Research										
Purchase			$45,000							
										Days until Renewal
Total			$55,000	$7,500		$7,500		$2,500		325

WRITER: Fred Samson

PAYMENTS Deal	Percentage	Amount	Reimbursable Amount	Partial Payment	Balance Paid	Amount Paid	Date Paid (Agent)	Amount Billed	Date Billed	Amount Collected	Date Collected	Days Outstanding
Total	100%	$55,000	$55,000									
Commence	18%	$10,000	$10,000			$10,000	8/25/92	$10,000	8/25/92	$10,000	10/1/92	
WGA		$1,250	$1,250			$1,250	8/25/92	$1,250	8/25/92	$1,250	10/1/92	17
1st Draft	36%	$20,000	$20,000			$20,000	9/15/92	$20,000	9/15/92			
WGA		$2,500	$2,500			$2,500	9/15/92	$2,500	9/15/92			17
2nd Draft	18%	$10,000	$10,000									
WGA		$1,250	$1,250									
2nd Revis.	18%	$10,000	$10,000									
WGA		$1,250	$1,250									
Polish	9%	$5,000	$5,000									
WGA		$625	$625									
Consult	5%	$2,500	$2,500									
Prod Bonus		$10,000	$10,000									
TOTAL		$64,375	$64,375	$0	$0	$33,750		$33,750		$11,250		
WGA P&W	12.50%											
Total P&W	$6,875											
Total Fee	$55,000											
Total Outstanding		$27,500										
Total Unreimbursed		$27,500										

Appendix G
Resources

BOOK FINDERS

Brand Bookshop
231 N. Brand Blvd.
Glendale, CA 91203
818-507-5943

For a $1 fee, the Brand Bookshop will search for a book through local dealers and contact you if they locate it.

The Book Shop
134 N. Citrus Avenue
Covina, CA 91723
818-967-1888

The Book Shop will only search for out-of-print books. A typical search can take more than two months.

International Bookfinder Inc.
P.O. Box 1
Pacific Palisades, CA 90272-0001
Contact: Rick Mohr

There is no telephone number. Send title, author, publishing information, and the amount you are willing to spend on the book.
Search time depends on the book.

Needham Book Finder
P.O. Box 3067
Santa Monica, California 90408
310-395-0538
Contact: Stan Kerman
Also try:

Books in Print
Available through CompuServe
1-800-848-8199

This is a database that gives information on books, and it is just one database available through CompuServe. A $3.00 search using the Books in Print Database retrieves up to 10 titles. Each title which you download to your computer costs an additional $3.00.

Bookfinder

This is a book that lists bookstores by location in the Los Angeles area. It indicates their specialty and if they perform book finding services. *Bookfinder* is available in new and used bookstores.

BOOKSTORES

B. Dalton Bookseller
210 N. Los Angeles Street
Los Angeles, CA 90012
213-687-3050
(located in the Los Angeles Mall and elsewhere)

Book Soup
8818 W. Sunset Blvd.
Los Angeles, CA 90069
310-659-3110

Brentano's—Century City Mall
10250 Santa Monica Blvd.
Los Angeles, CA 90067
310-785-0204

Dutton's Books
(four locations)
11975 San Vicente Blvd. (at Bundy)
Los Angeles, CA 90049
310-476-6263

5146 Laurel Canyon Blvd.
North Hollywood, CA 91607
818-769-3866

3806 Magnolia Blvd.
Burbank, CA 91505
818-840-8003

505 South Flower Street—Level C
Los Angeles, CA 90071
213-683-1199

Fowler Brothers
717 W. 7th Street
Los Angeles, CA 90017
213-627-7846
213-627-1410 FAX

The Samuel French Bookstores
(two locations)
7623 Sunset Blvd.
Hollywood, CA 90046
213-876-0570

11963 Ventura Blvd.
Studio City, CA 91604
818-762-0535
Offers an extensive collection of plays, as well as entertainment and theater books.

Larry Edmunds
6644 Hollywood Blvd
Hollywood, CA 90028
213-463-3273
The Larry Edmunds store in Hollywood sells a wide range of movie books, reference books, screenplays, old magazines, posters, and still photographs. Many of the Larry Edmunds items are antiques.

BOOK STORES—USED

Book City
6627 Hollywood Blvd.
Hollywood, CA 90028
213-466-2525
213-466-1049

Book City of Burbank
308 N. San Fernando Blvd.
Burbank, CA 91502
818-848-4417

Cosmopolitan Book Shop
7007 Melrose Ave.
Los Angeles, CA 90038
213-938-7119

BREAKDOWN SERVICES LIMITED
1120 S. Robertson Blvd.
Los Angeles, CA 90035
310-276-9166

CAR RENTAL

Beverly Hills Hotel
9641 W. Sunset Blvd.
Beverly Hills, CA 90210
310-276-2251
Concierge will arrange car leasing for guests.

Budget
9815 Wilshire Blvd.
Beverly Hills, CA 90210
310-274-9173

Exotic City Motor Cars
5250 W. Century Blvd.
Los Angeles, CA 90045
310-216-1183
(handles exotic and luxury cars)

Midway Rent-A-Car
2926 Wilshire Blvd.
Los Angeles, CA 90010
213-487-4700

Rent-A-Wreck
12333 W. Pico Blvd.
Los Angeles, CA 90064
310-478-0676

CELLULAR PHONES

American Way Cellular
1653 S. La Cienega Blvd.
Los Angeles, CA 90035
310-278-2007

Road And Show Cellular
13470 Washington Blvd., #308
Marina Del Rey, CA 90292
310-301-2121
(complimentary pick-up and delivery)

HAND-HELD COMPUTERS

Newton
A hand-held personal address and note system made by Apple Computer. It has no keyboard, but recognizes handwriting. Can communicate with desktop computers by infrared transmission (similar to TV remote control.)

DETAILING SERVICES

Hollywood Detail
6464 W. Sunset Blvd.
Hollywood, CA 90028
213-464-2524
(will pick up car from office)

Auto Spa
128 S. Western Ave.
Los Angeles, CA 90004
213-383-8130

GUILD AGENCY LINES

Writers Guild
310-205-2502
212-767-7800

Directors Guild
213-851-3671
212-581-0370

Screen Actors Guild
213-856-6737
212-944-6797

INFORMATION SERVICES

A.C. Nielsen Media Research
Nielsen is the ratings service for the television industry. They calculate viewership and demographics for every television show on the air and publish the results daily for their subscribers. The Nielsen service costs hundreds of dollars per month, so it may not be a worthwhile expense for a small production company. The Nielsen ratings are also published weekly in the trades. Their phone number is 213-386-7316.

Baseline
Baseline a comprehensive computerized database of entertainment industry credits and information. A subscriber to Baseline connects to the database through a personal computer (either IBM Compatible or Macintosh) and telephone modem. Once logged on to the system, the user can search for individual credits or complete credit listings for films and television shows. Baseline also gives up-to-date boxoffice information and headline news from The Hollywood Reporter. Baseline use costs from about $2.00 to $3.50 per minute, depending on the type of information being provided.

If you don't have a computer, or if you need to do extensive research, Baseline will do the research for you and bill your account. If you don't have an account, Baseline accepts credit cards. Baseline now offers film industry news over a pay-per-call, or 900 service: 1-900-230-FILM (1-900-230-3456) It offers callers the choice of hearing about boxoffice figures from the weekend, industry headlines, upcoming films, and the current week's video releases. It costs 95 cents per minute.Baseline's phone number is 213-659-3830 or 1-800-242-7546 outside Los Angeles.

CompuServe
5000 Arlington Centre Blvd.
Columbus Ohio, 43220
800-848-8199

CompuServe is an on-line database information service covering many different topics, with over 1,700 Databases available. Books-in-Print is just one of the many databases to choose from. Unlike Prodigy, which charges a flat monthly rate, CompuServe charges on a task-by-task basis, with different charges for each database accessed, and for each entry downloaded. To receive CompuServe, you must have a computer with modem capability. A membership kit is $39.95.

Entertainment Data, Inc. (EDI)
8350 Wilshire Blvd, Suite #210
Beverly Hills, CA 90211
213-658-8300

E.D.I. provides the industry with information about box-office grosses, release dates, distributor information on current and past feature film releases, overnight box-office tracking, 'Historical Data Bases' of box office release schedule, and grosses going back to 1980. E.D.I also provides custom research services for film marketing studies. Costs of services vary.

Genie
GENIE GE Computer Service
401 N. Washington
Rockville MD, 20850
800-638-9636

An electronic mail service providing job bulletin boards, research databases, an on-line Groliers encyclopedia, and multi-player games.
You need a computer with a modem. Genie is compatible with everything, but you need a communications software program—anything that allows you to dial telephone numbers through a modem.

Costs: $4.95 for a monthly subscription. Rates range from $6 to $18 per hour depending on time of day. No start up charges or kit.

Journal Graphics

Journal Graphics provides written transcripts of news shows such as WASHINGTON WEEK IN REVIEW. They charge one fee for mailing the transcript to you, but for a premium they also offer fax or Federal Express service on a same-day or next-day basis. Journal Graphics publishes a quarterly catalogue indexed by topic. Their phone number is 212-227-7323

NEXIS

NEXIS is a full-text database that contains magazine, newspaper, and wire service articles from hundreds of periodicals going back to the 1970s, as well as many other electronic data services. You connect to NEXIS through a personal computer and modem. You can search through NEXIS using key words. For example, if you were to enter the name "Donald Trump" as a key word to search for, NEXIS would list every article that contained the name "Donald Trump" in its text. You can then select the article you want to see, and it will appear in full on your screen instantly! Because it is a full-text database, NEXIS is extremely valuable in finding obscure articles and other information that would take hours to find in a library.

NEXIS also carries an entertainment information service, which includes Baseline's database as well as articles from trade publications, and film reviews from major newspapers. NEXIS is owned by Mead Data Central, Inc., of Dayton Ohio, and their phone number is 1-800-227-4908

Prodigy

445 Hamilton Ave
White Plains NY, 10601
800-PRODIGY

Prodigy is a joint venture between IBM and Sears. It is sold at Sears stores. Prodigy is another on-line computer service, with 800 services offered, including an on-line Groliers encyclopedia (33,000 articles updated quarterly), and other services such as EASY SABRE, which enables you to make airline reservations, access to stock market info, and on-line entertainment bulletin boards. You need an IBM or Macintosh compatible computer with a modem. It must be a Hayes or Hayes-compatible modem, 12, or 2400 BAUD. Start up kit is $19.95, with a $14.95 dollar flat rate per month, no matter how much or how little you use the service.

Santa Monica Public Library Card Catalogue

The Santa Monica Public Library makes its card catalogue available to people with a personal computer and modem. By accessing the card catalog, you can search for books using the title, author's name or the book's subject matter as key words. The card catalogue will give the you the book's call number in the library, and tell you whether it is currently in the library. It is a great, free service. To get information about the service, call 310-458-8600. If you have your computer all set up with a modem, the library's computer can be reached at 310-458-8990.

INSURANCE BROKERS

Albert G. Ruben
2121 Avenue of the Stars, Suite 700
Los Angeles, California 90067-5001
310-551-1101

Aon Entertainment, Ltd. (film completion guarantors)
10 Universal City Plaza
Suite 2200
Universal City, CA 91608
818-506-1500

Curland Peterson Insurance Associates, Inc.
15301 Ventura Blvd., Suite 435
Sherman Oaks, CA 91403
818-788-9810

Truman Van Dyke
6255 Sunset Boulevard, Suite 1401
Hollywood, California 90028
213-462-3300

LIBRARIES

Academy of Motion Picture Arts and Sciences (AMPAS) Library
333 S. La Cienega Drive
Beverly Hills, CA 90211
310-247-3035

AMPAS maintains a library at its Beverly Hills headquarters. The Academy library contains 6 million movie stills, books on film, major periodicals, microfilm of old periodicals, and movie-related clipping files from 150 newspapers and magazines. The library is open to the public free of charge, but only to those with legitimate research or professional work to do. Bring a picture ID to the library to get a day pass.

Academy of Television Arts and Sciences (ATAS) Library

Academy of Television Arts and Sciences
5220 Lankershim Blvd.
North Hollywood, CA 91601
818-754-2800

ATAS has a library in North Hollywood. The library contains reference books on television, directories of distributors of television shows, biographies of television figures, information on the Emmy Awards, still photos, and a clippings file.

American Film Institute (AFI) Library

American Film Institute
2021 N. Western Ave.
Los Angeles, CA 90027
213-856-7600

The AFI Library contains screenplays of many recent and old films, clippings, and books about the movie business. Unfortunately, the AFI Library is only open from 1-5 on Wednesdays and has no reference telephone line.

Beverly Hills Public Library

444 North Rexford Drive
Beverly Hills, CA 90210
310-288-2200

Burbank Public Library

110 North Glenoaks Boulevard
Burbank, California 91502
818-953-9737

Hollywood Public Library

1623 N. Ivar
Hollywood, CA 90028
213-467-1821

Los Angeles Public Library

Temporary location, until the summer of 1993:
433 S. Spring Street
Los Angeles, California
213-612-3200

New library, from the summer of 1993 on:
630 West Fifth Street
Los Angeles, California 90071
213-612-3200

Museum of Television and Radio Library
212-621-6780.

The Museum of Television and Radio in New York City (formerly the Museum of Broadcasting) has 40,000 old television and radio programs in its archives. They are available to the general public for viewing, though the Museum does not lend these programs. If you become a member of the Museum for a $125 fee, you can make a reservation to use the library.

Santa Monica Public Library
1343 Sixth Street
Santa Monica, California 90401
310-4458-8600

U.C.L.A. University Research Library

The University Research Library (U.R.L.) of the University of California at Los Angeles (U.C.L.A.) is one of the finest libraries in Southern California. It also has an Arts Library with extensive holdings in entertainment industry periodicals and publications. You can get library privileges at the U.R.L. by becoming a Sustaining Member of the Friends of the U.C.L.A. Library for a fee of $200. The Arts Library can be reached at 310-825-3817.

U.C.L.A. Archive Research Study Center

U.C.L.A. also maintains an extensive video library of old television programs in its Archive Research Study Center. One can request episodes of *Gilligan's Island, Ben Casey* or many other shows, and watch them on the premises through closed circuit television. This resource is useful for remakes. The Archive Study Center is open to the public at no charge. The Center's phone number is 310-206-5388

PAGERS

PageNet
11150 Santa Monica Blvd., #120
Los Angeles, CA 90025
1-800-762-7243

RADIO AND TV REPORTS
41 East 42nd St.
New York, NY 10017
212-309-1400

6255 Sunset Blvd.
Los Angeles, CA 90028
213-466-6124

A TV and radio electronic monitoring and clipping service. This research firm records everything on television and radio, but only keeps it for sixty days. They compile tapes tailored to specific needs for public relations, advertising and film research.

Costs:　　$85.00 for first clip up to ten minutes.

　　　　　$55.00 for each ten-minute clip thereafter on the same tape.

REFERENCE BOOKS

ACTORS

Academy Players Directory
This multi-volume set contains photographs of about 19,000 actors and actresses and the names of their agents. It is an absolute necessity for any office involved in casting. (*Published by the Academy of Motion Picture Arts and Sciences • 8949 Wilshire Blvd. Beverly Hills, CA 90211 • 310 247-3000*)

Film Actors Guide
Lists credits of over 4,600 actors who have worked in films over the last 10 years. (*Published by Lone Eagle Publishing • 2337 Roscomare Rd Suite #9 Los Angeles, CA 90077-1815 • 310-471-8066*)

Agents

Film Producers, Studios, Agents and Casting Directors Guide
by David M. Kipen & Jack Lechner

Lists agents and their agencies, as well as producers, executive rosters of studios and large production companies, and casting directors. Cross-referenced by film titles. (*Published by Lone Eagle Publishing • 2337 Roscomare Rd. Suite #9 Los Angeles, CA 90077-1815 • 310-471-8066*)

Hollywood Agents Directory
Lists literary, talent, theatrical, and commercial agencies and their agents. (*Published by Hollywood Creative Directory • 3000 Olympic Blvd. Santa Monica, CA 90404 • 310-315-4815*)

Below-the-line talent and Information

Cinematographers/Production Designers/Costume Designers & Film Editors Guide
Lists credits and contact information for these major technical artists. (*Published annually by Lone Eagle Publishing • 2337 Roscomare Rd. Suite #9 Los Angeles, CA 90077-1815 • 310-471-8066*)

LA 411
Lists production companies, technical people of all varieties, post production facilities, support services from animal training to computer software. Used mainly by people in commercial production. (*Published by LA 411 Publishing • 326 N. Detroit, Los Angeles, CA 90036 • 213-460-6304*)

Hollywood Reporter Blu-Book
Contains listings of production companies, support services for production, unions, studio and network executive rosters, and celebrity contacts, among other things. (*Published by the Hollywood Reporter • 5055 Wilshire Blvd, Los Angeles, CA 90036 • 213-525-2000*)

Motion Picture TV and Theater Directory
Comprehensive directory of physical production and support services for New York and other states. Also includes information about Canada and Europe. (*Published by Motion Picture Enterprises, semiannually*) • *PO BOX 276, Tarrytown, NY 10591 • 212-245-0969*)

Studio Directory
The telephone book for the motion picture industry. Contains listings of production services, rental services, production companies, advertising agencies, artist and writer representatives, and casting companies, among other categories. (*Published by Pacific Coast Studio Directory • PO BOX V, Pine Mountain, CA 93222 • 805-242-2722*)

Who's Who?—Qui Est Qui?
This is a Canadian's Who's Who of everyone involved in Cinema and Television in Canada, and is put together by their Film Commission. It is an invaluable guide helpful in finding out who is doing what, and where, in the growing Canadian film industry. (*Published by the Academy of Canadian Cinema and Television • 158 Pearl St. Toronto, Ontario, Canada, M5H1L3 • 416-591-2040*)

DIRECTORS

Director's Guild Directory
Names, contact information, and credits of 10,000 current DGA members. Also a good source for Unit Production Managers, Assistant Directors, etc. (*Published by the Directors Guild of America • 7920 Sunset Blvd. Los Angeles, CA 90046 • 310-289-2000*)

Feature Directors 1980-92, Their Credits & Their Agents
Credits and agency information on over 1,100 feature film directors. (*Published by Hollywood Creative Directory • 3000 Olympic Blvd. Santa Monica, CA 90404 • 310-315-4815*)

Film Directors—A Complete Guide
The most comprehensive listing of working film and television movie directors. Gives the name and phone number of director's agent, as well as title and year of release for produced films. Also indexed by title. (*Published by Lone Eagle Publishing • 2337 Roscomare Rd. Suite #9 Los Angeles, CA 90077-1815 • 310-471-8066*)

Television Directors Guide
Lists credits, agent information, and awards for directors of episodic television, movies of the week, and specials, cross-indexed by show title. Also includes listings of programs by genre and indexes of agents and managers. (*Published by Lone Eagle Publishing • 2337 Roscomare Rd. Suite #9 Los Angeles, CA 90077-1815 • 310-471-8066*)

Hollywood Distributors Directory

Lists over 350 domestic and foreign distribution and syndication companies and their current marketing, sales and acquisitions staff.
(*Published by Hollywood Creative Directory • 3000 Olympic Blvd. Santa Monica, CA 90404 • 310-315-4815*)

ENCYCLOPEDIAS, COMPILATIONS, AND DICTIONARIES

Complete Directory of Prime Time Network TV shows, 1946—Present

Lists every prime-time television series ever put on the air, excluding pilots that aired one time only. Provides a plot summary, casting information, air dates and network. Book also contains data on the television ratings history of many shows, and primetime schedules from every year since 1946. (*Published by Ballantine Books • 201 E. 50th St. New York, NY 10022 • 212-751-2600*)

Dictionary of Films

Credits, plotlines, and critical comments on 1,300 classics of world film, including many international films that are not usually listed in the current American directories. (*Published by University of California Press • 2120 Berkeley Way, Berkeley, CA 94720 • 510-642-4247*)

Dictionary of Film Makers

Bios and credits of 1000 international film directors. (*Published by University of California Press • 2120 Berkeley Way, Berkeley, CA 94720 • 510-642-4247*)

Film Encyclopedia

Over 7000 entries covering directors, films, actors, terminology, and history. (*Published by HarperCollins • 10 E 53rd St. New York, NY 10022 • 212-207-7000*)

Filmmaker's Dictionary

Over 1,500 Motion Picture and Television terms from technical to slang. (*Published by Lone Eagle Publishing • 2337 Roscomare Rd. Suite #9 Los Angeles, CA 90077-1815 • 310-471-8066*)

Halliwell's Film Guide

Contains information on thousands of films, including date of release, plotline, cast, major credits, and some critical comments. (*Published by Harper and Collins • 10 E 53rd St. New York, NY 10022 • 212-207-7000*)

Halliwell's Filmgoer's Companion and Video Viewer's Companion

Contains miniature biographies of famous movie personalities, movie trivia, and credits on well-known movies. (*Published by HarperCollins • 10 E 53rd St. New York, NY 10022 • 212-207-7000*)

Leonard Maltin's Movie and Video Guide

Lists title, plot summary, major casting and director of virtually every feature film and television movie ever made. (*Published by Signet Books • 375 Hudson St. New York, NY 10014 • 212-366-2000*)

Movies Made for Television

Lists every television movie and mini-series made from 1964 to 1986 and gives plot summaries, casting, technical credits and network information. Indexed by actors, writers, directors and producers. (*Published by New York/ZOETROPE • 833 Broadway, 4th Floor, New York NY 10003 • 212-254-8235*)

Program Book

Compilation of pilots, commitments for series, miniseries, and specials. Covers the four networks, cable, and syndication. Lists production company information for each series, as well as plotlines and formats. (*Published by Daily Variety • 5700 Wilshire Blvd. Suite 120, Los Angeles, CA 90036 • 213-857-6600 Los Angeles, CA*)

TV Movie Reference Guide '84-'89

Complete credits on over 637 television movies produced between 1984 and 1989. (*Published by Hollywood Creative Directory • 3000 Olympic Blvd. Santa Monica, CA 90404 • 310-315-4815*)

TV & Cable Movie Reference Guide '89-'91

Complete credits on over 300 movies made for network and cable television from 1989-1991, with cross-referenced names and their credits. (*Published by Hollywood Creative Directory • 3000 Olympic Blvd. Santa Monica, CA 90404 • 310-315-4815*)

Variety Anniversary Issue

Contains every feature film review published by Variety from October to October, unless the film never came out. Also includes summary box-office data on films released during the year. (*Published annually by Variety • 5700 Wilshire Blvd., Suite 120, Los Angeles, CA 90036 • 213-857-6600*)

Variety Movie Guide
Contains over 5000 movie reviews from Variety, from 1914 through the year of publication. (*Published annually by Prentice Hall/Simon and Schuster • 200 Old Tappan Road, Old Tappan, NJ 07675 • 515-284-6781*)

PRODUCTION COMPANIES, STUDIOS, NETWORKS

Film Producers, Studios, Agents and Casting Directors Guide
Lists producers, executive rosters of studios and large production companies, as well as agents and their agencies, and casting directors. Cross-referenced by film titles. (*Published by Lone Eagle Publishing • 2337 Roscomare Rd. Suite #9 Los Angeles, CA 90077-1815 • 310-471-8066*)

Hollywood Creative Directory
Lists name, addresses and phone numbers of production companies, networks and studios. For each company, the Creative Directory lists the current executive roster with titles.
(*Published by Hollywood Creative Directory • 3000 Olympic Blvd. Santa Monica, CA 90404 • 310-315-4815*)

PUBLISHING

Literary Market Place
The yellow pages of the publishing industry. Lists every book publisher and book agent in the country, among other things. Extremely useful for tracking down film rights to books. (*Published by A and I Bowker • 515 E 85th St., New York, NY 10028 • 800-334-3838*)

Master Plots
Multi-volume set contains two-page plot summaries of famous books and stories from world literature. Master Plots can provide instant coverage for classic books. (*Published by Salem Press • 580 Sylvan Ave. Englewood Cliffs, NJ 107632 • 201-871-3700*)

WRITERS

Film Writers Guide
Lists major working feature film writers, giving credits and agency information. Also indexed by title. (*Published by Lone Eagle Publishing • 2337*

Roscomare Rd. Suite #9 Los Angeles, CA 90077-1815 • 310-471-8066)

Television Writers Guide
Lists credits, agent information, and awards for writers of episodic television, movies of the week, and specials, cross-indexed by show title. Also includes listings of programs by genre and indexes of agents and managers. (*Published by Lone Eagle Publishing • 2337 Roscomare Rd. Suite #9 Los Angeles, CA 90077-1815 • 310-471-8066)*

Feature Writers 1980-92, Their Credits & Their Agents
Credits, awards, and representation information for more than 2,600 feature film writers. (*Published by Hollywood Creative Directory • 3000 Olympic Blvd. Santa Monica, CA 90404 • 310-315-4815)*

Writer's Guild of America Directory
Contains names, some credits, and agent information for Writer's Guild members. (*Published by the Writer's Guild of America • 8955 Beverly Boulevard, Los Angeles, CA 90048 • 310-550-1000)*

RESEARCH COMPANIES

Deforest Research
1645 N. Vine Street, #701
Los Angeles, CA 90028
213-469-2271

Marshall Plumb Research Associates, Inc.
4150 Riverside Drive, #209
Burbank, CA 91505
818-848-7071

SOFTWARE—STANDARD MACINTOSH PROGRAMS

Dinodex
A program set up to emulate a Rolodex. (*Published by Portfolio Systems • 800-729-3966)*

Filemaker Pro
A versatile database program. (*Published by Claris Corporation, Santa Clara, CA • 408-727-8227. Available at many computer stores.)*

Hypercard

A data management program designed specially for the Macintosh. It enables the user to access different nodes of information by pressing customized on-screen buttons. (*Published by Claris Corporation, Santa Clara, CA • 408-727-8227. Hypercard comes as part of the standard Macintosh package.*)

Macdraw II

Enables user to design graphics with precise drawing controls and a choice of over 16,000 colors and customized patterns. (*Published by Claris Corporation, Santa Clara, CA • 408-727-8227. Available in many computer stores*)

Microsoft Word

A menu-driven general word processing program. It has many features, including Spell Check, Thesaurus, and the ability to use style sheets. (*Published by Microsoft Corporation, Redmond, Washington • 206-882-8080. Available at most computer software stores.*)

Microsoft Excel

This is a spread-sheet program which can be used to set up tables and charts, and do detailed administrative tasks and statistical functions. It is advanced, and is used by professional accountants and people in finance. (*Published by Microsoft Corporation, Redmond, Washington • 206-882-8080. Available at most computer software stores.*)

Microsoft Works

Gives you the ability to integrate a word processor, spread sheet and database in a communications package. This is a less in-depth a program than Microsoft Excel, because it gives you a little bit of everything. This is a simple yet capable system with general tasks for the novice user. Designed for the small business and home office. (*Published by Microsoft Corporation, Redmond, Washington • 206-882-8080. Available at most computer software stores.*)

SOFTWARE—STANDARD IBM COMPATIBLE PROGRAMS

Lotus 1-2-3

This is a comprehensive spreadsheet program. The DOS version is still the industry standard spreadsheet used, because it is the most complete spreadsheet program available on the market. (*Published by Lotus Development Corporation, Cambridge, MA • 800-343-5414. Available at most computer software stores*)

Q&A
A database program designed for personal and small business use. (*Published by Borland International, Scotts Valley CA • 408-438-8400. Available at many computer software stores*)

Word Perfect
This is a general word processing program, widely used by businesses and legal firms. Good for letters, legal briefs, and preparing large mailings. (*Published by Word Perfect Corporation • 800-451-5151*)

SOFTWARE—SPECIALTY PROGRAMS
The following computer programs are available either through the **Lone Eagle Catalogue at 1-800-FILMBKS (1-800-345-6257)** or from

Writer's Computer Store
11317 Santa Monica Boulevard
Los Angeles, CA 90024
310-479-7774

Collaborator
Collaborator helps you write a better script by asking you questions about your main characters and story. It then generates a report with suggestions for how to improve your screenplay. Available for Mac and IBM Compatible.

Final Draft
Final Draft is a scriptwriting program, which automatically sets your script into a professional format, with "Cut to" and "Continued" in all the right places. For the Mac only.

Scriptor
A scriptwriting program for Mac or IBM Compatible.

Movie Magic Scheduling
Enables a production manager to break down a script and generate a shooting schedule, production board strips, call sheets, cast lists, and day out of days reports. Available for Mac and IBM Compatible.

Movie Magic Budgeting
Companion program to Movie Magic Scheduling. Allows production manager to estimate film production costs with a high degree of precision and speed. Can interface with accounting programs. Available for Mac and IBM Compatible.

SOFTWARE STORES

BEVERLY HILLS

MicroAge
9911 W. Pico Blvd.
Los Angeles, CA 90035
310-552-2211
(Adjacent to Beverly Hills)

Inacomp
9230 W. Olympic,
Beverly Hills, CA 90212
310-275-7430

HOLLYWOOD

Egghead Software
7162 Beverly Blvd.
Los Angeles, CA 90036
213-937-0401

SOS Computers
362 S. La Brea Ave.
Los Angeles, CA 90036
213-857-0371

SAN FERNANDO VALLEY

Software Supermarket
19317 Ventura Blvd.
Tarzana CA 91356
818-783-3233

Egghead Software
5608 Laurel Canyon Blvd.
North Hollywood, CA 91607
818-766-1767

WESTSIDE

Computer Business Center
2811 Ocean Park Blvd.
Santa Monica, CA 90405
310-452-2027

Egghead Software
2400 Barrington Avenue
Los Angeles, CA 90064
310-477-1577

MicroAge
9911 W. Pico Blvd.
Los Angeles, CA 90035
310-552-2211

Unitec
12024 Wilshire Blvd.
West Los Angeles, CA 90025
310-820-2400

Writer's Computer Store
11317 Santa Monica Blvd
Los Angeles, CA 90024
310-479-7774

This is a specialty store uniquely geared to people in the writing trade. A user friendly store with customized software and training available to writers.

TRADE PRESS

Billboard
5055 Wilshire Blvd
Los Angeles, CA 90036
213-525-2300

Daily Variety
5700 Wilshire Blvd. Suite 120
Los Angeles, CA 90036
213-857-6600

Electronic Media
6500 Wilshire Blvd.
Los Angeles, CA 90048
213-651-3710

Entertainment Law and Finance
Leader Publications
111 8th Ave, 9th Fl.
New York, NY 10011
212-463-5709

Covers Film, Music, Television, Cable, Theater, Art and Books. Latest case decisions, IRS regulations, contracts, royalties, corporate sponsorship and so forth.

The Hollywood Reporter
5055 Wilshire Blvd.
Los Angeles, CA 90036
213-525-2000

Weekly Variety
Variety Publications
475 Park Avenue South
New York, NY 10016
212-779-1100

TRAVEL AGENCIES

Bel-Air Travel, Inc.
612 N. Sepulveda Blvd.
Los Angeles, CA 90049
310-476-3053
818-901-9666

Hoffman Travel Service
11337 Ventura Blvd.
Studio City, CA 91604
818-508-7600

VIDEO STORES

BEVERLY HILLS

Music Plus
406 N. Beverly Dr.
Beverly Hills, CA 90210
310-275-3955

Videocentre
145 S. Beverly Dr.
Beverly Hills, CA 90212-3002 (1/2 block S. of Wilshire)
310-550-1092

Videotheque
330 N. Beverly Dr.
Beverly Hills, CA 90210
310-858-7600

HOLLYWOOD

Blockbuster
4470 Sunset Blvd.
Los Angeles, CA 90027
213-661-0791

Wherehouse Music, Movies and More
162 S. Vermont Ave.
Los Angeles, CA 90004
213-387-0558

SANTA MONICA

20/20 Video
2825 Santa Monica Blvd. Suite #104
Santa Monica, CA 90404
310-829-2020

Vidiots
(largest selection of foreign films)
302 Pico Blvd.
Santa Monica, CA 90405
310-392-8508

SAN FERNANDO VALLEY

Blockbuster Video
2420 W. Burbank Blvd.
Burbank, CA 91505
818-566-1193

Tower Records/Video
14612 Ventura Blvd.
Sherman Oaks, CA 91403
818-995-7373

Videowest
11376 Ventura Blvd.
Studio City, CA 91604
818-760-0096

Wherehouse Music, Movies and More
1551 W. Olive Ave
Burbank, CA 91505
818-842-2349

12123 Ventura Blvd
Studio City, CA 91604
818-769-1444

WEST HOLLYWOOD

Tower Records/Video
8844 Sunset Blvd.
West Hollywood, CA 90069
310-657-3344

Video Collection
470 N. Doheny Dr.
West Hollywood, CA 90048
310-273-7700

WESTSIDE

Blockbuster
12112 Santa Monica Blvd.
Los Angeles, CA 90025
310-447-2481

20/20 VIDEO
11663 Wilshire Blvd.
West Los Angeles CA 90025
310-208-4336

Odyssey Video
11910 Wilshire Boulevard
Los Angeles, CA 90025
310-477-2523
310-477-2524

Wherehouse Music, Movies and More
1095 Broxton Ave. (*Westwood*)
Los Angeles, CA 90024
310-824-2255

VIDEO—HARD TO FIND TAPES AND CLASSICS

Rocket Video
633 N. La Brea Blvd,
Los Angeles, CA 90036
213-965-1100
(*Classics, old films, also documentaries*)

Video France
2345 Westwood Blvd
Los Angeles, 90064
310-474-8078
(*French and Italian Movies*)

Videotheque
330 N. Beverly Dr.
Beverly Hills, CA 90210
310-858-7600

Video West
805 Larrabee
West Hollywood, CA 90069
310-659-5762
(*large selection of classics, musicals, westerns*)

Vidiots
302 Pico Blvd
Santa Monica, CA
310-392-8508
(*large selection of foreign films, cult films, and experimental films*)

Also see **Radio and TV Reports** for off-the-air videos of recent programs.

VISITORS AND CONVENTIONS BUREAU—CITY OF LOS ANGELES
515 South Figueroa 11th Fl.
Los Angeles, CA 90071
213-624-7300

Promotes tourism in L.A. County. Makes bookings for conventions in the L.A. area in convention centers and hotels. Also available for tourists to get information about L.A. county, and where to find things.

Appendix H
Guilds

American Guild of Variety Artists
4741 Laurel Canyon Blvd.
Suite 208
North Hollywood, CA 91607
818-508-9984

Costume Designers Guild, IATSE Local 892
13949 Ventura Blvd.—Suite 309
Sherman Oaks, CA 91423
818-905-1557

Directors Guild of America, Inc. (DGA)
7920 Sunset Blvd.
Los Angeles, CA 90046
310-289-2000

400 N. Michigan Ave.—Suite 307
Chicago, IL 60611
312-644-5050

110 W. 57th Street
New York, NY 10019
212-581-0370

Directors Guild of America/ Producers Pension & Health Plans
8436 W. Third Street—Suite 900
Los Angeles, CA 90048
213-653-2991

The Dramatists Guild, Inc.
P.O. Box 480092
Los Angeles, CA 90048
213-935-2686

The Dramatists Guild, Inc.
234 W. 44th Street
New York, NY 10036
212-398-9366

Producers Guild of America
400 S. Beverly Drive—Suite 211
Beverly Hills, CA 90212
310-557-0807

Production Office Coordinators & Accountants Guild IATSE, Local 717
13949 Ventura Blvd.—Suite 306
Sherman Oaks, CA 91423
818-906-9986

Publicists Guild
IATSE Local 818
13949 Ventura Blvd.
Suite 302
Sherman Oaks, CA 91423-3570
818-905-1541

Screen Actors Guild (SAG)
7065 Hollywood Blvd.
Hollywood, CA 90028-6065
213-465-4600

1515 Broadway
44th Floor
New York, NY 10036
212-944-1030

75 E. Wacker Drive
14th Floor
Chicago, IL 60601
312-372-8081

Screen Extras Guild, Inc.
3629 Cahuenga Blvd. West
Los Angeles, CA 90068
213-851-4301

Songwriters Guild of America
6430 Sunset Blvd.
Suite 1002
Hollywood, CA 90028
213-462-1108

Writers Guild of America (WGA)
8955 Beverly Blvd.
Los Angeles, CA 90048
310-550-1000

Writers Guild of America East, Inc.
555 W. 57th Street
New York, NY 10019
212-245-6180

INTERNATIONAL GUILDS

Association of Television and Radio Artists (Writers)
2239 Young Street
Toronto, Ontario, M4S 2B5 Canada
416-489-1311

WGA—Great Britain (Writers)
430 Edgeware Road
London, UK W21EH England
011-44-7-1-723-8074

Directors Guild of Canada
387 Bloor St. East, Suite 401
Toronto, Ontario, M4W 1H7 Canada
416-972-0098

Bectu (Directors)
111 Wardour Street
London, West 1 E6JZ England
011-447-1-437-8506